Contingent Convertibles [CoCos]

A Potent Instrument for Financial Reform

World Scientific–Now Publishers Series in Business

ISSN: 2251-3442

World Scientific – Now Publishers Series in Business: **Vol.5**

Contingent Convertibles [CoCos]

A Potent Instrument for Financial Reform

George M von Furstenberg

Indiana University, USA

now    World Scientific

Published by

World Scientific Publishing Co. Pte. Ltd.

5 Toh Tuck Link, Singapore 596224

USA office: 27 Warren Street, Suite 401-402, Hackensack, NJ 07601

UK office: 57 Shelton Street, Covent Garden, London WC2H 9HE

and

now publishers Inc.
PO Box 1024
Hanover, MA 02339
USA

Library of Congress Cataloging-in-Publication Data
Von Furstenberg, George M., 1941–
    Contingent convertibles [CoCos] : a potent instrument for financial reform / George M. von Furstenberg, Indiana University, USA.
        pages cm
    Includes bibliographical references and index.
    ISBN 978-9814619899 (hardcover : alk. paper)
    1. Convertible securities. 2. Convertible bonds. I. Title.
    HG4652.V66 2014
    332.63'2--dc23
                                        2014024087

British Library Cataloguing-in-Publication Data
A catalogue record for this book is available from the British Library.

World Scientific–Now Publishers Series in Business — Vol. 5
CONTINGENT CONVERTIBLES [CoCos]
A Potent Instrument for Financial Reform

Copyright © George M. von Furstenberg 2015

In-house Editor: Sandhya Venkatesh

Printed in Singapore

Acknowledgments

Development of the work presented here started in 2010. It was then greatly aided and advanced by research fellowships or visits at three institutions: (i) the Deutsche Bundesbank where I thank in particular Dr. Heinz Herrmann, its head of Research and Director of the Economic Research Centre, (ii) the Hong Kong Institute for Monetary Research where I thank Dong He, its Director, who is also the Executive Director (Research) for the HKMA, and (iii) the Risk Management Institute at the National University of Singapore, where I am much indebted to Professor Jin-Chuan Duan, Director of NUS-RMI and Cycle & Carriage Professor of Finance at the NUS Business School. He is also the founding Editor-in-Chief of *Global Credit Review*. Neither the institutions nor the individuals just named are responsible for the views expressed herein, of course, and they may not share them. My sincere thanks also go to Ben Garceau for proofreading the manuscript and to Ms. Sandhya Venkatesh of World Scientific Publishing for her superb editorial work. On a personal level I am very much indebted to my wife Gabrielle for being so lovingly supportive of me and my work and to our son Philip for his infectious zest and joy for life. Finally, I am grateful to the Department of Economics at Indiana University for facilitating this work in its congenial and stimulating research environment. Please contact me at vonfurst@indiana.edu, with "Cocos" in the subject line, to point out any needed corrections and improvements.

Abstract

This is the first book on CoCos, an innovative instrument that has attracted growing attention since it was first issued in 2009. Henceforth spelled cocos, they represent debt that is subject to being converted automatically into common equity under pre-specified terms of conversion if the chosen regulatory capital ratio falls to a level triggering conversion. Cocos are that subspecies of contingent capital that references regulatory (Basel III) concepts in its triggers. From 2014 on, trigger points are set by common equity (Common Equity Tier 1 [CET1]) in percent of risk-weighted assets [RWA] or of more complicated measures of total exposure to a variety of risks, particularly credit risk. CET1 trigger levels of at least 7% are generally activated to fortify institutions in transitory difficulties that are expected to continue as going concerns. Lower trigger levels, near 5%, are characteristic of bail-in cocos that are intended to facilitate resolution outside of bankruptcy, although the chances of recovery would also be improved if the cushion of such cocos were substantial.

This study is mostly concerned with going-concern 'recovery-' rather than 'resolution-' cocos, because avoiding failure and costly disruption of financial networks without government financing is the first order of business. Cocos hold a high promise of providing fully loss-absorbing equity capital when it is most needed and least available to financial institutions. Yet, having grown out of the 2007–2009 financial crisis, they are still an 'infant' reform instrument in many respects. Few of the instrument's design features (or even the rating, regulatory, and tax treatments) are entirely settled. This monograph seeks to help move the discussion toward the main decision points. These must be passed before cocos can live up to their promise and prove their value for contingency planning and self-insurance. They should do so not only in Europe and Latin America but also increasingly in North America, Australia, South Africa, the Middle East and centers of high finance in Eastern and Southern parts of Asia, including Singapore and Hong Kong—come the next financial crisis.

Contents

List of Tables

About the Author

George M. von Furstenberg is J.H. Rudy Emeritus Professor of Economics at Indiana University.

Before returning to Indiana University in 2002, he was the inaugural holder of the Robert Bendheim Chair in Economic and Financial Policy at Fordham University's Lincoln Center Campus. Work at the IMF (Division Chief in the Research Department, 1978–1983) and at US government agencies such as the US President's Council of Economic Advisers (Senior Staff Economist, 1973–76), the Department of State (1989–90) and the National Science Foundation (Economics Program Director, 2006–08) have alternated with his academic pursuits.

His research and teaching subjects have centered on international finance and open-economy macroeconomics, but he has also worked on a variety of public finance issues, the determinants of mortgage default risk, and aspects of financial reform. His latest book projects have dealt with *Regulation and Supervision of Financial Institutions in the NAFTA Countries, Learning from the World's Best Central Bankers*, and *Monetary Unions and Hard Pegs: Effects on Trade, Financial Development, and Stability*. He joined the G8/G20 Research Group in 1999 and in 2000 was President of the North American Economics and Finance Association.

Part I
Foundations

1

Introduction

Reacting to the severe financial crisis of 2007–2009, contingent convertible debt securities, abbreviated *CoCos* or *cocos*, were introduced as a promising new instrument of financial reform. They were to reduce bank failures and thereby cushion the next financial crisis more reliably and automatically than existing subordinated debt. After a slow start in 2009 that almost stopped in 2010, their issuance has been growing progressively. However, a number of their design features and uses are still experimental. This makes it exciting to assist with their evaluation, development and acceptance in the public interest and from capital market perspectives.

Banks headquartered in Western Europe, most notably in the United Kingdom and Switzerland, have been the main issuers of cocos, but investor demand can be found for them wherever they may be offered: in North and South America and in Southeast Asia as well. Hurdles that must be jumped when issuing cocos into the US are described by Oakes and Milonakis (2013). BBVA Citi Research (2013, p. 5), under the heading "lower total funding volumes but a clear preference for cocos" reported that cocos issuance by European Banks in 2013 had been running at 30% of their total subordinated funding and at about 4% of senior unsecured plus subordinated funding. If Citigroup estimates that European banks could raise as much as €65 billion ($88 billion at 1.35$/€) in 2014 should turn out to be correct, the latter percentage could rise to at least 15%.

The saving grace of cocos is that they get converted into common stock on pre-specified terms when a bank or investment bank becomes so thinly capitalized that a preset trigger level for a designated capital or leverage ratio is breached. For now it shall suffice to say that regulatory capital ratios typically have common equity in the numerator and risk-weighted assets in the

3

denominator, while leverage ratios have a somewhat broader equity-like sum in the numerator and a much larger, not risk weighted, asset aggregate in the denominator. Hence it is not unusual for capital ratios to be twice as high as leverage ratios for the same firm, with both customarily reported in percentages. Indicative of the role that the loss of equity capital by many banks plays in bringing on and propagating a banking crisis, Caprio (2013) identifies a banking crisis by whether much or all of bank capital is being exhausted in a troubled country. He finds that, by this criterion, there were 117 episodes of systemic banking crises in 93 countries between 1970 and 2002. These episodes are thus a recurring phenomenon and ubiquitous.

Severe banking crises are marked by the breakdown of the intermediation system between financial and non-financial sectors and between agents frozen out of fraying financial networks. As risk aversion mounts and illiquidity rises, the price of the least liquid assets plummets, starting with the riskiest. Mutual trust in the ability of counterparties to honor their financial commitments breaks down. Consequently, banking crises almost invariably metastasize into pandemics of general financial and economic crises. These crises have an increasingly global reach. As operating and revaluation (mark-to-market) losses mount in the banking sector, losses many times higher than those inflicted on unsecured creditors and stockholders of the banks afflict the national and international economy as a whole and its nonbank participants.

Banking crises may not be entirely endemic or precipitated solely from within by the managerial, cultural, regulatory, and political environment in which banks operate. Several types of outside disturbances could also play a part in fomenting a crisis. However, human agency is paramount and analogies with acts of god or with volcanic eruptions, tsunamis, or black swans are a cheap excuse. For instance, if black swans are so extremely rare, why are financial crises so common? Indeed, financial crises share broadly similar patterns in the lead-up and aftermath of such crises. Here is just one quote from Reinhart and Rogoff (2009, p. 224) on their employment and output effects, leaving aside the asset price declines and surging government debt which they also identified as typically associated with such crises:

> The aftermath of banking crises is associated with profound declines in output and employment. The unemployment rate rises an average [for severe systemic post-World War II financial crises that started prior to 2007] of 7 percentage points during the down phase of the cycle, which lasts on average more than four years. Output falls (from peak to trough) more than 9 percent on average, although the duration of the downturn, averaging roughly two years, is considerably shorter than that of unemployment.

For the US alone Atkinson, Luttrell, and Rosenblum (2013, p. 9) have since estimated that the total loss resulting from output remaining below trend from 2008 prospectively until 2020 would be equivalent to 65% to 165% of one-year's output or $10 to $25 trillion.

Outcomes for individual crises may of course differ greatly from the average even within the same group of countries as Montiel's (2014) case studies (which include 8 crises in emerging-market countries) vividly demonstrate. Two of these countries, Argentina and Turkey, appeared in 2014 to be lurching for somewhat different reasons toward crisis once again. Nevertheless the pathologies on the whole, in both emerging and advanced countries, are well known to crisis specialists and those who construct early warning indicators of approaching financial crises. Hence it is natural to wonder why banking regulators, supervisors, legislators, and international financial institutions which claim to know better cannot do something to break the pattern of recurring financial mayhem.

Here Reinhart and Rogoff (2009, p. 156) provide an important clue. They first cite evidence that inadequate regulation and lack of supervision at the time of liberalization may play a key role in explaining why deregulation and banking crises are so closely linked in developed countries and emerging markets alike. Then they conclude, "in the 2000s the United States, for all its this-time-is-different hubris, proved no exception, for *financial innovation is a variant of the liberalization process*" (emphasis added).

Sharpening the point, it can be said that financial innovation is a process by which the financial system continually tries to deregulate itself so that, unmoored, it can get back to trolling in dangerous waters. Barth, Caprio, and Levine (2012, p. 231) also blame the *Guardians of Finance* and those who appoint and then hobble them, for forever dashing hopes of lasting improvement. They find serious and chronic defects in the institutional apparatus that selects, implements, and reforms financial policies and conclude, "Through acts of commission and omission, major financial regulatory agencies repeatedly designed and [knowingly] maintained policies that increased the fragility of the financial system and the inefficient allocation of capital."

Just as financial crises are all too common, there are serial accommodations or outright bailouts of too-big-to-fail [TBTF] institutions caught up in them. Citibank (now Citigroup), for example, has had to be pulled back from the abyss many times in its over 200-year history. Counting back just a quarter century from the start of the 2007–2009 crisis, in 1982 Citibank almost failed because of bad loans made to Latin America, but of course it was TBTF for that to happen. In 1989–1991 it was in big trouble again largely on account of excessive lending on richly valued commercial real estate, not just in the United States. Then Citibank got drawn into the 1998 Long Term Capital Management disaster, falling victim to concentrated counterparty risk. This was followed by the residential mortgage credit, derivatives, and failure of risk management fiasco that led to a partial government takeover of up to 36% of Citigroup by early 2009. The average time between the onset of the institution's crises in this quarter century was about eight years.

The Schumpeterian usage of the term *creative destruction* intends to draw attention to the invigorating effects of bankruptcy because "creative" is meant to apply to the destruction and its aftermath and not to its perpetrator. Applied to banking, the meaning is different: Those who wreak havoc in banking have found ever more creative ways to do so, but the results have not been particularly creative in making way for something new and better. The remnants of one operation that has been shattered and reduced by a loss of network relationships eventually get picked up by another without compensatory benefits to the system as a whole. When Nick Leeson's outsized and unfortunate position taking in 1995 brought down Barings Bank, an institution 50 years older than Citibank, there was no indication that its business model was outmoded; still, it had obviously been ill-prepared to manage and appropriately limit some type of operational risk somewhere in its far-flung business. Such a whale of a loss has occurred in several TBTF banks since that time for exactly the same reasons, though so far not with quite such fatal consequences. Was there any healthy progress for investment banking hidden in the collapse of Lehman Brothers in the late summer of 2008? If so, it has yet to be pointed out.

Perhaps the main result of this collapse and its ugly consequences has been to make the implicit TBTF guarantee even firmer. This could help explain why maintaining a good reputation has become less relevant and dependable since TBTF became the norm. Unless supported by professional pride and a few grains of professional ethics, reputation becomes instrumentalized. It is then viewed as an institutional asset that is not to be piled up and treasured but used and abused in dealing with unwary loan, wealth-management, underwriting and consulting-business clients. Self-restraint by managers in the interest of preserving their institution's—and their own—good name may be too much to hope for in the shadow of TBTF.

1.1 The Operative Principles Applied in this Monograph

Five working principles for the choices made in this book follow from these considerations and polite reservations:

1. Financial innovations originally proposed from outside the financial industry are more likely to be beneficial than those developed entirely within that industry. However, the industry should not be forced to adopt any proposed instrument innovations, least of all if their optimal benefit-cost relations

and the proper scale and scope of their application still need to be found out and pre-tested. Incentives to adopt that are commensurate with the expected public benefit may be justified by arguments similar to those used to justify infant-industry tariffs, but cocos mandates should be avoided.

2. Instrument innovations should focus on increasing bank capital and access to equity capital before an institution enters the acute stage of any crisis that has already reduced capital ratios to dangerously low levels. Going-concern cocos with triggers based on regulatory capital ratios provide such a service. True to their insurance rationale, cocos should be issued in good times to be available for providing capital support in bad times. There has been a worrisome tendency to do the opposite, particularly in Iberian bailouts, by attaching upside conversion or repurchase options to cocos that were sold to the government rather than to private parties.

3. Neither regulators nor bank managers should be allowed to interfere with the automaticity of high-trigger cocos conversion when triggered, provided that the trigger is set at or above the level at which the institution is regarded as adequately capitalized by its national regulator. In those cases, cocos trigger activation and conversion should not be subject to the dubious agency of government regulators or the managers of the banks that have issued cocos. The cost of issuing high-trigger cocos would needlessly be raised, and their credit rating would be reduced, by providing for discretionary override of a going-concern cocos trigger. Furthermore, if regulators can play fast and loose with trigger activation and the accounting measures and conditions surrounding conversion, they could prevent the legal system and civil law suits from safeguarding the accurate, timely and transparent application of the built-in conversion mechanism.

4. Apart from the definition of the trigger and the level at which it is set, the recovery or 'replacement' rate of cocos that is afforded by the common stock received in conversion is a crucial strategic variable. If that value is zero, as with write-down-only cocos, their holders are set to lose the entire principal invested when cocos are triggered while from debt write-off pre-existing shareholders gain what cocos holders lose. Since shareholders have the upper hand, this incentive structure is toxic and militates against the future issue of such cocos.

5. If cocos holders are direct or indirect loan clients of banks, for instance via hedge funds, their losses could spill back. Hence the replacement rate should be closer to 1 than to 0 to reduce prospective losses for cocos holders and to lower the yield they require. A second reason is that pre-existing shareholders and managers should not stand to gain more from conversion than would suffice to keep them interested in cocos being issued in the first place. A replacement rate of about 0.8 would provide for the appropriate apportionment of relatively small gains and losses to the two parties without undue spillovers to third parties.

1.2 Orientation and Summary for Parts I–IV

Part I lays the foundations that are needed for the subject matter of this study by first outlining the regulatory environment into which cocos must fit in order to make a recognized contribution to some parts of regulatory capital. Because cocos convert into common equity outside of bankruptcy they are part of a long—though not unchallenged—tradition in Europe and the United States of trying to preserve going-concern value by offering struggling entrepreneurs occasional forbearance and a second chance to succeed. However, cocos are not the only currently available instrument that may be suitable for this purpose; reverse convertible securities and loss equity puts will be considered and contrasted with cocos as well. Because cocos came to be used in response to the financial crisis of 2007–2009, some knowledge of the muddled history of bailouts and rescue efforts mounted on behalf of individual institutions during this period is part of the background that will need to be laid out. Monetary and fiscal exposures and policy objectives in these rescue missions and their aftermath will be discussed as well, again mainly from a US perspective. Because banks headquartered in the United States have yet to issue cocos, the focus in the next two Parts will shift to what Europe has done with cocos.

Part II will try to make the case for cocos by taking on some of their challengers. First it will distinguish high-trigger from low-trigger cocos and then contrast them from non-viability contingent capital and other "bailinable" debt. It will then discuss what each of these hybrid securities, when converted, can do for the survival or prompt resolution of an institution compared with simply having a larger equity cushion in the first place. The third comparison will be with trying to negotiate a restructuring that meets with debt holders' approval of a substantial write-down of their non-cocos claims. This will involve working through a recent actual restructuring with numbers that facilitate comparison with what might have been different had there been cocos to convert on the balance sheet. Hence the third paired comparison will pit cocos not against alternative financing instruments but against restructuring procedures which turned out to be very costly and time consuming without them.

Part III will deal with varieties of cocos design and their pricing and rationales. It will provide a baseline estimate of the conversion risk premium controlling for the level of the 'riskless' interest rate, the annualized probability of conversion, and the replacement rate. These estimates will be based on the assumption of risk neutrality, meaning that the conversion risk premium only has to cover the loss expected from the sale of stock obtained from conversion without requiring additional compensation on account of risk aversion. Actual yields required on write-down-only cocos with varying trigger levels and credit ratings will then be confronted with the baseline estimates and other model-based estimates such as of the annualized premium rate in percent of 'nominal' required on credit default swaps written on non-cocos bonds with otherwise similar characteristics. Attention will then shift to the somewhat perverse use of bailout cocos by governments wanting to help rescue their TBTF banks without ending up as the owners of all or substantial parts of them and having to take the acquisition costs on-budget. With interest rates set at 10% by the acquiring government agencies of Ireland, Portugal, and Spain, these cocos were meant to be repurchased within a few years, hopefully with the proceeds of new stock issues in the market, before their mandatory date of conversion by the government was reached. The government of Ireland instead managed to remarket these cocos and sell them to private holders with a small accounting gain. Two surviving Greek banks balked at going through with expensive cocos issues which they had already announced when they managed to meet the higher capital requirements imposed on them without cocos.

Part IV will emphasize that for cocos to be able to compete in the capital market they must satisfy three conditions which are not yet readily reconcilable in a number of national jurisdictions: They must (1) qualify to meet some part of regulatory capital requirements, (2) be rated investment-grade rather than high-yield debt by the major rating agencies of cocos, Standard & Poor's (S&P) and Fitch, and (3) pay interest that is tax-deductible in most jurisdictions and preferably also in the United States. Because satisfying any one of the three conditions may very well conflict with one or both others under present conditions, cocos issuance has been made unnecessarily expensive and is being held back. The first three chapters in this Part will thus attempt to show how cocos must be structured, and to what extent regulators must rein in some of their assertions of unbridled discretion, in order to reconcile these conflicting requirements. Doing so would clear the way for cocos to be issued on terms attractive for financial institutions and investors. Chapter 16 will contain discussion informed by excerpts taken from the rating guidelines issued by S&P and proposed by Moody's. Chapter 17 will excerpt regulations from European and

US sources that are organized into seven documents. These documents bring authenticity to the discussion of what regulators propose under Basel III and what EU and US regulators then require from cocos. The last chapter in this Part will combine conclusions with concrete recommendations for making cocos—on account of their merit for greater financial responsibility and self-insurance—more of a success.

2

Overview of Basel III Implementation Most Relevant for Cocos

The Basel Committee on Banking Supervision [BCBS], or "Basel Committee" according to its new charter (BCBS, 2013a), is the primary global standard-setter for the prudential regulation of banks and provides a forum for cooperation on banking supervisory matters. Since its establishment in 1974, the Basel Committee's mandate has been to strengthen the regulation, supervision and risk management practices of banks worldwide with the purpose of enhancing financial stability and contributing to "a level playing field" among internationally active banks. The current set of standards, first proposed in 2010–2011, is known as Basel III. The Committee's Secretariat is located in Basel, Switzerland, at the Bank for International Settlements [BIS]. The BIS is an International Financial Institution [IFI] founded in 1930. It now provides a coordination platform and technical support for central banks, and has regulatory and supervisory authority in drafting financial standards and regulations. Once finalized and adopted by the relevant committee such as the BCBS, these standards and regulations are proposed for adoption both by national regulators and for implementation by internationally-active financial institutions under their jurisdiction.

The Basel Committee's decisions thus do not have legal force. To become binding, its proposals need to be transposed into national, and, if appropriate European Union [EU] regulations with some permissible variances, especially for smaller and less complex national financial institutions. This process of formal adoption and supporting legislation requires a timetable that may take years to pass and then more years to implement. In the United States, for example, the Federal Reserve Board approved the final rules to implement the Basel III capital reforms only in July 2013 for fulfillment by the various built-in BCBS deadlines. The last of these is January 1, 2019. However, for reasons of reputation and with official encouragement, major banks have sought to meet Basel III requirements "fully loaded" (as they would be in 2019) well before the deadline.

In Europe the process of transposing the Basel III Accord put forward by the BCBS into law has been formalized in the Capital Requirements Directive IV [CRD IV]. This Directive had been proposed by the European Commission [EC] in July 2011 with the assistance and advice of the European Banking Authority [EBA], and it was accepted by the European Parliament and the Council on April 16, 2013. The EBA is a regulatory financial agency of the EU; it is headquartered in London and commenced operations at the beginning of 2011. The EBA prides itself as being the center of a hub-and-spoke network of EU and national bodies safeguarding the stability of the financial system. It has conducted stress tests—initially feckless—of banks and put forth proposals, consultation papers, and drafts of numerous Regulatory Technical Standards [RTS] regarding the translation of Basel III into EU and national legislation under CRD IV. It has also helped prepare the accompanying body of Capital Requirements Regulation [CRR] which took effect in EU member countries immediately upon adoption by the European Parliament and Council as part of "the single rule book."

2.1 Regulatory Capital Requirements

The BCBS has developed a succession of international regulatory frameworks and agreements for subsequent adoption by members and willing non-members. The underlying documents have been compiled in BCBS (2013c). One of the more important of these evolving agreements is the Basel Capital Accord of 1988 which was implemented in subsequent years as Basel I. It was followed by Basel II which was proposed and adopted with successive revisions during the years 1999–2009 including Basel 2.5 (2005–2009). The capital and liquidity framework generally referred to as Basel III, or B3, was first documented in BCBS (2010 and 2011c) and is still evolving. All these regimes focused on the minimum required level and quality of "capital," i.e., equity and equity-like instruments, which banks should have in percent of their risk-weighted assets in order to be regarded as *adequately capitalized*.

The capital requirements make reference to Tier 1 [T1] and Tier 2 [T2] capital in percent of the risk-weighted asset of a financial institution. T1 capital is paid-in and retained common equity or non-common and still equity-like capital. T2 is normally senior to T1 capital and less immediately loss-absorbing. T1 capital is known as *core* or *going-concern* capital, while T2 subordinated debt and preference shares are often viewed as gone-concern capital in that T2 capital may become loss-absorbing only when bankruptcy resolution is already impending. T2 capital is no longer divided into upper and lower slices, but T1 capital is a composite of tangible Common Equity Tier 1 [CET1] and Additional Tier 1 [AT1] capital. Together T1 plus T2, expressed in percent of Risk Weighted Assets [RWA] yield the *total* capital percentage. Its minimum level, specified by regulators, sets the least amount of total regulatory capital in percent of RWA which a financial institution has to maintain at all times. To keep well away from that minimum which could bring on regulatory intervention, banks tend to target capital ratios that are several percentage points higher by adding a voluntary buffer. Like the *total* regulatory capital of financial institutions, their *own funds* include CET1, AT1, and T2 capital, net of specified deductions from these different types of capital, and transitional provisions for *own funds* in terms of grandfathering.

Regulators are not only setting this total, however, but also its composition by prescribing what contribution the higher-quality components of regulatory capital, CET1 and AT1, must make to the total capital percentage. Even within these categories there are limits to how much an individual instrument may be relied upon to meet capital requirements. Furthermore, since January 1, 2013, certain instruments, such as cumulative preferred stock and subordinated debt that cannot be bailed-in outside of bankruptcy at regulators' discretion have been phased out of regulatory capital at the rate of 10% a year. Complete Basel III definitions of all the components of regulatory capital mentioned so far are provided in BCBS (2011a). These definitions are not necessarily applied consistently over time. The EBA (2011a and 2011b), for instance, established a "temporary" capital target, of 9% of RWA, first to be met by the end of June 2012 and then extended until banks have shown regulators how they plan to meet the tough Basel III rules taking effect later this decade. It called this percentage *Core Tier 1* [CT1] but then excluded all Buffer Convertible Capital Securities [BCCS] from the numerator even if they are structured exactly like cocos that are eligible for AT1. Furthermore, the risk-weighting, taken from an older version of "Basel," tended to result in almost 50% lower measures of RWA than would have been assigned to the same asset portfolio under Basel III. Hence, crudely translated into Basel III terminology and metrics, the 9% target imposed by the EBA, $T1/RWA_{Basel2.5}$, is actually equal to a $CET1/RWA_{Basel3}$ percentage that is only about half as large and not far from the rock-bottom minimum of 4.5% imposed under Basel III.

The appearance of toughness by regulators operating in a jumble of risk weightings can be deceiving. For instance, in mid-2010 the CEO of Credit Suisse, Brady Dougan, reported that RWA would rise by 76% from $233 to $410 billion under Basel III from the then-current Basel 2.5 rules. Comparable figures for UBS, reported by then-CEO Oswald Grübel, showed a rise of 100% from $205 to $409 billion before taking account of "mitigating steps" to reduce assets classified as having high risk weights under Basel III. Under the Internal Ratings Based [IRB] approach, RWA can be computed by multiplying 12.5 by the total amount of the capital estimated to be required to cover various types of risk. Hence if this required amount of capital amounts to less than 8% of total assets [TA], RWA is less than TA. Under the standardized approach, the calculation is more direct and certainly more transparent as assets are assigned to a limited number of buckets with pre-assigned risk weights. Then any asset with a risk weight of less than 100% would contribute to RWA being less than TA. In actuality, aggregate risk weights for the most important component, credit risk, may be no more than 20%. Both the EBA (2013a) and the BCBS (2013b) have struggled with variances in risk-weighting between countries and institutions, only about half of which are plausibly attributable to different risk profiles of banks' portfolios. Hence, regulatory convergence in both the rules and their interpretation and application likely were lagging.

2.2 The Leverage Ratio Requirements

The minimum that has been set for the three basic capital ratios in percent of RWA under Basel III is 4.5% for CET1, 6% for T1, and 8% for (T1+T2) which is called *total capital* under Basel III and *own funds* in EU regulations. The minimum *Tier 1 leverage ratio*, calculated as the ratio of T1 capital to net consolidated balance sheet assets, is 3% under Basel III. If the net assets just before are approximately equal to TA, the leverage ratio, T1/TA, divided by the T1 capital ratio, T1/RWA, yields the average risk weight, RWA/TA. If that weight were around 0.5, as is characteristic for banks based in the United States, a minimum T1 capital ratio of 6% would imply a minimum leverage ratio of 3%. But if the average risk weight were only 0.2, as is common in Europe, a minimum T1 capital ratio of 6% would imply a leverage ratio of only 1.2%. Then the 3% minimum on the leverage ratio would be binding and require a T1/RWA ratio of 15% to be satisfied. Admati and Hellwig (2013, pp. 176, 189) appear to have missed the force of this implication when they characterize a leverage ratio of 3% as "outrageously low" while later praising the setting of a CET1 conservation buffer equal to 2.5% of RWA on top of the 4.5% CET1/RWA minimum requirement as "[going] in the right direction."

For the reasons just explained, banks in Europe tend to be much more concerned than banks—and banking agencies—in the United States about keeping down the level of the leverage ratio required. As currently planned (BCBS, 2013d), the Basel III leverage ratio would become binding at the beginning of 2018. US banking regulators have proposed a 2% add-on for eight bank holding companies [BHCs] that have been identified by the FSB (2013) as global systemically important banks [G-SIBs]. These

BHCs are identified in the notes to Table 1. Similar to the graduated constraints imposed for underfunding the conservation buffer, a covered BHC that does not maintain a combined (also called *supplementary*) leverage ratio of at least 5%—i.e., a buffer of at least 2% on top of the 3% Basel III minimum—would be subject to restrictions on making capital distributions and bonus payments. Their severity would depend on the size of the shortfall from 5%. For Insured Depositary Institutions [IDI] the US add-on is even higher at 3%. Hence each IDI subsidiary of a BHC must maintain a 6% Basel III supplementary leverage ratio to be considered well capitalized after January 1, 2018.

Until the Basel III leverage ratio receives Pillar 1 (minimum capital requirement) treatment in bank regulations, much still needs to be decided about both its numerator and denominator. During the transition period ending January 1, 2017, the BCBS (2013d, point 9) "will collect data ... to track the impact of using either total regulatory capital or Common Equity Tier 1 as the capital measure" instead of Tier 1. This undertaking was reaffirmed in BCBS (2014, point 11). The final decision on how capital is measured in the numerator of the leverage ratio is important for cocos since, of course, they are not CET1 prior to conversion but part of AT1 and therefore T1 in most countries. Qualifying cocos may become part of T2 and hence of total regulatory capital in all countries; that will be of no help in meeting leverage ratio requirements anywhere, however, since total regulatory capital that includes T2 does not seem to be in the running for the numerator.

The denominator, as currently proposed, would be a simple sum of total on-balance-sheet exposures, total derivative exposures, total securities financing transaction exposures, and other off-balance sheet exposures. The content and calculation of the resulting "total exposures" may yet be modified as well. However, the basic goal remains to preserve the leverage ratio, constructed without risk-weighting of its denominator components, as a backstop to the traditional Basel capital measures which are expressed in percent of risk-weighted assets. If the risk weights were 'gamed' and risk systematically understated in application, reported regulatory capital ratios, unlike the leverage ratios, would be overstated and could provide false comfort.

If IDIs subject to the Advanced Approaches Rule let any of the ratios that are then in effect fall below their minima, they would be classified as *undercapitalized* and thus be subject to restrictions on capital distributions, the need to file a capital restoration plan, and enhanced supervisory oversight demanding Prompt Corrective Action [PCA]. If the shortfall in any category is more than 2 percentage points (1 percentage point in the leverage ratio) they would be classified as *significantly undercapitalized* and restrictions on interest payments on subordinated debt could kick in, while they would be *well capitalized* if they held 2 percentage points or more capital than the minimum required (OCC & Fed, 2013b, p. 62040).

2.3 Drivers and Evolution of Reforms Affecting Cocos

The set of measures proposed under Basel III were driven by the financial crisis of 2007–2009. During that crisis, the BCBS (2011b) noted, a number of banks were rescued by the public sector injecting funds in the form of common equity and other forms of T1 capital. This meant that T2 capital instruments (mainly subordinated debt), and in some cases T1 instruments, did not absorb losses incurred by banks that would have failed in the absence of public sector support.

In view of this, the Basel III reforms have specified that the terms and conditions of all non-common T1 and T2 instruments issued by an internationally active bank must have a provision that requires such instruments, at the option of the relevant authority, to either be written off or promptly converted into common equity upon the occurrence of the trigger event. This applies unless the inclusion of such a provision in the instruments themselves is redundant because the governing national jurisdiction of the bank requires this treatment already. The trigger event is the earlier of (1) a decision that a write-off, without which the firm would become non-viable, is necessary and (2) the decision to make a public-sector injection of capital, or equivalent support, without which the firm would have become non-viable. In all of this, non-viability is a judgment call by the relevant authority.

These "minimum requirements to ensure loss absorbency at the point of non-viability" for instruments to be included in AT1 or T2 capital are in addition to other characteristics required to assure that such instruments fully absorb losses before taxpayers are exposed. In particular, to be eligible for inclusion in AT1, an instrument must be "perpetual," having no maturity date. It can only be called or redeemed through discretionary repurchases with the prior approval of the banking organization's primary government supervisor. If called, as may happen after 5 years from the date of issue at the earliest, the instrument would normally have to be replaced by an instrument of equal or higher loss absorbency. In addition, dividends and interest payments on instruments qualifying for CET1 and AT1 must be at the discretion of the issuer as well as its supervisor, and non-payment must be irrecoverable. Hence any preferred equity included in AT1 would have to be both perpetual and non-cumulative except that preferred equity that is scheduled to be converted to common equity would satisfy both requirements automatically since conversion would be to a more loss-absorbing capital component, CET1, that is itself perpetual. Components of T2 capital are senior to AT1 components which in turn are senior to CET1 in the event of bankruptcy. However, any pre-authorized common equity issued at conversion must be identical to pre-existing common equity so that all distinctions of seniority would then be lost. Debt instruments with fixed maturity of no less than five years from date of issue and preferred equity that is cumulative may be included in T2 if regulators can still stop interest and dividend payments at the point of non-viability without triggering bankruptcy.

These restrictions and requirements aim to improve the banking sector's ability to absorb shocks arising from firm-specific as well as systemic financial and economic stress and to improve risk management and governance.

The 1988 Accord, which continued to evolve until 1992, focused exclusively on credit risk until market risk was added in

1996–97 as a risk factor (with later modifications) to be considered in determining capital adequacy. Although many financial institutions are most concerned about credit risk, market risk is paramount for others, particularly those that engage in massive maturity transformation with high leverage such as Real Estate Investment Trusts [REITs]. Hatteras Financial Corp. [HTS], for instance, invests only in fully insured (federal mortgage) *agency* securities whose insurance is backstopped by the US Treasury. Hence there is no appreciable credit risk even though securities guaranteed by Fannie Mae and Freddie Mac receive a 20% risk weight under the current "standardized" approach to risk weighting further described below. HTS is however strongly exposed to market risk combined with basis risk that cannot easily be hedged. Thus the company reported on p. 34 of its Form Q-10 for the second quarter of 2013 that "interest rates and prices changed more on agency securities than on US Treasury securities or interest rate hedges with similar average lives." As a result, book value per share of common stock plunged from $28.18 at the end of the first quarter 2013 to $22.18 of the second (or by 21%) and the ratio of debt to shareholders' equity jumped from 7.4:1 to 9.3:1 while the average haircut under its repurchase facilities rose from 4.3% to 4.5%. In spite of these worrisome developments, HTS kept its quarterly dividend initially unchanged at 70 cents per share though it dropped to 55 cents by the third quarter.

Returning to the calculation of assets that are weighted by credit risk, there have been significant improvements from Basel I to III. Initially a fixed weight of 0 was assigned to claims on OECD (Organisation for Economic Co-operation and Development, based in Paris) central governments and central banks, with Mexico included after it had become a member in 1994. On the other hand, a fixed weight of 100% of the book value of assets was assigned to claims on their non-OECD counterparts like Korea which became a member only two years later. Both the 0% and the 100% weights rewarded membership in the OECD but they set back the cause of sovereign risk assessment and encouraged the build-up of government debt and sovereign risks in OECD member states. Similarly, a uniform 50% risk weight on claims fully secured by mortgages on residential properties appears untenable in retrospect. This called for greater differentiation in risk assessments. For sovereign debt a more risk-sensitive treatment has since been provided by linking risk weights to the Country Risk Classification measure produced by the OECD.

Risk weights on residential mortgages are now also based on several criteria including loan characteristics and loan-to-value exposure. A "category 1" conventional mortgage, for instance, would get a risk weight of 35% if its loan-to-value [LTV] ratio at origination were 60% or less and 100% if LTV were above 90% (OCC, Fed & FDIC, 2012a, p. 47). That risk differentiation is most welcome but not nearly enough. Results obtained in my first article (von Furstenberg, 1969, esp. p. 474) suggest that if default rates on FHA-insured home mortgage cohorts originated at an LTV of 90% are represented by an index value of 100, then that value would be 264 if the LTV had been 95% (standing for "above 90%") and 12 if it had been 55% (standing for "below 60%"). Hence default rates predicted on 95% LTV home mortgages would be 264/12, or 22 times as high as on 55% LTV mortgages, and not just 100/35, or 3 times as high as the Basel risk weighting implies. The result implies that default rates rise at a rapidly increasing rate as the initial equity-to-value ratio at the time of mortgage origination—which is similar to the down-payment ratio—falls below 10%. The Basel II revised capital-adequacy framework embodying such changes to the standardized approach to risk-weighting of assets also included other reforms. The new framework rested on three pillars. The first continued to consist of minimum capital requirements but with refinement of the standardized rules set forth in the 1988 Accord. The second pillar strengthened supervisory review of an institution's internal risk assessment process and capital adequacy. The third pillar provided a basis for the effective use of public disclosure to strengthen market discipline as a complement to supervisory efforts. The official history of the BCBS, www.bis.org/bcbs/history.htm, provides details.

Under Basel III, fixed risk weights have survived in the "standardized" approach but internal ratings based [IRB] approaches to credit risk also began to be permitted for deriving risk-based asset totals. A greater number of risks and additional ratios—such as a minimum liquidity-coverage and net-stable-funding ratio, and a leverage ratio—were proposed for consideration or are already in force. The objective of one of the planned selective buffers that would impose higher capital levels on Systemically Important Financial Institutions [SIFIs] is to reduce the funding advantage enjoyed by those institutions that are judged to be too big to fail [TBTF]. Furthermore, a Capital Conservation Buffer for all banks and a Countercyclical Buffer for "advanced approaches" institutions, including more than just SIFIs, are being phased in and will reach their final level by the start of 2019. The advanced internal ratings-based approach for credit risk and the advanced measurement approach for operational risk in general apply to core banks that have consolidated total assets of $250 billion or more, have consolidated on-balance-sheet foreign exposure of $10 billion or more, or are a subsidiary of a core bank. Somewhat smaller, non-core banks may be allowed to apply voluntarily the advanced approaches rule that is mandatory for the core banks.

Finally, Basel III aimed to raise the quality of regulatory capital by providing the first detailed specification of the features required for a capital instrument to be classified from the most loss-absorbing component, CET1, to AT1 capital and then down to certain forms of hybrid capital qualifying for T2. The exact definitions and specifications proposed by the BCBS are documented in Chapter 17. They were put down to help reduce differences in the specifications set by national regulators, thereby promoting international regulatory convergence. Basel III also reconsidered which features an instrument would need to have to qualify for inclusion in any of the three categories of regulatory capital above. In particular, because subordinated debt had generally failed to be loss-absorbing outside of bankruptcy, its qualification as capital, limited to 50% of T1 capital under the original Accord, was limited even more. The maximum was cut back to 1.25% of RWA for banks using the standardized approach and 0.6% of RWA for those using the IRB approaches. While these caps were taken off in the final rule issued in 2013 (OCC & Fed, 2013a, p. 121), newly subordinated debt had to be explicitly "bailinable" if it was to qualify for T2. That is, it had to be written off or converted into common equity automatically when triggered without setting off repayment accelerations or bankruptcy. Advanced approaches banking organizations also have to phase out their Trust Preferred Securities [TruPS] from T2 by the end of 2021, beginning in 2016.

Table 1 provides an overview of the various additive components that, when fully implemented by 2019, may get as high as 16.5% for SIFIs, or 13% for those not subject to the SIFI surcharge, and 10.5% for those institutions not using the "advanced approaches" to the measurement of operational risks and hence not subject either to the on-again, off-again countercyclical buffer. Still, 16.5% by 2019 is twice as much as the highest possible minimum total capital ratio of 8% for all financial institutions still prevailing in 2015. For relatively small institutions using the standardized approach the increase would be far less, from 8% to 10.5%, over the same period. Hence big institutions are at a disadvantage to offset the benefits from the TBTF free-riding they enjoy. Only the Capital Conservation Buffer [CCB] that will rise to 2.5% of RWA by 2019 for all institutions is neutral in this regard. The CCB will be used to buffer a financial firm against violation of its CET1 requirements that would precipitate Prompt Corrective Action [PCA], meaning that the CCB will be available for use when needed. The cost of such use will be automatic restrictions on the payment of dividends and on other distributions, such as through stock buybacks. These restrictions rise with the extent to which the 2.5% buffer is reduced by a decline in CET1 below its 7% minimum. For instance, if the conservation buffer were down to 2% of standardized or advanced RWA, 60% of eligible income at most could be paid out, but the payout ratio would be only 20% if the buffer had been down to 1% of RWA. However, prudent financial firms might well choose to cut or suspend dividends under such conditions anyway, even if distributable funds are still

Table 1. Basel III Regulatory Capital Requirements in % of Risk-Weighted Assets for SIFIs

01/01 of year:	2015	2016	2017	2018	2019 & thereafter
Capital Conservation Buffer [CCB]—met by CET1		0.625%	1.25%	1.875%	2.5%
Minimum Common Equity Tier 1 [CET1] + CCB	4.5%	5.125%	5.75%	6.375%	7.0%
Minimum Tier 1 + CCB—met by CET1 and up to 1.5% by Additional Tier 1 [AT1]	6.0%	6.625%	7.25%	7.875%	8.5%
Minimum total capital + CCB (met by CET1) = CET1 + AT1 ≤ 1.5% + T2 ≤ 2%	8.0%	8.625%	9.25%	9.875%	10.5%
Individual SIFI[a] surcharge—met by addit. CET1		0.25%– 0.625%	0.50%–1.25%	0.75%– 1.875%	1%–2.5% Eventually 1%–3.5%
Countercyclical Buffer[b]—met by additional CET1		0%– 0.625%	0%–1.25%	0%– 1.875%	0%– 2.5%
Highest possible total min. in % of RWA	8.0%	9.875%	11.75%	13.625%	16.5%
Leverage Ratio[c]—met by existing T1		Ratio report begins	Implementation Decision	Basel III 3% ↔ US 5%–6%	5% for US G-SIBS, 6% their IDIs

[a] There were 8 US Global Systemically Important Banks [G-SIBs] among the 29 identified by the FSB (2013): JPM with 2.5% and Citigroup with 2% eventual bucket surcharge; Bank of America, Goldman Sachs, and Morgan Stanley with 1.5%; and Bank of New York Mellon, State Street Corp., and Wells Fargo with 1%. Nine Global Systemically Important Insurance Companies, G-IIs, incl. AIG and Metlife, have also been identified. National regulators are to identify D(o-mestic)-SIBs for imposing buffer surcharges.

[b] This buffer requirement is imposed with 12 months' notice at the discretion of national regulators to curb excessive credit growth. The buffer requirement can be met by CET1 and "other fully loss absorbing capital."

[c] "Advanced approaches" banking organizations face supplementary leverage ratios higher than the 3% minimum Basel III T1 leverage ratio proposed for all banks. Its denominator is the average of 3 month-ends total exposures. IDIs are Insured Deposit Taking Institutions.

available. Then such restrictions may add little to costs, particularly since the adverse signaling effect otherwise attaching to dividend reductions may be lessened when they follow automatically from the published CET1 ratio falling below 7% of RWA after 2018.

Looking at Citigroup's recent accounts reproduced in Table 2 can help make some of these relations more concrete. Under the pre-Basel III regulations still in effect for the second quarter of 2013, Citigroup reported T1/RWA of 13.3% and estimates that this ratio would be 17% lower, or 11%, if the post-transition Basel III regulations had been applied both in the estimation of CET1, the largest component of T1, and in that of the denominator, RWA. Since the weighted-average risk weight, RWA/TA, was 0.646, the leverage ratio with total assets [TA] in the denominator came out as 7.1%, more than 2 percentage points above the 5% that will eventually be required. Furthermore, comparing the actual data in Table 2 with the required levels of CET1/RWA, T1/RWA, and (T1+T2)/RWA in the second to fourth rows and last column of Table 1, shows that Citigroup's PCA ratios were all 2 percentage points or more above the required minimum. This made it appear "well capitalized" on all counts. Hence the point of these multiple minima, which differ in (risk) weighting and by coverage, may be to induce financial institutions to show that they can comfortably meet all of them. Hopefully each of these minima provides distinct safeguards that are needed in their own right and are not redundant.

Table 2 lists some deductions that are made from the book value of equity, to arrive at the regulatory CET1 total. The most important and controversial of these are (i) disallowed deferred tax assets [DTAs] from federal, state and local tax loss carry-forwards and (ii) timing differences implicit in the establishment of general loss reserves between the recognition of income for generally accepted accounting and tax purposes and net deductions that have not yet been taken on tax returns. These assets are clearly not immediately loss-absorbing for loss corporations in difficulties, but they could prove valuable when these difficulties pass before the loss carry-forwards have expired. The DTAs could also be valuable after an ownership change if the acquiring company can use

Table 2. Capital Ratios and Components under Prior and Basel III Regulations: Citigroup as of 06/30/2013

In billions of dollars	Regs as of 06/30/2013	Basel III Regs
Common Equity from Balance Sheet	192	192
Less: Disallowed deferred tax assets	40	45
Less: Goodwill and other disallowed intangible tax assets	27	30
Less: Omitted items (net)	(7)	(–)
Common Equity Tier 1 [CET1]	132	117
Additional Tier 1 Capital [AT1]	12	12
• Qualifying perpetual preferred stock	4	4
• Qualifying trust preferred securities	7	7
• Qualifying non-controlling interests	1	1
Tier 1 [T1] Capital ("Core Capital") T1 = CET1 + AT1	144	129
Tier 2 [T2] Capital	32	32
• Allowance for credit losses	14	14
• Qualifying subordinated debts	18	18
Total Capital (T1 + T2)	176	161
Total Risk-Weighted Assets [RWA]	1,084	1,168
Total Assets [TA] ($1,884 minus items excl. from T1)	1,824	1,809
Capital Ratios: CET1/RWA	12.2%	10.0%
T1/RWA	13.3%	11.0%
(T1 + T2)/RWA	16.2%	13.8%
Leverage Ratio: T1/TA	7.9%	7.1%
Avg. Risk Weight: RWA/TA	59.4%	64.6%

Notes: For advanced-approaches banking organizations—including all SIFIs—cumulative perpetual preferred stock, trust-preferred securities, and subordinated debts that are not automatically converted to equity or written off outside of bankruptcy when a specified trigger event occurs will no longer qualify as regulatory capital to any degree past year-end 2015 under Basel III. The phase-out process on eligibility is to leave time for replacement with more equity-like instruments meeting the Basel III requirements for AT1 and/or T2. Because AT1 and T2 were only reported under the (then) still prevailing standard, Basel 2.5, their Basel 2.5 values were adopted for Basel III without change. All other data are from Citigroup's Quarterly Report for the period ended June 30, 2013, pp. 40, 42. They show that all capital ratios are about 20% larger when estimated under Basel 2.5 than Basel III. Under the Advanced Measurement Approaches [AMA] applicable to Citigroup, banks develop their own empirical models and analyses to quantify the capital required for operational risk of loss resulting from inadequate or failed internal processes, people and systems, or from external events.

them to reduce its income taxes. However, Section 382 of the IRS Code, 26USC§382, strictly limits the net operating loss that can be claimed or carried back or forward after an ownership change. Hence there is ample justification for barring all or most of the DTA components from inclusion in CET1, as Basel III requires.

Because tax issues and inconsistent rulings also beset cocos, it is already useful here to segue to the related question of how such issues get resolved and what can be learned from an override of Section 382. According to that Section, "the Secretary [of the Treasury] shall prescribe such regulations as may be necessary or appropriate to carry out the purposes of section 382," and equally "to issue such regulations and other guidance as may be necessary or appropriate to carry out the purposes of EESA" (IRS, 2010). The latter is the Emergency Economic Stabilization Act of 2008 that included the Troubled Assets Relief Program, TARP, and another dose of executive-branch empowerment. The US Department of the Treasury has made full, and ultimately unchallenged, use of these authorities to promote the sale of the Treasury's one-third stake in Citigroup and to raise the value of its shares. It did so by having a notice issued that this sale, contrary to the exact terms specified in Section 382, did not constitute a change of ownership and that Citigroup thereby could keep roughly $38 billion of its DTAs. Notice 2010-2 in IRS (2010) describes this disappearance act as follows:

> For purposes of measuring shifts in ownership by any 5-percent shareholder on any testing date occurring on or after the date on which the issuing corporation redeems stock held by the Treasury that had been issued to Treasury pursuant to the [ESSA] Programs, the stock so redeemed shall be treated as if it had never been outstanding.

The take-away from this episode for Chapter 15 later on is that the Treasury can exercise broad authority to bend the tax code to its will to serve a 'higher' calling than equal treatment under the tax code across cases and its uniform application over time.

2.4 Basel III's Narrow Opening for Cocos

Having surveyed the components of regulatory capital required under Basel III finally leads up to the question of how cocos would fit into any of them. The cancellation of the cocos debt in conversion contributes to retained earnings or to reduced losses and thereby raises CET1 whether or not new shares of common stock are issued in conversion. The question that remains is whether cocos can contribute to AT1 and/or T2 when issued, so that they can help satisfy the "tier-1" and/or "total" capital-ratio requirements. We start with the position taken by the three US bank regulatory agencies (OCC, Fed & FDIC, 2012b, p. 52) on this matter:

> The agencies recognize that instruments classified as liabilities for accounting purposes could potentially be included in additional tier 1 [AT1] capital under Basel III. However... an instrument classified as a liability under GAAP would not qualify as [AT1] capital. The agencies believe that only allowing the inclusion of instruments classified as equity under GAAP in tier 1 capital would help strengthen the loss-absorption capabilities of [AT1] capital instruments ...

In the following year, these agencies (OCC & Fed, 2013a, p. 116) firmly rejected commenters' request to revise the rules to provide that contingent capital instruments will qualify as AT1, regardless of their treatment under GAAP. While cocos thus are disqualified for AT1 in the United States, it does appear that cocos of a particular design could satisfy the requirements for T2, and do so without being subject to quantitative limitations. For the agencies (OCC, Fed & FDIC, 2012b, p. 56) have proposed that there be "no limit on the amount of tier 2 capital that could be included in a banking organization's total capital" and that "existing limitations on term subordinated debt... within tier 2 would also be eliminated." However, "the agencies recognize that over time, capital instruments that are equivalent in quality and loss-absorption capacity to existing instruments may be created... and are proposing to consider the eligibility of such instruments on a case-by-case basis." It appears therefore that cocos with a remaining term to maturity of at least 5 years (that are callable and replaceable only after a minimum of 5 years from issuance and then only with permission of the relevant agency), and have one or more risk-based-capital and/or leverage-ratio triggers in addition to the non-viability trigger, would pass muster for being fully included in T2. The last of these triggers must be subject to activation by the US bank regulatory agencies and lead to cocos being written off or converted promptly into pre-authorized newly-issued shares of common stock.

While it appears from the discussion above that cocos are to be excluded from AT1 and hence T1 capital *in the United States*, it is nevertheless possible that they will be found qualified to contribute to the countercyclical buffer capital if "fully loss absorbing capital" other than CET1 should be identified by the BCBS as suitable for that purpose at the end of its ongoing review. However, unless such further guidance is provided, the countercyclical buffer will have to be met by CET1 only (BCBS, 2011c, pp. 58–59, incl. fn. 51) just like the Capital Conservation Buffer [CCB] and the SIFI surcharge, as shown in the first column of Table 1. Then, in the United States, cocos could contribute to meeting regulatory capital requirements only through T2, whose share in the total capital requirements *minimum*—though not in the total capital ratio to the extent it is above the minimum—is limited to 2 percentage points. In fact, the BCBS will "support the use of contingent capital to meet higher national loss absorbency requirements than the global requirement, as high-trigger contingent capital could help absorb losses on a going concern basis" (BCBS, 2011d, pp. 19–20).

Now the target level of the total capital ratio which a US global systemically important bank [G-SIB] might seek could well be 2 percentage points above the minimum so that it may be classified as "well capitalized." Then cocos might provide 4 percentage points of this above-minimum total capital ratio expressed as percentage of RWA. Expressed in percent of total assets [TA], 4 percentage points would shrink to a mere 2.6 if the average risk weight for US SIFIs under Basel III is like Citigroup's 64.6% (see Table 2). Hence the opening for cocos in the United States is quite narrow: They could amount at most to 2% to 3% of the balance sheet total of major financial institutions. Indeed, there may be no official welcome at all: in the United States, the Financial Stability Oversight Council (2012), established by the Dodd-Frank Wall Street Reform and Consumer Protection Act of 2010, had to submit a study to the US Congress regarding the feasibility, benefits, costs and structure of a contingent capital requirement for non-bank financial companies supervised by the Fed and for large, interconnected bank holding companies [BHCs]. That work declined to assign any place at all to cocos in the US regulatory capital framework, recommending "further study" by regulators instead.

Both the BIS and the EU do not share the US regulators' zeal for keeping cocos categorically out of AT1, ostensibly because they are not treated as equity under US Generally Accepted Accounting Principles [GAAP]. BCBS (2011c, p. 17) specifically defuses this issue by listing classification as liabilities for accounting purposes as compatible with including otherwise qualified cocos in AT1 capital:

> Instruments classified as liabilities for accounting purposes must have principal loss absorption through either (i) conversion to common shares at an objective pre-specified trigger point or (ii) a write-down mechanism which allocates losses to the instrument at a pre-specified trigger point. The write-down will have the following effects:
>
> a. Reduce the claim of the instrument in liquidation;
> b. Reduce the amount re-paid when a call is exercised; and
> c. Partially or fully reduce coupon/dividend payments on the instrument.

In addition, BCBS (2011c, p. 16) implies that gone-concern cocos are to be treated at least as equity- and not debt-like for "[t]he instrument cannot contribute to liabilities exceeding assets if such a balance-sheet test forms part of national insolvency law." The EU implementing regulations repeat the provisions just quoted almost verbatim except that they also allow for instruments being written down on a temporary, and not just permanent, basis (see EC, 2013, L176/49 Article 52: Additional Tier 1 Instruments, items (n) and (m)). Since contingently reversible write-downs act like a tax on recovery and recreate debt overhang and excessive leverage when write-up is activated in recovery from a crisis, we will not comment on this EU divergence any further or consider cocos with such a design feature. In all other respects, EU regulations, unlike US regulations, have faithfully implemented Basel III with regard to cocos.

Indeed, around May 1, 2013, the Spanish bank BBVA became the first European bank to sell cocos that qualified for AT1. Within less than a year, three banks headquartered in Australia, two each in Singapore, Canada, and France, one in Switzerland, the United Kingdom, and Brazil, and one more in Spain had followed as AT1 issuers; Moody's (2014) provides an overview. They qualified by being perpetual bonds paying interest that is discretionary and non-cumulative without defaulting, converting to common equity when triggered by one of their built-in triggers or under the point-of-non-viability trigger, and satisfying requirements for being classified AT1 capital in all other respects. US refusal to recognize T1 cocos leaves room for T2 cocos only so that the entire contribution that cocos can make to the minimum required total capital percentage is capped at 2 percentage points of RWA in the United States. The maximum contribution to the basic total regulatory capital percentage which cocos may make is quite limited even outside the United States. It amounts to 3.5% of RWA as the text table below shows. If the sum of the AT1 and T2 capital percentages filled by cocos is less, CET1 will have to be that much higher to bring the total capital percentage up to at least 8%.

**Components of Regulatory Capital Requirements
to be Met by January 1, 2019**

T1 = CET1+AT1	6% minimum	Tier 1 or Core Capital
CET1	4.5% minimum	Common Equity Tier 1
AT1	1.5% maximum	Additional Tier 1 Capital
T2	2% max., now unlimited	Tier 2 Capital
Total = T1 + T2	8% minimum	Total Regulatory Capital

The text table above has listed the components of regulatory capital discussed so far and their minimum or maximum in percent of RWA currently proposed for implementation by 2019. To be Basel-III compliant, national regulators and organizations such as the European Banking Authority [EBA] may set higher, but not lower, minimum capital requirements. The Swiss Financial Market Supervisory Authority [FINMA], for instance, has imposed a minimum CET1 requirement equal to 10%, by adding a 5.5% capital conservation buffer to the basic CET1 capital requirement of 4.5%. Countries such as Switzerland have argued that setting national capital requirements well above the Basel III levels is necessary because their banking system is so large relative to GDP as to create intolerably high fiscal exposure in a crisis. At year-end 2010, Switzerland's two dominant banks with global reach, Union Bank of Switzerland [UBS] and Credit Suisse [CS], together had bank assets—mostly globally booked—equal to about 425% of Switzerland's GDP and 38% of Switzerland's domestic credit market (FSB, 2012, p. 9). This made the two institutions TBTF if global and domestic economic stability was to be preserved but also too-big-to-save for the Swiss government and taxpayer. Hence the potential fiscal cost of the government's implicit TBTF guarantee had to be lowered to an affordable (and hence credible) level by taking much more drastic steps to reduce the probability of failure and the cost per failure than required in countries less specialized in the business of global finance.

Requiring financial institutions, in particular UBS and CS, to exceed the Basel III requirements and to invest in more self-insurance by holding more of their liabilities in a form that would yield assured loss absorbency outside of bankruptcy would serve this objective from the Swiss government's perspective. On the other hand, subsidiaries of foreign banks may shun establishment in Switzerland, and UBS and CS may shift more of their business to their subsidiaries elsewhere to evade the higher capital requirements of Switzerland. Conversely, foreign banks may begrudge their Swiss competitors' extra layer of prudential provisions and the resulting aura of super-safety known as "the Swiss finish." They may charge that Swiss banks, like UK banks now as well, may be using their national obligation to meet much higher capital requirements than mandated under Basel III to "unfair" reputational advantage. Another familiar argument for regulatory convergence is that banks are exposed to each other so that one bank's choice of exceptionally high capital ratios still leaves it exposed to counterparties' choice of lower ratios. Within Europe, however, national regulators are already able to impose systemic risk buffers of 1% to 3% of RWA for all exposures without seeking prior approval from the European Commission [EC]. In addition, national regulators may set their own countercyclical buffer percentages because the rate of credit growth and cyclical conditions may well differ between their countries. Thus a balance has been struck between the desire for a level playing field for banks and allowing for national differences in systemic risk exposure. Of course, individual financial institutions are always free to target much more than the obligatory minimum for their own reputation, resilience, and credit rating. Indeed the amount of capital in excess of required levels plays a crucial role in rating decisions as will be discussed and documented in Chapter 16.

Additional capital requirements have been proposed under Basel III for implementation at later dates. Some of these are intended to address the TBTF problem by depriving TBTF institutions of the funding advantage conferred by their status by imposing additional reserve requirements that must be met solely by CET1. Others are buffer capital requirements that may be drawn upon when financial institutions are in difficulty individually or collectively and regulators have issued the required findings and permissions. The three proposed additional capital requirements, only touched on so far, are

• A Capital Conservation Buffer equal to 2.5% of RWA. This buffer is mandatory for all financial institutions in that its decimation brings progressively more severe restrictions on discretionary distributions—such as dividend payments and stock buy-backs—and enhanced supervisory oversight.

- A *progressive* CET1 requirement for almost 30 current Global Systemically Important Banks [G-SIBs] that have been identified by the Financial Stability Board [FSB] each year since 2011 on the basis of their size, global cross-jurisdictional activity, complexity, and substitutability for the financial infrastructure provided. The FSB coordinates at the international level the work of financial authorities and international standard setting bodies and is hosted by the BIS in Basel, Switzerland. The G-SIB requirement may be viewed as a selective add-on to the capital conservation buffer of 2.5% which applies to all banks. The add-on ranges from 1% to 2.5% of RWA depending on the bank's systemic importance as judged by the four criteria listed above. An additional 1% could be applied to banks facing the highest G-SIB surcharge as a disincentive to increase their global systemic importance in the future, but this proposal may yet be withdrawn. Any G-SIB surcharge that survives would be intended to reduce the benefits of being TBTF by raising the cost of capital for the affected institutions and lowering the prospective costs to taxpayers to bail them out.

- The countercyclical CET1 buffer requirement may fluctuate in a range of 0 to 2.5% of RWA. It is applied *pro rata* by national authorities to all banks, foreign and domestic, having credit exposure in their jurisdiction. This countercyclical buffer requirement can be turned on or raised with 12 month notice or pre-announcement by national regulators, but switched off with immediate effect when regulators desire. That regulatory buffer capital may then be drawn upon in any subsequent downturn.

As expressed by Bolton and Samama (2012, p. 283), the concern is that "as the costs of building or maintaining a capital buffer fall in boom times and rise in recessions, bank lending may amplify … boom-and-bust cycles." In a downturn capital ratios tend to decline as profits and retained earnings fall off and provisions for identified future losses rise, crimping additions to CET1 in the numerator. Although this effect on the capital ratio is likely to dominate, assets become more risky and reclassifications of assets prompted by illiquidity and delinquency may boost RWA by increasing risk weights in the denominator. Hence capital ratios will decline, but it remains unclear whether the countercyclical buffer requirement can do much to reduce undesirable pro-cyclical effects.

If the capital ratio targeted by banks is 3 or more percentages above its "permanently" required level, they do not need to react to transitory changes in the countercyclical buffer requirement at all. For instance, if the countercyclical requirement is raised from 0 to say 2% in a particular national jurisdiction, well-capitalized banks could simply let the excess capital ratio above the required level shrink from 3 percentage points or more to 1 percentage point or more without feeling pressured to reduce lending. Since these banks would know that the countercyclical buffer requirement will come off in a downturn, they need not react to its imposition in an upturn. When that requirement does in fact come off and the targeted excess capital ratio of 3 or more percentage points is restored, there would be no special effort to increase lending.

Since all of these additional requirements as now proposed must be met by CET1 they do not provide an opening for cocos, although regulators' arguments for not allowing cocos to contribute to the *progressive* requirement for G-SIBs appear particularly peremptory. National regulators in some countries—such as the Swiss financial market supervisory authority FINMA—have begged to differ on the exclusion of cocos both from buffer capital and from the progressive component. FINMA requires Switzerland's two largest banks to maintain high-trigger cocos, which convert when CET1 has fallen to 7% of RWA or less in an amount equal to 3% of RWA, and low-trigger cocos in an amount of 6% of RWA. Given that FINMA requires CET1 holdings of at least 10% if dividend restrictions and other imposed capital conservation measures are to be avoided, conversion of all the high-trigger cocos would restore the financial firm to adequate capitalization. Should it nevertheless come later to conversion of gone-concern cocos with a low 5% trigger, the firm would get yet another lease on life, becoming again adequately capitalized as the CET1 ratio would jump from 5% to 11%. The write-off of the cocos debt in conversion would yield a boost to equity just when it is needed in a cyclical downturn to counter the decline in CET1/RWA stemming from industry-wide operating losses subtracting from the numerator and increased average risk weights adding to the denominator even while assets are being liquidated to reduce it.

Cocos would thus live up to their self-insurance rationale and contribute to *stabilizing* CET1 across the credit cycle in a way that merely requiring more CET1 to be built up on the upside in order to be drawn upon on the downside could not do. In addition, substituting cocos for otherwise comparable non-cocos debt would raise the leverage ratio when using T1 as the capital measure of the leverage ratio (see EC, 2011, Article 482, Sec. 2(d), p. 149) and if cocos were included in AT1. Also, compared with issuing more shares in lieu of cocos, the number of shares to be issued in a contingent conversion would not be considered in reporting fully diluted earnings until the remote contingency had materialized. This is correct to avoid distortions in financial reporting since it is the cocos debt cancellation that produces the increase in equity when conversion leads to newly-issued shares.

3
Cocos and the Struggle to Preserve Going-Concern Value

Contingent Convertible debt instruments are debt which comes with a contingent obligation to convert to common stock at a loss. This potentially costly obligation, to accept equity for more than it is worth when a designated trigger point for conversion has been reached, relegates cocos to the class of downside convertibles. Holders of Reverse Convertible Securities [RCS] and of catastrophe bonds and makers of Loss Equity Puts [LEP] share this downside exposure with investors in cocos: should bad things happen which they do not control, they lose.

To place cocos among a multitude of convertibles it is helpful to contrast them first with conventional upside convertibles, which are much more common than downside convertibles, and then to contrast cocos with RCS instruments and LEP options in this special class.

The conversion feature of upside convertibles is valued rather than feared by investors because it is an option that is not exercised unless it becomes profitable for them to do so prior to the maturity of the debt. Conversely, the automatic conversion of downside convertibles that occurs upon reaching a pre-specified trigger point relieves their issuers while causing holders some distress. The interest yield required on downside convertibles must therefore be higher than on otherwise comparable straight debt, while the opposite applies to upside convertible debt instruments. To be comparable in all major respects other than the holders' option to convert, the two types of debt would have to have the same or similar credit rating, (lack of) seniority, effective maturity, and liquidity.

Cocos are very different: they are essentially the reverse of the upside convertibles just described. Their purpose is to provide automatic debt relief to a company that is struggling after having fallen on hard times. Investors in these downside convertibles stand to lose when mandatory conversions are triggered by capital ratios falling below critical levels, as the replacement value of the common stock received will tend to be less than the face value of the cocos converted. Investors therefore require an interest rate on cocos that is higher than on otherwise comparable straight debt by the amount of the premium payable for accepting this unpleasant conversion risk. At given probabilities of conversion write-off-only cocos, which leave investors with nothing if triggered, would make this risk as costly as it can get.

Issuing cocos amounts to a company's purchase of some limited capital-access insurance against bankruptcy resolution. By this analogy, the conversion risk premium in the coco coupon payments is the periodic insurance premium payable by the company to investors in its cocos; the cancellation of the cocos debt in the event of conversion is analogous to an insurance settlement for the company. That settlement boosts the loss-absorbing equity capital just when such a boost is most needed to steer the company away from bankruptcy, but other means of raising capital are unavailable or at least highly dilutive. Upon conversion, ownership is initially divided between pre-existing shareholders and shareholders by conversion but the class of shares outstanding remains one and the same.

By comparing and contrasting other types of convertibles, all of the major features of cocos will be outlined in this chapter. This will be done to keep building up the Foundations by adding a portfolio perspective on cocos to Part I. Subsequent Parts will explore the rationale and design of each of these features and the controversies surrounding them. The final chapters will gauge the tax treatment, rating outcomes, and multinational regulations that will shape the future of this innovative, but still underutilized, instrument of financial reform.

3.1 Downside Convertibles:
Managing Conversion Price and Replacement

Because cocos represent the opposite of upside convertible debt with an embedded call option for investors, they resemble reverse convertible securities with an embedded put option for the management of the firm. Hence even though RCS are short-term coupon-bearing notes and cocos are long-term bonds, they otherwise have several features in common. Both types of downside convertibles may use a reference price based on the stock market price [MP_i] close to the time of cocos issue [subscript i] and both require a conversion price [CP] that is usually fixed at that time. For RCS, CP is equal to the reference price MP_i, and conversion [subscript c] is triggered when MP_c falls to the knock-in level, usually set at 70% to 80% of MP_i. Thus a 20% to 30% decline in the share price of common would bring on conversion that would leave the RCS holders 20% to 30% short of receiving the face value of the RCS from the shares received in conversion. This result would be anti-dilutive for pre-existing shareholders in that book value per share would rise when the RCS are converted and this debt is written off.

For some of the cocos actually issued, CP is equal to the market price per share of common stock at or around the time of issue, MP_i. The market price in the adverse time of cocos conversion, MP_c, is bound to be much lower than MP_i especially since cocos are best issued when the firm's balance sheet is strong, its stock price is high above book value per share, and capital insurance is cheap. Hence cocos holders can expect to suffer substantial losses years later in the unlikely event that conversion is eventually triggered. In this example, their actual loss upon conversion would equal $(1 - MP_c/MP_i)$ percent of the face amount of the cocos converted, where MP_c/MP_i is the replacement rate when $CP = MP_i$.

More generally, depending on the cocos covenant, issuers may set the CP not only at MP_i, but also at MP_c—whatever it may turn out to be after the public notice of conversion—or at a minimum level, CP_{min}. This minimum could be set to become binding when MP_c has fallen perhaps 50% below MP_i. In all of these cases, the number of common shares issued in conversion [N_c] is given by the face value [FV] of the debt instrument subject to conversion divided by the designated conversion price per share. Hence

N_c = FV/CP and FV = CP(N_c). Now the market price of these shares upon conversion is $MP_c N_c$, and their value relative to FV is $MP_c N_c$/FV = MP_c/CP after substituting for FV and cancelling N_c. Hence the higher the conversion price relative to the market price at conversion, the smaller the actual *replacement rate,* also called *recovery rate,* represented by MP_c/CP.

Contingent write-off-only debt securities issued in recent years have been classified as cocos, perhaps because their complete write-off amounts to the same as conversion at a CP that approaches infinity. True to the formula for N_c = FV/CP above, the outcome is that conversion yields no shares at all and the recovery rate is at its lower limit of zero. At the upper limit, if CP equals $E_i(MP_c)$, which is the value of MP_c based on expectations formed at the time of cocos issue [E_i], the originally expected replacement rate is 100%. That rate might occasionally even exceed 100% after the fact when the actual value of MP_c turns out to be greater than both $E_i(MP_c)$ and CP.

The trigger level aside, only a single policy-management variable, CP, is involved in setting the terms of conversion for any cocos to be issued, but CP sets N_c, the number of shares to be issued in conversion, and hence influences $E_i(MP_c)$. Financial communications tend to highlight CP rather than N_c; specifying either is sufficient since one implies the other, given FV. Anti-dilution provisions, when activated, provide for offsetting changes in CP and N_c from their initial setting, but cocos conversion does not trigger such adjustments nor is it necessarily dilutive in the value (rather than ownership) sense. Dilution of the value of the stake of pre-existing shareholders occurs only if conversion terms are such that equity grows proportionately less rapidly from the write-off of the cocos debt than the number of common shares outstanding increases from conversion.

Both of the two types of downside convertibles considered so far, RCS and Cocos, also contain a trigger whose level is chosen in part as a barrier against conversions not brought on by a pronounced deterioration in fundamentals but precipitated by transitory downturns and market "noise" instead. For RCS that trigger is usually 20–30% below the reference price, but the chosen drop percentage may be set higher for stocks with persistently above-average price volatility.

Conversion of cocos is not triggered by a specified minimum stock price decline below its reference level, although such a trigger has sometimes been recommended. If investors in cocos are to be attracted by a high expected replacement rate such as 80% of the face value of the cocos converted, it might be tempting to add an option for cocos holders to put their cocos for shares of common on conversion terms when the firm's MP_c has fallen to 0.8CP or less. Instead, the trigger can only be activated for now by a decline in the firm's capital ratio, derived from regulatory accounting, to or below a critical level. For going-concern cocos, the high-trigger level of the capital ratio defined as CET1/RWA has been set most often at 7% although levels up to 10% may become common for high-trigger cocos issued by G-SIBs after 2014. The minimum CET1 ratio to be maintained permanently from 2019 on by all other types of banks remains 7%. When that level is breached, the bank is likely to be under intense pressure to reduce leverage and the size of its balance sheet and exposure to risky assets. Nonetheless, conversion of cocos by itself does not change either RWA or TA. Hence capital and leverage ratios with these denominators are raised by conversion at the same percentage as the write-off of converted debt contributes to CET1.

3.1.1 *Comparative Advantages of Cocos vs. RCS*

These two downside convertibles both serve the purpose of helping the corporation brace for adversity. They do so by prepositioning contingent equity support from debt that is written off outside of bankruptcy when it must be converted into common equity according to its trigger and conversion terms. Cocos, like RCS, thus would provide supplementary capital self-insurance for the bank. Still there are differences in what each instrument does best.

RCS generally have conversion prices that are based on a short trailing average of market prices prevailing just before the time of issue, MP_i. Their mandatory conversion into common stock is triggered by stock market prices that are set 20% to 30% lower than that conversion price, i.e., equal to 0.7 to 0.8 of MP_i. Hence if a quick sale of the shares received in conversion is possible without moving the market price, the recovery rate is a reliable 70% to 80%. With cocos, CP can be set in such a way that the *expected* recovery rate, $E_i(MP_c)/CP$, is also equal to any chosen recovery-rate target. However, even an unbiased estimate of MP formed at the time of cocos issue may prove to be far off at the time of conversion. This makes the actual recovery rate on cocos after the announcement of conversion highly uncertain.

On the other hand, cocos are better equipped to directly address and meet the concerns of regulators about capital ratios that are in urgent need of being restored to at least adequate levels. Because the correlation between changes in the stock price and the capital ratio of a firm is only weakly positive, cocos have a clear advantage in this regard: They connect with the measures and system by which they are regulated and called to account.

3.1.2 *Connecting Cocos and LEPs*

Loss Equity Puts [LEPs] give the buyer the right to sell a fixed number of shares at a predetermined price if losses surpass a specified trigger level. A large decline in the bank's own share price around the time of exercise or conversion [MP_c] to a small fraction [s] of the stock market price prevailing at acquisition of the LEP and cocos issuance [MP_0] could be the trigger event that would allow the bank to put shares at an exercise price [XP] that is higher than $sMP_0 = MP_c$. To reveal the price relations that prevail between Cocos and LEPs, it is useful to simplify the exposition by assuming that the riskless interest rate is zero and that the conversion price on cocos is set equal to the strike price on the LEP, so that $XP = CP$, and both are then set equal to MP_0, as they could well be in practice. If the bank then had issued cocos contingently converting into N_c shares which had been put at MP_0 upon conversion, there would have been a net gain of $(MP_0 - MP_c) = (1 - s)$ MP_0 per share from the put that would have hedged the conversion loss to cocos holders of $(MP_c - MP_0) = -(1 - s)MP_0$ per share.

If arbitrage possibilities were perfect and financial markets complete, the implication would be that the bank's cost of buying the protection afforded by the LEPs under given conditions would be equal to the cost of the conversion risk premium paid to investors, a risk which exercise of the LEP would fully offset. However, this ability is based on cocos and LEPs being triggered at a common low market price of these shares whose level could be influenced appreciably by the actions of the bank buying LEPs for its own shares. More importantly, a stock price trigger would put cocos out of sync with Basel III and unable to perform predictably and reliably when needed to ward off regulatory intervention. Hence until the loss event referenced in LEPs is triggered by the same Basel III measures and contingencies as applied to cocos, their performance cannot realistically be compared.

3.2 History of Approaches to Bankruptcy Prevention and Resolution

The evolution of modern bankruptcy law and bankruptcy resolution practices that started in the Middle Ages shows how historical precedent, ideological predispositions, and strategic political objectives have shaped the contest between debtors and creditors in bankruptcy proceedings. Sgard (2013) has masterfully laid out the shifting balances that have been struck between the different interests during the formative stages of capitalism in 17th and 18th century Europe. If the economic order as a whole or "the whole population of market participants" as Sgard (2013, p. 223) puts it, is considered the most important,

> then bankruptcy should work, first of all, on an *ex ante* basis; i.e., it should make clear that bad decisions involve high costs, so that managers think twice before adding more risk to their balance sheets. The harsher the treatment of bankrupts, the better; market discipline would be stronger, microeconomic decision closer to optimum, and welfare higher; or so the argument runs.

Alternately, lawmakers have also pursued a laissez-faire approach that leaves individual debtors and creditors in charge of resolving insolvencies. They are allowed to bargain *ex post* and adopt the solution to their own default that best suits their interests, and they may even agree on a clean slate affording a fresh start. The downside risk is that the expectation of an easier way out of default may cause moral hazard, hence a weakening of market discipline and a looser pattern of capital allocation (Sgard, 2013, p. 223).

The *ex post* approach was supported in France by traditional acceptance of judicial confirmation of majority votes among creditors as a means of controlling holdout investors. This reduced transaction costs and offered alternatives to the destruction of going-concern value such as forbearance, partial debt forgiveness, and other means of continuation and restructuring, well before collective-action clauses were formalized in debt contracts. Providing a judicial platform for private bargaining "assumed that supporting continuation arrangements was positive both in private and collective terms" (Sgard, 2013, p. 224).

Even without the support of such a platform, a debtor could avoid being adjudicated as a bankrupt and shielded from further arrest and seizure in seventeenth century France if she ceded all her goods and assets to her creditors *voluntarily*. The creditors then proceeded to sell them and share the return among themselves on a *pro rata* basis (Sgard, 2013, p. 227). Whether or not the sales proceeds more than covered the face value of the debt, all sales proceeds would accrue to the new owners under this cession; the original owners would be wiped out, but would be free to start afresh. If any residual surplus had to be returned to the original owners instead, the replacement rate on the converted debt would have been capped at 100% and ownership after conversion would be apportioned between the original owners and the new owners. The same outcome for the former cocos holders and pre-existing shareholders would result outside of bankruptcy from the conversion of cocos under the method that sets the conversion price per common share equal to its market value around the time of conversion. This would yield a 100% replacement rate on cocos as previously described.

In seventeenth century England, on the other hand, Sgard (2013, pp. 224, 228) continues, bankruptcy became a single-entry, single-exit process that led exclusively to liquidation. "It worked, therefore, as a debt collection instrument, often a harsh one, that did not support businesses that had suffered a liquidity shock while remaining intrinsically solvent. Entrepreneurs had to be careful and limit risk-taking." Unpaid debt remaining from any bankruptcy liquidation would not be forgiven and would hang over any new resource acquisition.

Skeel (2001, p. 43) claims that "the generally debtor-friendly approach to bankruptcy, and the primacy of lawyers rather than an administrator distinguish US bankruptcy law from every other insolvency law in the world." He further notes that "rather than a creditor collection device, as most previous bankruptcy laws had been, the first permanent US law would be as sympathetic to debtors' interests as to those of creditors... In contrast to England, where a governmental official plays a pervasive role, the referees under the 1898 act would have little incentive to get actively involved; and the process would be left largely to the parties themselves." Skeel thus describes as exceptional a US approach to debtors' workout from bankruptcy whose basic characteristics Sgard found to have prevailed already in France two centuries earlier.

Set against this background, going-concern cocos combine the purpose of the *ex post* approach, which is to help avert bankruptcy, with some of the prospective deterrent effect expected from the unrelenting creditor-rights enforcement of the *ex ante* approach. Thus the holders of write-down-only cocos have contracted to lose everything outside of bankruptcy, and before all other claimants, when their claims are cancelled in conversion. Self-interest will thus make them highly vigilant. This helps preserve going-concern value and lower risk for all others both *ex ante* and through cancellation of the cocos debt should their holders be wiped out after all. At the other extreme, conversion terms can be such that cocos holders are promised the full face value of cocos in the form of common shares when conversion is triggered, unless the market price per share after the announcement of conversion is less than a specified minimum. Assuming the minimum is not binding at conversion, the *ownership* stake of pre-existing shareholders could stand to be severely diluted, being largely assumed by the former cocos holders. Cocos holders get the principal repaid with interest in the form of common stock, and all other debt holders benefit from having cocos on the balance sheet, because cocos debt is the most junior—and hence ahead of them to convert—when misfortune strikes. Cocos with a recovery rate for their holders away from either extreme may thus combine the best elements of what Sgard characterized as *ex ante* deterrence and *ex post* survival approaches.

In between these extremes where cocos holders in the event of conversion lose everything ($\rho = 0$) or nothing ($\rho = 1$), there are more incentive-compatible conversion terms. These involve actual conversion into a specified number of common shares that is set so that cocos holders can expect to suffer a substantial haircut at conversion of around 20%. Investors in cocos would demand a conversion risk premium that is greater as the replacement rate expected from the number of shares received in conversion is lower and the probability of conversion is higher. Once invested, they would use their influence on management to temper risks so as to bring down, or at least stabilize, the probability of conversion. Pre-existing shareholders, on the other hand, would benefit from any excess of the percentage increase in equity value in the firm over the percentage increase in the number of shares outstanding after cocos conversion. They would therefore obtain some relief from the downward spiral that had triggered conversion in the first place. This would keep them interested in having cocos issued by the firm on capital-insurance grounds in the first place, and even more so if cocos can be issued at an interest rate that lowers the after-tax cost of capital overall.

If such an interest rate is accepted in the market, cocos holders and all holders of more senior debt—as well as pre-existing shareholders—could come to agree among themselves to the issuance of cocos and to the conditions of settlement in the event of their conversion. There would be no owner and creditor committees confronting debtors in continuation negotiations and proceedings that may drag on under court supervision while going-concern value declines. Instead, the non-negotiable pre-arranged automaticity of cocos conversion is supposed to mean that help from an equity injection is sure to be available when needed, provided its trigger level has been set high enough for timely debt relief that avoids dismemberment or other wasteful enforcement of bankruptcy.

However, if even the cancellation of all of the bank's outstanding cocos debt would be patently insufficient to save the company, that immediate and complete write-down may come into question as bankruptcy protocols take over. In the United States, contemporary adjudications tend to focus on 'equitable' burden sharing by stockholders and a wide range of creditors of the firm with only limited respect for contractual seniority of debt claims and degrees of subordination. Hence the disciplining effect of an instrument like write-down-only cocos—that appears strong *ex ante*—is undercut when its provisions are regarded as not fully credible because judges and regulators introduce time-inconsistency *ex post*. As the next chapter will demonstrate, preservation of going-concern value may not be their paramount concern.

4

The Treatment of TBTF Financial Institutions in the Last Crisis

When Systemically Important Financial Institutions [SIFIs], then called Too Big to Fail [TBTF], get into trouble as they periodically do, there are a number of ways to deal with them. Several of these approaches to problem resolution have been applied during the financial crisis of 2007–2009 with varying degrees of success to SIFIs and lesser institutions in the United States. Among the past resolutions scrutinized for clues to improved practices are those of the Investment Banks Bear Stearns, Lehman Brothers, and Merrill Lynch, and Savings Bank and S&L Association Holding Companies principally engaged in mortgage banking, Countrywide, Wachovia, and Washington Mutual.

4.1 Disorderly Fragmentation before Liquidation

Lehman Brothers' emergency filing for Chapter 11 bankruptcy protection on September 15, 2008 represents the worst approach to resolution of those considered here. "What makes things break up like they do?" asks Ralph in *Lord of the Flies*. Deliberate break-up into newly formed entities may be feasible in quiet times to reduce the size and number of financial institutions that are TBTF. Crisis resolutions tend to have the opposite effect of increasing concentration in banking; it is next to impossible, however, to preserve going-concern value in failing companies when parts of them are hastily excised and thrown on the block in death-bed negotiations. As former Treasury Secretary Henry Paulson said to Ross Sorkin in an interview published in the *New York Times* on August 27, 2013:

> No bank should be too big or too complex to fail, but almost any bank is too big to liquidate quickly, particularly in the midst of a crisis.

Even worse than expected, Lehman's disorderly collapse desta-
bilized counterparties and disrupted business networks and the
normal functioning of financial markets. Commenting on the debacle five years later on September 15, 2013, Alan Blinder—Vice
Chairman of the Federal Reserve Board of Governors in the mid-
1990s—said on National Public Radio (US-NPR) that "the beginning of the Great Recession was the day Lehman failed." Since
then there has been much revisionism from those who would shun
responsibility by describing the crisis events as having an unstop-
pable and unforeseeable "tsunami" cause. It took Lehman Brothers Holdings, Inc. until March 2012 (42 months) to emerge from
bankruptcy. It did so as a liquidating company whose main activity was paying back a total of about $65 billion to its creditors who
have asserted more than $300 billion in claims. As reported by
Reuters on March 6, 2012, the recovery rate from a series of distributions—the first of which took place in April 2012 and the fifth in
April 2014 —may eventually reach a paltry 21%, or a little more
in individual cases depending on the seniority of the debt. In the
meantime, the monthly outlay for lawyers, advisers, and managers
has been as high as $150 million (Reuters, January 31, 2013), or
about $7 million per business day, a comfortable retainer.

The direct loss of value that may be attributed to the workout
under bankruptcy alone—not counting the losses leading up to it,
or the potentially huge indirect industry and economy-wide losses
that followed—can be triangulated crudely in a few steps. The
first is to consider the book value of $20 billion, which is the dif-
ference between the $639 billion in assets and $619 billion in debt
reported in the bankruptcy filing of Monday, September 15, 2008.
The other two pieces of information are the actual or 'fair' market
values of Lehman Brothers just preceding the bankruptcy filing.
At the end of August 2008, Lehman Brothers gave 691 million as
the total number of its diluted shares outstanding. The stock price
had fallen from over $65 in January 2008 to $3.65 at the close on
September 12. Hence the actual market value of Lehman Brothers
on that day was about $2.5 billion. A few days earlier, Lehman
Brothers' CEO Dick Fuld had rejected the adequacy of a share

price in the "low single digits" by cursing: "Bear Stearns got $10 a share, there is *no* [expletive here omitted] way I will sell this firm for less" (Sorkin, 2009, p. 230). Hence combining the actual with the "fair" market price (or at least Fuld's notion of it) would yield an estimate of between $2.5 billion and $6.9 billion as the value of Lehman Brothers on the verge of bankruptcy.

Losses did not stop there. Even before the resolution process had run its multi-year course, the remaining equity value had turned negative as indicated by the above-mentioned deficiency of about $235 billion in the repayment of credits. This huge shortfall, which amounted to 37% of the total assets of $639 billion reported at the bankruptcy filing, may be attributed in large part to the unfortunate choice of the resolution process least suitable for SIFIs in difficulties: disorderly break-up and piecemeal liquidation.

Quoting from the FDIC *Resolutions Manual* (FDIC, n.d., pp. 68–69) shows how little has changed in the delays and outcomes of resolution when following the Lehman Brothers' track, except that FDIC-insured deposits are now fully protected up to the coverage limit and available without long waits.

> In general practice, between 1865 and 1933, depositors of national and state banks were treated in the same way as other creditors—they received funds from the liquidation of the bank's assets *after* those assets were liquidated. On average, it took about six years at the federal level to liquidate a failed bank's assets, to pay the depositors, and to close the bank's books... Even when depositors did ultimately receive their funds, the amounts were significantly less than they had originally deposited into the banks. From 1921 through 1930, 1,200 banks failed and depositors got [on average about 60%] of their deposits back.

Paulson (2010, p. 209) claims that the Fed had no way to do better due to a lack of authority to guarantee Lehman's liabilities or to undertake other effective rescue measures. As an investment bank, Lehman's supervisor was the United States Securities and Exchange Commission [SEC]. Its Chairman until January 2009 was Christopher Cox. Ben Bernanke was about to enter his second term as Chairman of the Board of Governors of the Federal Reserve System, and Tim Geithner, before becoming Secretary of the Treasury in January 2009, was President of the Federal Reserve Bank of New York which conducts the US Government's financing operations for the System. At this pivotal moment of the financial crisis, Bernanke and Geithner chose not to broaden their appeal for emergency powers to extend credit to a systemically important investment bank even though such authority might have been derived from Section 13(3) of the Federal Reserve Act. The Fed had stretched the limits of its authority earlier, in March 2008, when assisting with JPMorgan Chase's absorption of Bear Stearns and would do so again when bailing out the American International Group [AIG] on September 16, 2008, the day after the official beginning of Lehman Brothers' bankruptcy debacle. For the latter, however, the Federal Reserve in New York and Washington declined to fund either a takeover or an orderly winddown process. It had decided by September 14, 2008, as the post-bankruptcy strategy was being formulated, that it could and would lend directly to the Lehman broker-dealer arm to enable it to unwind its repo positions (Paulson, 2010, pp. 215–216).

Even though the federal government provided only limited short-term help to buy a little more time for Lehman to dispose of itself, taxpayers did not remain unscathed. Rather, they were burdened certainly no less than they would have been by the cost of a bailout or subsidized merger that would have preserved going-concern value. Letting Lehman abjectly fail deepened the economic damage wrought by the financial crisis. That set off automatic effects and fiscal policy responses that greatly increased government deficits at all levels. As reported by the US Bureau of Economic Analysis, the federal government's net borrowing alone surged from $355 billion in 2007 to $1,510 billion in 2010. The cumulative increase in net borrowing outstanding from the end of 2007 to that of 2010 was $3,768 billion. If only 10% of this increase in net federal government debt—debt that burdens current and future generations—is attributable to the way Lehman's insolvency was left to play out, it would have been highly profitable for the government to rescue Lehman instead. $377 billion in bailout outlays on Lehman would surely have been enough several times over: it would have been more than double the $182 billion dispensed in the most expensive US government bailout of a financial firm, that of AIG (see http://en.wikipedia.org/Maiden_Lane_LLC).

Most of the government's emergency capital injections were eventually recovered, after being converted from cumulative to non-cumulative preferred stock and then to common-equity, as was the practice with the "rubber contracts" under the Treasury's Troubled Asset Relief Program [TARP] (see von Furstenberg, 2009, pp. 71–72). TARP became law on October 3, 2008 originally with the authority to spend up to $700 billion. $431 billion of this was actually disbursed according to the Congressional Budget Office (CBO, 2012), though not to purchase troubled assets but to make capital injections. When the total amount recovered began to exceed the amounts originally disbursed after four years, the program was trumpeted as having made an *ex post* accounting "profit" for the government, falsely implying that there was no subsidy cost. The program in fact provided TBTF subsidies to financial institutions from start to finish as they got credit or equity injections that would not have been available from any other source on such easy, successively sweetened, terms. Hence the government's risk bearing was not sufficiently compensated *ex ante*, and therein lies the subsidy cost to the government and the benefit doled out to private financial institutions.

4.2 FDIC Receivership: A Superior Resolution Model?

In an institutionally self-serving (but fairly convincing) feature article, staff of the FDIC (2011) attempted to cost out a counterfactual under which Lehman Brothers Inc. would have been resolved by the FDIC as receiver. Assigning this task to the FDIC would have been in line with the Dodd-Frank Act which was signed into law in July 2010. Under Title II of that Act, summarized in ABA (2010b), Federal authorities will be able to place covered financial companies, in particular large Bank Holding Companies [BHCs] and Significant Non-Banks, in receivership under Federal control rather than leaving them to be resolved under Chapter 11 reorganization or Chapter 7 liquidation under the US Bankruptcy Code. Under Title II, the Federal Reserve and the FDIC are responsible for deciding whether to recommend to the Treasury Secretary that the FDIC be appointed as receiver for a troubled financial company. If so appointed, the FDIC is given a wide range of powers and accorded significant deference to carry out its receivership and resolution functions and to decide what the resolution approach will be.

In deciding on the disposition of assets, the FDIC is to be mindful of the objectives of maximizing the net present value obtained from any sale or disposition while also mitigating the potential for serious adverse effects to the financial system as a whole and ensuring fair treatment of bidders. For instance, to facilitate prompt acquisition by a single party most able to benefit from maintaining the going-concern value of an institution in receivership, the FDIC may agree to loss-sharing on defined pools of assets, or to an acquisition which excludes these pools of bad assets.

The FDIC study (2011, pp. 15, 18) thus reported that the troubled assets of Lehman Brothers had been valued at between $50 and $70 billion (say $60 billion) in book value prior to markdown by potential acquirers conducting due-diligence assessments. Potential acquirers balked when they realized that losses on these troubled assets could be around $40 billion. The FDIC would therefore have to make Lehman Brothers fit for sale out of receivership by cleaning up its balance sheet at no cost to the taxpayer. It could have done so by reducing the book value of Lehman's troubled assets from $60 billion to $20 billion while also reducing its liabilities by $40 billion via bail-in. The Dodd-Frank Act requires that losses in receivership are to be borne by equity holders and unsecured creditors so that there will be no bailout. Thus, in the FDIC study, existing shareholders would have absorbed $20 billion of losses, holders of subordinated debt also would have lost their entire stake, of $15 billion, and general unsecured creditors would have lost the remaining $5 billion out of

$175 billion in face value. After marking the troubled assets of $60 billion down to fair value, the assets of the company would have fallen from $210 billion to $170 billion, just enough to allow assumption of the surviving $170 billion of general unsecured debt by an acquiring company.

If a potential acquirer from among the several candidates who had conducted due diligence on Lehman had been willing to pay anything at all for its going-concern value after its balance sheet had been cleaned up and shrunk, the FDIC would have realized value that could help cover its administrative expenses as receiver. Its claims have the highest priority among unsecured claims against the covered financial company. Hence in this telling, Lehman Brothers and its shareholders would still be gone and so would its subordinated debt and a small percentage of its unsecured debt, but neither taxpayers nor the FDIC would have to absorb any losses. Under FDIC receivership, Lehman Brothers could have been sold and liquidated at no cost to the government and with a much higher recovery value for general unsecured creditors than achieved under bankruptcy. Since, as portrayed above, there would have been no equity in the corporation to be acquired, the capital ratio of the combined entity, after the takeover, would have been depressed. To succeed, the corporate acquirer would, therefore, have to be in a position to raise equity capital quickly in order to adequately capitalize the new behemoth just created.

If preserving the going-concern value of Lehman in FDIC receivership would have cost investors and creditors $40 billion while the government—and hence the taxpayers—would have saved perhaps as much as $377 billion by avoiding the fiscal fallout from its disorderly break-up, the conjectural benefit to cost ratio would have been over 9. This number would rise by several multiples if not only the fiscal savings but some of the economic savings from avoiding the disorderly break-up of Lehman were counted as benefits. To get down to $40 billion assumes, however, that Lehman needed to be strengthened only by so much as to be fit for takeover by a stronger bank. Otherwise, $40 billion might not be nearly enough to disperse the cloud of suspicion hanging over Lehman and threatening its continued funding. Potential acquirers, Barclays Bank and Bank of America among them, had serious and rapidly escalating problems of their own. Hence it is unclear whether the assisted acquisition of Lehman by another SIFI—rather than shoring up the going-concern value of what had been Lehman as intended—would not have dragged both of them down.

In fact, the record of resolution through government-brokered whole mergers is mixed. Several bailouts of large US financial institutions principally involving the Federal Reserve Chairman, the Secretary of the Treasury, and the Treasury's Office of the Comptroller of the Currency [OCC] avoided breakup by facilitating the takeover of most or all of the institution that was to be kept from failing. Some of the takeover deals were not honored when a better offer was received for the company, such as the acquisition of Wachovia Corporation by ailing Citigroup, where the government would have covered any losses on Wachovia's mortgage portfolio in excess of $42 billion. Thus on October 3, 2008 Wells Fargo clinched a deal to buy Wachovia for $15.4 billion without requiring a backstop by the FDIC, paying $7 per share, while Citigroup had intended to spend only two-thirds as much on this deal.

Other hasty mergers proved disastrous for the acquirer. As the *New York Post* reported on January 8, 2013, the $4.1 billion cost of Bank of America's acquisition of Countrywide and its toxic portfolio on January 11, 2008 had ballooned to $47 billion by January 2013 and these costs were still growing. It was also reported that "Bank of America was threatened with the firings of the management and Board as well as [damage to] the relationship between the bank and federal regulators if Bank of America did not go through with the acquisition of Merrill Lynch" (en. wikipedia.org/wiki/Merrill_Lynch). In September 2012, Bank of America agreed to settle with shareholders who accused it of misleading them on the financial health of Merrill Lynch when it was purchased pursuant to an agreement reached on September 15, 2008. While unexpected losses initially mounted on this acquisition, Merrill Lynch has since proved "somewhat fruitful" for the bank according to *Forbes* Magazine and not comparable to Bank of America's acquisition of Countrywide. The same article in the September 28, 2012 issue described the latter as "arguably the worst acquisition in history."

What all these government-brokered mergers have in common is non-transparent, inconsistent, crude, cunning, and potentially corrupt price discovery under intense pressure from various quarters. There was an agreement to pay $2 per share of Bear Stearns, but JPMorgan chose to raise that price to $10 per share in a hurry. What would have been left of Wachovia after the cherry-picking by Citigroup was estimated to be worth about $2 per share according to the *Wall Street Journal* of October 4, 2008, but it was ultimately acquired by Wells Fargo for $7 a share. Bank of America's federally strong-armed acquisition of Merrill Lynch occurred at a price of $29 per share. One need not get too exercised over such government tactics since SIFIs try to browbeat and co-opt federal regulators all the time, using the clout that comes from being too big, too interconnected, too irreplaceable, etc. to fail. Yet $29 per share represented a premium of 70% over the September 12, 2008 closing price and 38% over Merrill's book value of $21 a share. Such large premiums appear extravagant and suspicious when paid for the stock of a failing company.

The FDIC has delivered more acceptable results in some of these regards. This may explain why the resolution procedures envisaged in the Dodd-Frank Act lean toward receivership rather than the bankruptcy model. When a chartering authority closes a bank and appoints the FDIC as receiver, the clash of competing public/private interests, the chaos of heated negotiations with changing partners, and the room for gamesmanship through legal interventions are much reduced. In particular, as the FDIC's *Resolutions Handbook* (FDIC, n.d., pp. 67–75) continues to explain, courts are prohibited from issuing injunctions or similar relief to restrain the FDIC as receiver from completing its resolution and liquidation activities. Federal and state executive agencies may not interfere with these FDIC activities either.

A receivership is designed to market the assets of a failed institution, liquidate them, and distribute the proceeds to the institution's creditors which include uninsured depositors. A receiver also has the power to merge a failed institution with another depository institution and to transfer its assets and liabilities *without the approval of any other agency, court, or party.* Furthermore, a receiver may form a new institution, such as a bridge bank, to take over the assets and liabilities of the failed institution.

Equipped with these powers and privileges and a mandate to seek resolution at the least direct and follow-on costs to the deposit insurance fund—a fund backstopped by a $100 billion line of credit from the US Treasury Department—the FDIC has performed well not only with small and medium-sized FDIC-insured institutions, but has showcased resolution through receivership even for large institutions such as Washington Mutual Bank which was seized by the FDIC on September 25, 2008. Its holding company, Washington Mutual Inc. [WMI], stripped of its main asset, filed for bankruptcy the next day. JP-Morgan Chase acquired the assets, assumed the qualified financial (i.e., derivative) contracts, and made a payment of $1.9 billion. According to the FDIC's press release of September 25, 2008 on the matter, "WaMu's balance sheet and the payment [made] by JPMorgan Chase allowed a transaction in which neither uninsured depositors nor the insurance fund absorbed any losses." Prompt resolution thus was achieved by wiping out stockholders of WMI and subordinated debt holders of the bank without any of the visible costs of a federal bailout of either the bank or of the FDIC Deposit Insurance Fund on account of any assistance to the Bank. Hence the main elements of the storyline in the FDIC's counterfactual account of Lehman Brothers resolution under receivership can be corroborated.

5

Strategic Policy Objectives in Privatizing the TBTF Backstop

For centuries most major economic crises in financially developed countries and principalities have been preceded and/or accompanied by financial crises—including waves of default and loss of capital—affecting banks and their counterparties. Over time, these crises and their disruption of financial intermediation and capital flows have spread far beyond their point of origin and afflicted entire regions, even the world economy. This has saddled policymakers with the task of guarding against and attempting to counteract financial crises of both foreign and domestic origin with the limited fiscal and monetary policy resources at their disposal. Cocos would be a useful addition to this arsenal because they could provide contingent capital infusions without undesirable side-effects or after-effects, although their sustainability through timely replacement after conversion remains a challenge. Continued issuance is likely to be least available for write-down-only cocos once they have left their holders badly burnt.

The combined result of financially triggered and amplified economic crises has been an increase in the central government's debt load. Reinhart and Rogoff (2009a, p. 471) found that such debt on average had grown by 86% over the three years following the onset of deep financial crises that occurred between the end of World War II and 2006. The financial crisis that started in 2007 was not included in that average; what happened in that crisis will now be compared with what happened on average before.

5.1 The 2007–2009 Financial Crisis:
Portfolio and Policy Responses

Between year-ends 2007 and 2010, the US gross federal debt outstanding increased by 51% to 94.3% of GDP. The portion held by government entities rose by 15% and the portion held by the public by 79% to 62.9% of GDP, all based on nominal dollars. According to the *Economic Report of the President* (2013, Tables B-78 and B-79), US government receipts fell by 16% over this period to 15.1% of GDP, while outlays rose 27% to 24.1% of GDP. The main contributors to the yawning federal government deficit, which had peaked at 10.1% of GDP in 2009 before dropping to 9% in 2010, were the automatic effects of recession that were reinforced by discretionary policy measures such as tax cut and stimulus-spending programs. Assuming 2% real economic growth and 2% inflation, the deficit would have to fall to 4% of GDP or less for the debt-to-GDP ratio to stop rising and begin to decline. In addition Reinhart and Rogoff (2010, p. 575) and Reinhart, Reinhart and Rogoff (2012, p. 81) found, and continue to maintain after making corrections, that median growth is about 1 percentage point less for countries with debt-to-GDP ratios of more than 90% than those with ratios below that threshold.

Worse yet, this reduction in the growth rate is likely to persist. Once the gross federal debt ratio has remained in excess of 90% of GDP for at least 5 years, as it has in the United States already for 2010–2014, debt overhang becomes recalcitrant and forbiddingly difficult to tackle politically. The Reinhart, Reinhart and Rogoff (2012, pp. 78–81) sample of 26 historical episodes from different countries suggests that such a debt overhang may well last another 15 to 20 years before fiscal sustainability is restored. This persistence is not generally due to continuing out-year bailout costs because the bailouts do not provide up-front cash grants so much as loans and equity injections by the government. These give rise to debt repayments and receipts from re-privatization for the government when the bailout has succeeded in saving a TBTF institution.

Quantitative Easing [QE] is another legacy principally brought on by policy responses to the 2007–2009 financial crisis which will take many years to unwind, assuming there is sufficient pressure from sharply rising inflation to do so at all. The first wave of QE was started by the Federal Reserve [Fed] in January 2009, one month after the Federal funds rate had been brought down essentially to zero in the United States; the UK began QE purchases of gilts later that year. These operations have taken off the market a substantial part of the net issue of both medium-term and long-term government securities, capped at 70% in the UK, and most of the flow supply of (residential) mortgage-backed securities [(R)MBS] guaranteed by US government agencies. The US agencies most involved, government-owned since September 2008, are known as Fannie Mae and Freddie Mac. From the end of 2007 to year-end 2013, the balance sheet of the Fed quadrupled from around $1 trillion to $4 trillion, with the increase of $3 trillion about equally split between longer-dated Treasury notes (5-years or more) and bonds and MBS. The European Central Bank [ECB] added about €1.5 trillion ($2 trillion), thereby doubling its total assets from the end of 2007 to the summer of 2012 before pulling back, with most of the increase taking the form of claims on euro area depository institutions in part due to the on-going euro crisis. By the end of 2013, the Bank of England had acquired about £0.375 trillion ($0.6 trillion) through gilt purchases net of redemptions by its Asset Purchase Facility. The Bank of Japan accelerated its purchases of government debt in 2013 to reduce interest rates on long-term obligations even further and to depress the exchange value of the yen. Especially for countries other than the United States, the interest rate intervention and long-term interest rate depression intended by QE cannot neatly be separated from un-sterilized exchange-rate intervention designed to induce depreciation—or resist appreciation—of the domestic currency against the US dollar and currencies of major trading partners.

The inflationary potential of QE at least until 2014 was restrained by the willingness of member banks to hold ever larger excess reserves, many times more than required, with the central bank. This could only happen in an environment of very low inflation in which safely deposited or lent liquid balances denominated in the leading currencies paid hardly any nominal interest at all. To maintain this willingness of member banks to keep their reserves idle, the Fed would have to keep the rate it pays on them very close to the federal funds rate, which is what major banks get on overnight loans to each other as long as there is no appreciable repayment risk. Excess reserves have risen from next to nothing at year-end 2007 to $2.4 trillion by the end of 2013.

Given the maturity mismatch between the Fed's reserve liabilities to member banks and its holdings of long-term government-related debt, any rise in the federal funds rate that may become necessary to restrain inflation would reduce the Fed's earnings spread by raising its cost of funds. That spread has allowed it to gross close to $100 billion in 2012 alone, $89 billion of which was transferred in quarterly installments classified as "miscellaneous receipts" to the US Treasury for 2012. A little less, $78 billion, was transferred for 2013. Taking this figure and dividing by the average of daily figures for "securities held outright" for the week ended January 1, 2014 in the Fed's H.4.1 release yields 2.07% as the low estimate of the transferable earnings spread of the Fed. Dividing by the corresponding year-end 2012 rather that 2013 figure instead, which is also only about 7% below the figure for "reserve bank credit" and now approximated by the average of daily figures for the week ended January 2, 2013, the percentage is 2.93% for the high estimate. Hence the earnings spread of the Fed on the securities it held in 2013 was 2% to 3%.

If the Fed needs to raise the federal funds rate from almost 0% to a normal level of 4% or more to keep the rate of inflation in the neighborhood of 2% and the real interest rate positive, the term structure of interest rates will rise unevenly and flatten out. Given the previous range of estimates of the Fed's net earnings spread, such a development could leave it with a politically unpopular operating deficit after meeting its own expenses. The Fed's unaccustomed and most unwelcome contribution to increasing—rather than decreasing—the government deficit could then undermine its reputation; it could become dependent on Treasury subsidies, jeopardizing its independence. A prospective Fed deficit might also stoke fears that it would raise its inflation target, or simply tolerate or seek higher inflation unannounced, although raising the expected inflation rate would not be effective in addressing the Fed's (or the nation's) fiscal sustainability issues.

The Fed would have to realize capital losses on sales of any of the medium and long-term assets acquired under its 2009–2014 series of QEs, if such assets had to be disposed of prior to maturity to help shrink its bloated balance sheet by reducing member bank reserves faster than originally expected. This is unlikely to become a problem, however, since the Fed's tentative exit policy of not replacing maturing and amortizing or prepaid mortgage (pass-through) securities will most likely be more than sufficient to deliver any intended contractionary impulse.

All the same, by setting up a very large maturity mismatch in its portfolio and engaging in activities similar to those of a mutual fund for long-term governments and of an unhedged Real Estate Investment Trust [REIT], the Fed is obviously getting its monetary policy enmeshed in risky intermediation and institutional self-interest considerations. These are likely to get in the way of its mandate to help assure future financial stability and reasonably low unemployment consistent with low or moderate inflation rates. For instance, the Fed's frequently avowed policy of holding its outsized portfolio to maturity so as to avoid having to mark its portfolio to market or to realize capital losses depends on being able to live with the consequences of member banks eventually turning to aggressively increasing the supply of credit in order to reduce excess reserves faster than the Fed is inclined to let them. If the rate at which the Fed plans to shrink its $4 trillion balance sheet, (presumably from 2015 on) should turn into a firm political commitment, it would detract from its ability to contribute to prudent and well-timed economic management. Hence it is not just the high amount of federal government debt outstanding, but the market and policy risks associated with holding it in private and government portfolios and funds that determine how much the high level of debt is likely to retard economic growth.

Disregarding outliers such as the Republic of Cyprus and

Slovenia from the euro-crisis of 2011–2013, several estimates of cumulative net fiscal costs of the bailout about five years after the onset of the last global crisis have been in the range of 10% to 15% of the respective GNP. Some estimates for Ireland 2007–2012 have been markedly higher while those for the United States, by 2013, have been quite a bit lower on account of the rapid repayment of loans and divestiture of equity investments originally undertaken by the US government in 2008–2009. Thus Reinhart and Rogoff's (2009a, p. 471) assessment—that the direct fiscal bank-bailout costs are a "much ballyhooed" but in several cases only relatively minor contributor to post-crisis debt burdens—has proved to be a fitting characterization for the United States. But it does not fit a number of other countries quite as well, including Mexico (see Black, 2008), Ireland (Whelan, 2012), and the United Kingdom (see National Audit Office, 2011; Curtis, 2011), which have all experienced financial crises during the last 20 years. It is also proper for governments that in a crisis effectively confiscate and write down part of their banks' deposit liabilities—as did Argentina in 2000–2001 and Cyprus in 2013—to be viewed as if they had taxed the owners of these deposits and spent the proceeds on bank bailouts, thereby adding to their fiscal costs.

Netting of outflows and inflows is often done incorrectly. Take for instance the government's total capital injections of $188 billion into Fannie Mae and Freddie Mac during 2008–2011. The government first set an interest rate of 10% on the preferred shares issued by these 'GSEs' and then modified its agreement with them in 2012 to require that essentially all of their profits be paid to the US Treasury for the benefit of the US government, their owner. While a total of $185 billion had already been paid by year-end 2013 and much more is on the way, all the government-owned enterprises did is start paying dividends duly owed after they returned to profitability in 2011. So far there has been no repayment of principal at all. Furthermore, re-privatization is impeded by the perennially deferred desire to have the agencies wither on the vine first so as to allow the private-label mortgage securitization business to revive. Hence there is no telling how much value has been preserved under their "conservatorship" and whether that value would hold up when the agencies have lost their TBTF guarantees as intended.

The point of dwelling on the extraordinary fiscal and monetary responses to a major financial and economic crisis is to show that they are both unsustainable and difficult to undo. Even tax cuts that are originally intended to be temporary are not easy to reverse on schedule, and thus time inconsistency may well triumph. On the spending side, temporary stimulus programs are equally hard to deliver punctually and then to turn off politically. Moreover, pressures to get on with essential infrastructure and human capital investments may grow stronger the longer such government-funded investments have been deferred. Neither can monetary policies that appreciably alter the composition of the public's balance sheet, portfolio composition, and yield spreads be readily reversed without harming politically vociferous holders of particular sets of assets or of financial interests in what they finance.

According to Reinhart and Rogoff's (2009b, p. 170) summary of results, the real stock of public debt almost doubles within three years after the onset of a banking crisis. Since that debt tends to rise faster than GDP for several more years, the time it takes to return to fiscal sustainability, defined as the pre-crisis fiscal condition, may be measured in decades if it succeeds at all. Shrinking the balance sheets of central banks and the excess bank reserves held with them back to pre-crisis levels (adjusted for normal economic growth) will also take over a decade of grueling monetary retrenchment if the plan is to allow most of the long-term assets acquired under the QE policy simply to run off.

Fiscal and monetary policies both will thus be pre-occupied with debilitating debt-management issues. Their ability to effectively confront new problems and tensions, some of which will be of their own making, will be very much curtailed. Thus the palliatives so richly applied to the present crisis for 6 to 7 years already carry the seeds of future financial crises, as often happens. The probability of such crises and the potential severity of those that still occur could be reduced—and room to maneuver through the next crisis gained—by encouraging banks to invest in their own capital insurance by issuing cocos. This would help strengthen debt discipline on management for which cocos are well equipped. Because cocos holders are debt holders junior even to stockholders first, and potential stockholders by conversion with equal rights second, they can counterbalance the excessive risk-taking incentives of pre-existing shareholders *ex ante* while at the same time taking a potential owner's interest in the health of the firm. Cocos holders have no upside in good times while pre-existing shareholders do not bear the full economic costs of their high-risk return seeking on the downside. Hence cocos have both a supporting microeconomic-management and corporate-governance rationale and can contribute to macroeconomic stabilization by making the choices facing policy makers in a major crisis a little less dire.

5.2 The Development and Growth of Cocos through 2014

Leaving a fuller recapitulation of the relevant regulatory categories and prescriptions for Chapter 17, regulatory capital is divided into fully loss-absorbing equity-like T1 components—i.e., Common Equity Tier 1 [CET1] and Additional Tier 1 capital [AT1]—and T2 instruments that are more debt-like, hence senior to T1 instruments, and less available to absorb losses. Over the 10 years starting from January 1, 2013, T1 and T2 instruments not containing this "point of non-viability" [PONV] bail-in trigger are to be successively replaced. PwC (2011, p. 4) has estimated that $1 trillion more CET1 will have to be raised, and between $400 and $800 billion in non-common instruments issued, over the 10-year course of this refinancing operation. If $20 billion of AT1 and $45 billion of T2 cocos are going to be issued in 2014 mostly in Europe for a total of €65 billion ($88 billion) as Citigroup has projected, that annual amount would be sufficient to cover much of the $400 to $800 billion just mentioned over 10 years. EMC (2013) notes that "some investment banks [are] predicting as much as €50 billion ($67 billion) in gross ... issuance in 2014," but even this lower annual total is still about as much as the entire gross issuance from 2009 through 2013. Gross and net issue will increasingly diverge as cocos age because they can be called after 5 years under certain conditions specified in the Documents included in Chapter 17. Since cocos are still relatively new, dating back to 2009, their annual issuance volume compares more favorably with the volume of other instruments being issued in the same time frame than when comparing total stocks outstanding.

The concept of cocos was incubated by a few academics, most notably Raviv (2004) and Flannery (2005; 2009). Flannery (2005, pp. 190–191) elaborates on the pedigree of this reform idea. These pioneers were followed by other contributors whose work was characterized and extended by Calomiris and Herring (2011, pp. 41–46). My own publications, (2011a–2013b), listed in References, identify more recent contributors and their works. There were also brief flurries of endorsements from bank supervisors and central bankers in 2009–2010. I have detailed these endorsements in (2011a, pp. 13–19) while later noting with regret (in 2013a, p. 96), that by 2010 such interest and support appears to have peaked. Since 2011, interest in capital markets has nevertheless picked up.

Cocos were named *Enhanced Capital Notes* [ECNs] by Lloyds Banking Group [LBG] in 2009, and almost every regulator and first-time issuer has since come up with a new name. Internationally active European banks have had only a few issues per year although activity has increased markedly since 2010. For 2009–2013, the annual European issuance volume has ranged from $4 billion in 2010 to an estimated $17 billion in 2013, with the cumulative five-year total only about €39 billion ($53 billion). The BIS (2013, p. 46) estimated a higher total of "some $70 billion" issued by banks since 2009 in the world as a whole. The earlier figure amounts to roughly 10% of the estimated $550 billion of non-cocos subordinated debt issued over the same period and to 1% of the $4.1 trillion of senior debt issued since 2009 that is also mentioned in Deutsche Bank (2013). The estimated actual European cocos issuance volume of $53 billion through 2013 includes cocos placed with government entities in recapitalization operations described in Chapters 13 and 14. Amounts reported include cocos issued in currencies other than the USD, mostly the euro, here using an exchange rate of 1.35 USD/EUR. BBVA Citi Research (2013) has charted the annual European issuance volume of cocos since 2009 in EUR bn. The $17 billion figure for 2013 is from ECM (2013).

The two big Swiss banks, UBS and Credit Suisse [CS], and Barclays Bank and LBG in the United Kingdom together accounted for more than half of the stock outstanding at year-end 2013. However, one or more banks headquartered in Ireland, the Netherlands, Belgium, France, Italy, Greece, Cyprus, Spain, Portugal, and, outside of Europe in Australia, Singapore, Canada, and Brazil among others have also either already issued cocos or announced a date for it. All of Asia, including banks in financial centers such as Hong Kong, Singapore, and Shanghai have been less active as issuers than as wealth managers and investors in cocos, as have the UAE and all of North America. In Europe, German and Scandinavian banks are finally coming forward with cocos issues though not with the preferred high-trigger version offering substantial recovery rates. Thus Deutsche Bank in May 2014 placed three tranches of AT1 notes with write-down and optional-write-up features and a low CET1 trigger of 5.125%. This benchmark issue raised the equivalent of €3.5 billion in three currencies with a coupon rate of 6% on the euro, 6.25% on the USD, and 7.125% on the GBP tranche. Scandinavian regulators have allowed banks to issue T2 cocos that would help with the solvency standard by being credited with raising the already high probability that a bank will survive for at least another year. The only cocos that have actually been converted into equity so far, though by a circuitous route, were issued by the Bank of Cyprus Group in 2011. They were first exchanged for Mandatory Convertible Notes with conversion terms sweetened to accelerate conversion. I have given more details in (2012a, p. 56).

Part II
Why Cocos?

6

High-Trigger Cocos
Compared with Other Bailinable Debt

This part lays out specific rationales for having financial institutions choose to put cocos on their balance sheets by considering several alternatives. It also seeks to show how cocos must be designed and (not) regulated to live up to their promise.

In January 2011, internationally active banks were put on notice that subordinated debt instruments, to be counted as part of regulatory capital, would soon have to have a provision that requires them, at the option of the relevant authority, to either be written off or converted into common equity upon the occurrence of the trigger event. After the beginning of 2013, all such newly-issued instruments were to be fully loss-absorbing by being subject to bail-in, or *bailinable*, when triggered. The metaphor behind this bail-in terminology needs brief clarification because bailing into a sinking boat would not be a way to save it. But if bailout is understood to characterize a situation in which the taxpayer is called upon to save a bank without creditors having to take losses, then bail-in provides for the opposite distribution of loss-absorption: it spares the taxpayer while hitting the bank's creditors whose debt is either cancelled outright or converted to common equity of lower value. The debt write-off would boost retained earnings, and hence equity, in either case.

6.1 Features Distinguishing High-Trigger Cocos from Bail-in Capital

To show that cocos deserve a place on the liability side of the balance sheet particularly of major financial institutions, cocos will first be compared with other bailinable debt. If the past is any guide, regulators in a crisis will be most reluctant to actually bail in such debt. They are generally averse to making matters worse by driving up haircuts and otherwise interfering with the continued funding and rollover of the short-term borrowings and repos that would likely occur once they have marked a bank as one whose longer-term subordinated debts may be headed for bail-in. Investors, then experience heightened uncertainty on account of regulators' arrogation of discretionary authority even before continued viability becomes an issue. OSFI's (and any other national regulator's) assertion of full discretionary authority to cancel the protection which the conversion of cocos might otherwise provide is disconcerting in this regard, particularly if it is meant to apply also to high-trigger cocos:

> Canadian authorities will retain full discretion to choose not to trigger NVCC [non-viability cocos] notwithstanding a determination by the Superintendent [of Financial Institutions] that a DTI [Deposit Taking Institution] has ceased, or is about to cease, to be viable. Under such circumstances, the DTI's creditors and shareholders could be exposed to losses through the use of other resolution tools or in liquidation. (OSFI (2011) as quoted in Osler (2011, pp. 8–9)).

The automaticity of high-trigger cocos conversion for thus reinvigorating a going concern would be highly preferable to waiting for regulators to impose a bail-in. To help further answer the central question of this Part, the automatic conversion of cocos— when triggered by their own internal mechanism and not by order of regulators—will be compared to the regulatory bail-in of other debt, as well as to the simple building up of a higher cushion of common equity in relation to total assets and choosing to operate with lower leverage before the next crisis. The final comparison will be to a recent actual voluntary restructuring of a non-financial corporation, SolarWorld AG. Unlike cocos which have been issued almost only by banks and an occasional insurance company, voluntary restructuring is not unique to financial institutions, of course. The ravishes of bankruptcy resolution with disorderly dismemberment followed by drawn-out liquidation proceedings require no further comment: this "Lehman" option was already dismissed as the worst of all possible approaches to a problematic resolution in Chapter 4.

In spite of their similarities with other types of bailinable debt that may be triggered either by a regulatory finding that an institution has reached the point of non-viability or by breach of the trigger specified in the instruments themselves, cocos have characteristics that set them apart from other hybrid debt. PwC (2011, p.2) explains:

> The terms "bail-in capital" and "CoCos" are often used inter-changeably, but it is useful to make a distinction and to define bail-in capital as instruments where write downs are triggered by the regulator at the point of non-viability (when capital ratios are close to the regulatory minimum); CoCo instruments are those that convert to equity when a pre-specified trigger point (such as a higher Common Equity Tier 1 capital ratio) is passed as a going concern—not at the point of resolution. The issues arising from both types of capital are broadly the same, as ... the only real distinction is that the conversion trigger for bail-in capital is at the discretion of the regulator whereas for CoCos it is a fixed trigger.

Low-trigger cocos triggered by regulators from the outside, or by their own terms at risk-weighted capital ratios of 5.125% of RWA or less, are often defined as gone-concern 'resolution' cocos in contrast to the high-trigger 'recovery' cocos issued at risk-based capital ratios of 7% or more—now up to 10%. So far only LBG in 2009 and a few banks including UBS, CS, and Société Générale in 2013 have issued low-trigger cocos; the quote above is not wrong, therefore, in assuming that most cocos going forward will be high-trigger, going-concern instruments. One of OSFI's "Principles" is also on the mark, namely that "[it] has determined that conversion is more consistent [than write-off without conversion into equity] with traditional insolvency consequences and reorganization norms and better respects the legitimate expectations of all stakeholders" (see Osler, 2011, p. 2, n.4).

What is distinctive about cocos relative to other bailinable debt is that they are subject to conversion by their own high triggers and not by regulators whose discretionary *modus operandi* is difficult for investors to model and to price in. Assume the Null hypothesis is that there is no cause for alarm: regulators may well be less concerned about committing Type II errors by not rejecting this hypothesis when false than Type I errors from rejecting it when the Null is in fact true. For by having been wrong in the former case they will be in good company, while in the latter case they risk being blamed for bringing on a crisis by sounding an alarm that turns out to have been uncalled for in retrospect. They are thus inherently conflicted when it comes to fending off a financial crisis by insisting on prompt corrective actions by any bank under their jurisdiction that is big enough for its collapse to rattle the market and financial system. Regulators' non-performance during the financial crisis of 2007–2009 shows that they tried to assuage rather than sound the alarm for years leading up to 2007 until well after the crisis had begun. Perhaps they feared getting blamed for drawing attention to the emergence of a crisis which their public expressions of dismay could have made self-fulfilling.

With prescient dissents especially from Eric S. Rosengren, President of the Federal Reserve Bank of Boston since July 2007, the minutes of the Federal Open Market Committee [FOMC] meetings from January 30–31 to December 11 of 2007, show a large majority seeing only a temporary slowdown in economic growth ahead. During this entire year the FOMC wrestled with little apparent sense of impending reality over getting the target for the federal funds rate down from 5.25% to 4.25% as if just a little easing would be good enough. Hence counting on regulators to take timely discretionary action—particularly if the point of non-viability is reached by a number of financial institutions at around the same time—may well mean waiting in vain. This is why the automatically activated, accounting based, and legally enforceable trigger of high-trigger cocos is so valuable. Cocos holders have an interest in hastening *and not stalling* conversion when they sense that the otherwise progressive erosion of replacement value lies ahead.

What functions cocos play in the liability portfolios of their issuers depends not only on the trigger level of the individual instruments, but also on the quantity issued, and an institution's suite of cocos issues—like Rabobank's and Credit Suisse's—with different trigger levels. In addition, because issuing high-trigger cocos raises the quality of any low-trigger cocos that may already be outstanding by making them less likely to convert, high-trigger cocos should be issued, or at least announced and expected, before low-tier cocos are issued by the same institution. Otherwise there would be windfalls for the holders of low-trigger cocos and of other bailinable debt, because these instruments would then be better protected than expected.

Furthermore, if conversion of all its low-trigger cocos would restore an institution to being adequately capitalized they could be regarded as 'recovery' cocos just as surely as a smaller amount of high-trigger cocos whose conversion at one time would achieve the same result. For instance, if an institution had cocos equal to 4% of RWA outstanding that had a risk-based capital ratio trigger of 5%, and cocos with a 7% trigger in the amount of 2% of RWA, their conversion in succession would return its capital ratio to 9% each time. Thus the fixed trigger features of individual cocos issues open up special portfolio management choices that are made *ex ante* to assist with informed pricing. Conditional predictability through contract fidelity is essential to effective self-insurance. Debt that is bailinable at the discretion of bank supervisors in groupings, on terms, and at times of regulators' choosing does not offer such calculability.

High-trigger 'recovery' cocos that are set up to convert well before the point of non-viability has been invoked thus have important features that set them apart from other bailinable debt. Being triggered automatically by their built-in trigger mechanism obviates the need to negotiate over the terms of restructuring and saves time to fend off insolvency and the ravishes of bankruptcy. Regulators have no business undermining the automaticity of high-trigger cocos conversion, or even that of low-trigger cocos, if such conversion would restore the institution to being at least adequately capitalized. Indeed

Documents 3 and 5 in Chapter 17, excerpted from the BCBS and the EBA respectively, contain injunctions against introducing anything into the covenant or the management of cocos that would interfere with the automaticity and promptness of conversion. Under "Conversion Period" Document 3 thus states that "the provisions to be included shall not undermine the conversion features of the instrument and *shall not* in particular *restrict the automaticity of conversion*" (Annex 3: Conversion Period, emphasis added here and below). Under the heading "Procedures and Timing for Determining that a Trigger Event has Occurred," Document 5 states further that "when the institution has established that the [CET1] ratio has fallen below the level that activates conversion or write-down of the instrument … the institution shall without delay determine that a trigger event has occurred and *there shall be an irrevocable obligation* to write-down or convert the instrument" (Art. 14, Sec. A). Regulators should not exempt themselves from these prudent injunctions against discretionary fine-tuning or suspension of the cocos-conversion recovery mechanism which they themselves helped devise.

7

Self-Insurance with Cocos Compared to Common Equity

Admati and Hellwig (2013) have recently published a much noted plea for higher CET1 requirements, pure and simple, and lambasted at every turn "the bankers" who chafe at raising them. My basic view is that the combination of capital and leverage requirements currently supposed to be phased in by 2019 (see Table 1) is about adequate. Their *de facto* implementation is already being moved up as banks compete in wanting to show that they already meet, or more than meet, the Basel III capital standards 'fully loaded,' i.e., at the final levels set for January 2019. The most that Admati and Hellwig (2013, p. 188) are willing to grant about cocos is that "they may be better at protecting the safety of the bank than simple debt." But they see "no valid reason for non-equity alternatives to be considered instead of equity when using equity would be simpler and more effective in achieving the goals of a stable and healthy financial system." They have not looked very hard to see any such reason; hence there is a challenge to demonstrate that cocos, which get just 2 out of almost 400 pages in their book, have some valuable features that distinguish them from common stock and make them suitable to be both part of and a supplement to the increased capital and leverage requirements ahead.

Regarding the extent to which cocos may qualify for meeting part of the regulatory capital requirements, the question is not just about their eligibility for AT1 and T2; it is also about the weight they should receive if their ability to absorb losses were judged to be less than 100%. Banks could then choose to meet growing capital requirements in whatever way they prefer within certain limits, providing valuable information on cocos' market rate of substitution with CET1 and their overall portfolio fit. As will be detailed in Chapter 16, whether cocos get partial or full credit as capital that is comparable to CET1, according to S&P, depends on their characteristics. Cocos could therefore be a less than 1:1 substitute for meeting CET1 regulatory capital requirements at the margin. That would not make them "inferior" to CET1 except on a one-dimensional scale that assumes that equity-content is their only valued characteristic. The focus here is not on how cocos should be weighted in this regard but on whether or not having cocos on the balance sheet could yield a range of benefits—some of which are special and not at least equally well available from having more CET1 instead of adding cocos.

Obviously something could be said for cocos if, as the Financial Stability Oversight Council attributes to them, they had "the potential to provide these benefits [of strengthening financial institutions' capital positions and ability to withstand losses during times of financial stress] at a lower cost of capital than additional common equity issuances" (2012, p. 19). A company's cocos are priced as a hybrid that turns from being debt-like in good times to becoming more equity-like when the fall in its capital ratio raises the risk of conversion. Hence their rate of interest should be between that of non-cocos subordinated debt that is senior to cocos and the required rate of return on equity for that company. Of course, this does not mean that adding cocos to the balance sheet has lowered the cost of capital overall from what it would be if an equal amount of common equity had been issued instead. For instance, if cocos are priced mainly as subordinated debt, as they may be when issued by a company with a very strong balance sheet, the rate of return required on its equity will rise on account of the increased leverage. "The leveraging will indeed raise the expected earnings per share on the equity, but not by [any more than just] enough to compensate the shareholders for the risks added by the leverage" (Miller, 1995, p. 486). Hence observing that the interest rate on debt-like instruments is below the rate of return required on equity is not sufficient to conclude that debt is less expensive than equity or that the cost of capital can reliably be reduced by increasing leverage.

Granting all of this, matters are a little more complicated with convertible hybrids like cocos which can turn from fish to fowl. For instance, cocos may be part of an acquisition strategy that simply buying a reportable minority share of a company's stock would not satisfy. Sovereign wealth funds, private-equity funds, and other strategic investors have already shown interest in concentrated holdings of a few privately-placed issues of cocos, perhaps as a cheap option to gain control in the event of conversion depending on the richness of the conversion terms. Adopting a conversion formula and setting the conversion price so as to allocate the losses and gains from conversion expected by cocos holders and pre-existing shareholders in a way that strengthens corporate governance is another (potentially beneficial) activity not applicable to the single-minded pursuit of only more CET1 issues. Cocos—especially those of the high-trigger variety—are supposed to be triggered well before the point of non-viability has been reached and supervisory intervention is called for, and are thus junior to pre-existing common equity prior to conversion and ranked equally (*pari passu*) afterwards. Pre-existing shareholders have reason to welcome such an arrangement. Issuing a suite of cocos with staggered trigger levels could even ensure the availability of equity infusions that could give a bank more than one lease on life after suffering a series of setbacks. Even if repeated dilutive stock issues were a feasible alternative to cope with such a situation, cocos conversion is distinctive in that it must avoid being dilutive in the value sense for pre-existing shareholders. In other words, the stock's price should not fall but rise on account of conversion, even though their ownership share will inevitably decline, write-down-only cocos excepted. As stated above, this implies that the percentage increase in the number of shares outstanding through conversion will not be larger than the percentage increase in equity due to the cancellation of the cocos debt that comes with it.

Bolton and Samama (2012, pp. 280–284) have provided other reasons why issuing equity can be freighted with several obstacles and high costs. Hence the issue of choosing an appropriate debt-equity ratio for a firm and the conversion features of its debt is not adequately disposed of by reference to the irrelevance proposition associated with the Modigliani-Miller theorem.

There also are purely opportunistic reasons for keeping an eye on the developing market for cocos. These instruments do not yet have a well-established preferred habitat with either fixed-income investors or any others. A number of issues have involved exchanges for similar types of non-cocos debt or preference shares. Arbitrage focused on the conversion risk premium has been impeded by lack of liquidity and the paucity of cocos exchange listings; Credit Default Swaps [CDS] and options on the respective issues would also have to be involved. Under such unsettled circumstances in incomplete markets, there may be opportunities to find terms of financing on cocos hybrids in the market that appear advantageous relative to issuing either more non-cocos subordinated debt or common equity, particularly if interest paid on cocos is deductible in the relevant jurisdiction. Although Admati and Hellwig see no reason for looking at non-equity alternatives, markets and calculated attempts at arbitrage cannot function without looking around.

7.1 Debating the Merits of Cocos

Here are several other points made by the Financial Stability Oversight Council (2012, p. 5) with regard to the potential benefits of going-concern cocos, with comments added:

1. Generating additional common equity capital to strengthen the firm's ability to absorb losses on its balance sheet (while it is a going concern). *Comment:* Having more common equity outstanding could achieve the same effect as getting more equity from cocos conversion unless having more equity all along would encourage excessive risk taking. Calomiris and Herring (2011, p. 12) want cocos in the mix in part because they would reduce managerial agency issues. These can arise when a thick equity cushion and managers' asymmetric information advantage enable them to take excessive

risks and to represent their own interests over those of (long-term) shareholders unchallenged.

2. Improving incentives for management to raise capital when needed (*i.e.*, before the instrument converts). *Comment:* Management will have difficulty raising capital when cocos conversion is widely expected to be imminent. But this difficulty does not arise *because* cocos conversion is imminent but because capital ratios have declined to a dangerously low level. This difficulty will affect high-trigger less than low-trigger cocos. To prod management to apply itself to timely capital provision, letting it come to cocos conversion would have to send a strong message of no-confidence in existing management and lead to its prospective replacement.

3. Heightening market discipline on management from common-stock holders and contingent capital investors, particularly if such instruments are issued in place of debt. *Comment:* Both pre-existing common-stock holders and investors in cocos anticipating conversion will welcome timely conversion when they see the fortunes of a company progressively decline and want to see it survive. If they want to pull out instead, pre-existing stockholders can presumably sell right away if they are willing to sell at market but holders of illiquid cocos may be locked-in until conversion. These holders might welcome cocos being converted into something much more liquid, like common stock. Defensive measures—such as naked short sales of the common equity expected from a future conversion or the purchase of put options—could help prevent further losses for apprehensive cocos holders. However, their sudden interest in put options with a strike price nearest the conversion price would signal to the market that they sense trouble ahead. Hence these put options would be expensive, perhaps forbiddingly so. By contrast, cocos conversion on its built-in terms adds no adverse information on the bank that was not already contained in its reported Basel III capital-ratio level and its

automatic, conditional, fully-anticipated consequences. In fact conversion raises that capital ratio, strengthens the company's balance sheet, and enhances its chances of survival.

Admati and Hellwig's (2013, p. 188) apprehensions about "panic in the markets for these securities or for the bank's shares" when conversion (even of high-trigger) cocos appears imminent would therefore not be well-motivated. Ongoing de-capitalization of a company can at some point create panic as the company is seen to approach insolvency. Cocos conversion can arrest or reverse that potentially fatal deterioration and forestall a panic, not cause it. If it is fear of progressive loss of capital that causes panic, having sufficient cocos on the balance sheet is the prophylactic that may calm investors.

Pressure on management to avoid undue risk is likely to be strongest if cocos conversion leads to the issuance of a greater number of shares than were already outstanding, or results in new concentrated holdings, so that effective control passes to the new shareholders from cocos conversion. The new controlling group may want to replace management on account of the losses they are likely to have suffered from the negative dynamic leading to cocos conversion and from a share price headed well below the fixed conversion price. Issuing cocos rather than non-cocos subordinated debt could thus increase inhibitions for management to take excessive risks. Even if "the suggestion [by Rajan (2010) and others] that debt disciplines managers [because of the need for issuers, particularly of short-term debt, to submit to frequent scrutiny to secure renewed financing] is not supported empirically" (Admati and Hellwig, 2013, p. 317), the broader coalition of interests that would be affected by high-trigger cocos conversion might exert some disciplining effect.

4. Generating increased liquidity at times of stress by a reduction in required debt service payments. *Comment:* This is a welcome—and even more valuable—addition to the suspension of dividends occurring at the same time. Because debt is cancelled upon conversion without the possibility of a

future write-up, leverage falls and book equity rises by the full amount of the debt forgiveness, and not just of the current interest forgiveness, outside bankruptcy.

5. Providing more flexibility for satisfying regulatory capital requirements (where contingent capital may be included in regulatory capital). *Comment:* Calomiris and Herring (2011, p. 29) favor the phasing in of a regulatory cocos *requirement* (of around 10% of book assets) in part to avoid signaling adverse self-selection that could be associated with *voluntary* cocos issues. Such issues could be taken as revealing management expectations of impending losses. However, giving cocos credit toward meeting regulatory capital requirements would reduce investors' ability to extract such negative signals. The reason is that each bank would then have to raise its regulatory capital by either equity or cocos or a combination of both to meet capital-ratio targets along with all other banks. Hence cocos mandates would not be needed to avoid unfavorable inferences that could discourage cocos issues.

Having discussed special features of cocos compared to common equity, I return to the issue of fractional regulatory CET1 credit for cocos that was raised at the beginning of this chapter. For the sake of illustration, if regulators were choosing between imposing (i) a minimum CET1 capital ratio of 6% or (ii) a total capital ratio of 8%, up to half of which could be met by cocos, the implied average rate of substitution between CET1 and cocos would be 1:2 or minus one-half. Once cocos amount to the maximum 4% of the relevant denominator, such as RWA or TA, the marginal rate of substitution of CET1 for cocos in regulatory capital would be zero: No amount of cocos above their maximum of 4% for regulatory purposes could do anything to reduce the required minimum amount of CET1, which is also 4% in this example. A company could enter any value for cocos in the {0, 4%} range into the following equation to determine the required minimum percentage of CET1, which is 6% − 0.5 cocos, and of the total capital ratio, CET1 + cocos:

$$\min (\text{CET1} + \text{cocos}) = 6\% + 0.5 \text{ cocos}, \ 0 \leq \text{cocos} \leq 4\%$$

If cocos should not be treated as 1:1 substitutes for CET1, perhaps a marginal tradeoff of more than 1 cocos for 1 unit of CET1 would be beneficial. Issuing two $10,000 cocos bonds in lieu of raising $10,000 in new equity, for example, and not refinancing $10,000 of non-cocos subordinated debt—to keep the size of the balance sheet the same in the alternative financing programs—could be an attractive package to make access to capital more secure in bad times.

8

Automatic Cocos Conversion
vs. Voluntary Restructuring

Reaching agreement on voluntary restructuring is much more costly and time consuming than converting bailinable debt into common stock. To illustrate the difficulties and losses that arise, the recent restructuring of a non-financial company, SolarWorld AG, can serve as a case in point that you do not have to be a financial company to benefit from having cocos on the balance sheet. Once Germany's largest solar producer, this public company has operations in a number of countries; it had even boasted of having America's largest and most advanced solar photovoltaic [PV] production facility (in Hillsboro, Oregon). Like most of its competitors, the company had been struggling with declining sales and with operating losses that escalated in 2013. Early in the year it started meetings with three groups of creditors holding promissory notes and loans, and two publicly traded bonds: (i) 7-year bonds or global notes totaling €400 million issued in January 21, 2010 at a fixed coupon rate of 6⅛%, and (ii) 5-year bonds totaling €150 million issued July 27, 2011 with a 6⅜% coupon. These two bonds could conceivably have been issued as cocos with a simple 10% leverage ratio trigger defined as book equity in percent of total balance-sheet assets. Such a trigger level would be very low for firms in most non-financial sectors; it was 27.5% (614.6/2,235.8 with data in millions of euros) for SolarWorld (2013, p. 40) as recently as January 1st, 2012.

By the end of 2012, this leverage ratio had declined to 8.8% (117.3/1333.8) and conversion of the two classes of bonds, had they been cocos, would have been triggered. The conversion price used to calculate the number of common shares issued in conversion might have been set at €5 per share on the first bond of €400 million when it was issued, and at €4 per share on the second bond of €150 million. Thus €550 million of debt would have been cancelled and 117.5 million new shares would have been issued in conversion to the former cocos holders in conversion. Because there were 111.72 million shares outstanding prior to conversion (SolarWorld, 2013, p. 5), the new shareholders would have acquired a little over half, 51.26%, of the company. Annual interest savings would have been €34 million, and the boost to book equity from the start of 2013 to mid-year, including the €550 million gain from debt forgiveness, would have been €567 million. The leverage ratio which had dropped below 3.0% (37.4/1,251.1) by June 30, 2013, would have thus been raised to 48.3% (604.4/1,251.1), *ceteris paribus*, assuming total assets would have declined as much as they did even with cocos conversion. In any event, the book value of SolarWorld's equity would have been restored almost to what it had been at the start of 2012, €614.6 million compared to €604.4 million, winning the company time to reinvent itself. As of January 2014, the company was again very much in the business of trying to fight off China Solar and other principal competitors with market means and countervailing duties.

These results help gauge the expected effects of conversion on three classes of investors: pre-existing shareholders, holders of cocos debt, and debt senior to cocos. Book value per share would have been €2.637 (€604.4 million divided by 229.22 million shares outstanding post-conversion), with shares valued at €294.6 million held by pre-existing shareholders and €309.8 million by the holders of new shares from conversion. Without cocos in the picture, book value per share would have been a mere €37.4/111.72 or €0.335 per share for the pre-existing shareholders when there were no others. Coincidentally, shares of SWVG.DE hit a 52-week low of €0.37 on June 27, 2013, making market price approximately equal to book value per share in this instance. As pre-existing shareholders had actual equity claims of only €37.4 rather than €294.6 million in book value as of June 30, 2013, they would have been vastly better off by that time had they had cocos to convert beforehand. Conversion would have been strongly anti-dilutive for them in a value sense. For giving up €567 million (€550 million in principal and €17 million in interest), the former cocos holders would obtain shares with an estimated market value of €310 million in conversion, making their calculated recovery rate 55%. While cocos holders lose, senior creditors and holders of short-term debt would stand to gain from the cocos conversion, restoring the capital of SolarWorld to a more than adequate level. Pre-existing shareholders would also benefit as the book value of equity would rise—from €37.4 million held by themselves alone—to €604.4 million shared, in this case roughly equally, with the new shareholders by conversion.

8.1 Voluntary Restructuring of a Non-financial: SolarWorld

SolarWorld's sales peaked in 2010 and losses started to pile up in the following year. By the middle of 2013, the amount of book equity had shrunk from 27% of total assets at the start of 2012 to less than 3% of total assets and insolvency was imminent. Starting in January 2013, the company proposed to rebuild equity by restructuring its liabilities and selling a share of itself to two strategic investors. Three classes of debt holders had to agree to take what amounted to a 55% haircut—or rather beheading—reduced to 40% only in the case of an outstanding loan from the European Investment Bank. The company described the 55% debt reduction implicit in the new debt instruments issued in the restructuring as a debt-to-equity swap because it was partly to be compensated by around 7 new shares per €1,000 bond. There was also a cash component amounting to 5% to 6% of the nominal value of the bond prior to its restructuring. The new shares were worth about as much as the cash component assuming their value was €8 per share which is what the strategic investor, Qatar Solar, had agreed to pay. Hence the effective debt reduction net of compensation was at least 43%, consisting of a new bond, cash, and new shares achieved in the restructuring. The corresponding replacement rate of 57%, derived with the data assembled in Table 3, is very close to the 55% estimated for cocos holders in the alternative resolution scenario. Drawn-out negotiations with debt and stockhold-

Table 3. SolarWorld AG Before and After its 2013 Restructuring (in millions of euros)

	New Bond	Cash	New Shares[a]	Total	Ownership[b] %
Bonds & other Debt 06/30/13	1)	2)	3)	1)–3)	
€139mm 6⅜ mat. 07/13/2016	61	8	8	77	6.8%
€387mm 6⅛ mat. 01/21/2017	175	21	21	217	17.6%
€404mm bank loans, pr. Notes	190	20	26	236	22.1%
€930mm and other Totals	**426**	**49**	**55**	**530**	**46.5%**
Cash Injections:					
€9.75mm Co. Founder Asbeck					19.5%
€36.25mm Qatar Solar S.P.C.					29.0%
€46mm and other Totals					**48.5%**
Pre-Existing Shareholders:					**5.0%**

Source: Calculated from SolarWorld (2013) and related company publications.

[a] The value of the 14.896 million new shares issued in the debt restructuring is speculative. It is assumed to be €8 per share, the same as Qatar Solar had paid, for a total stock market capitalization, at the time of €119 million. Of this amount, 46.5% (or €55 million) is allocated to creditors here. Since then, after a 1:150 reverse stock split that took effect on 01/27/2014, the then outstanding 744.8 thousand shares were quoted at €30.45 two days later under the new symbol SWVK:GR. The market capitalization of Solar World had thus shrunk to €22.7 million by that date. This may indicate that the 2013 restructuring was accomplished too slowly, and came too late to succeed.

[b] The ownership percentages shown in bold type add up to 100.

ers, however, during which the value of the business was shrinking, made the former outcome (without cocos) very difficult and
time-consuming to achieve.

Table 3 shows that the total recovery that might be expected
on three classes of debt claims that were still outstanding as of
June 30, 2013—totaling €930 million—is €530 million, or 57%.
Two strategic investors provided a total cash infusion of €46 million for a combined ownership share of 48.5%; this cash was used
by SolarWorld in partial compensation for the debt restructuring.
Raising cash through new stock issues and then applying the cash
to reduce debt promotes deleveraging and reduces debt overhang
by making the remaining debt smaller and less risky. But cancellation of debt through repurchase as otherwise also through cocos
conversion, interest savings aside, does not leave any new money
for investment in the business.

The distribution of loss absorption agreed to after several
rounds of (eventually successful) negotiations in the summer of
2013, for final implementation by February 2014, will now be
compared to what it might have been had cocos been available for
conversion at the end of 2012. The three groups of debt holders,
strategic investors, and pre-existing shareholders are the groups
most affected from the side of owners and creditors, not considering workers, customers, or suppliers. The distribution of gains
and losses from voluntary restructuring—after long delays during
which value was shrinking—was roughly as follows, with a
comparison of cocos conversion presented in italics:

• The three groups of debt holders on average gave up 43% of
  the estimated nominal value of their claims. Judged by the
  occasional transaction prices registered prior to the restructuring but after the acceptance of the restructuring plan by
  creditors and stockholders in August 2013, expected losses
  remained much greater: The two publicly traded bonds, due
  in 2016 and 2017, were trading at 30.5% (09/27/2013) and
  32.7% (09/24/2013) of par, respectively, even though both
  were only a few years away from maturity. *Had the two bond
  issues previously identified been cocos, their face value of*

*€550 million would have been cancelled in return for shares
that would have had an estimated market value of €310 at the
start of 2013. Hence the losses for these two groups of bond
holders would have been roughly €240 of principal (43% of
€567) but through conversion they would obtain a controlling
interest of 51.26% in the company. (The corresponding euro
amounts shown in Table 3 for debts that were still outstanding
on June 30, 2013 are somewhat lower.) There would be no
losses for the third group of holders of more short-term or
otherwise senior debt that could not consist of cocos in this
comparison. Unlike the holders of bank loans and personal
notes shown in Table 3, these holders would not participate in
the restructuring.*

* Pre-existing shareholders lost all but 5% of the company they
  owned. The market cap with 111.72 million old shares outstanding at a share price of €0.80 around the end of September 2013
  was about €89 million, 5% of which would be a mere €4.5 million. Even though the restructuring could be a 'done deal,' and
  stock markets are supposed to factor that in, a somewhat higher market capitalization may yet be achieved by February 2014
  when the restructuring is scheduled to be complete. *By contrast,
  pre-existing shareholders would have a book value gain of €276
  (= 0.4874 of €567) million from timely cocos conversion even
  though their ownership share would fall from 100% to 48.74%
  when the cocos were converted. Pre-existing shareholders would
  thus in essence gain what the cocos holders lose (€240 million)
  from cocos conversion. Dilution for existing shareholders in both
  a value and ownership sense has two consequences: (i) book value per share is reduced and (ii) the ownership share of pre-existing stockholders declines. Thus a pro rata rights issue by a company, if granted to its registered shareholders only, dilutes the
  value per share but not of the ownership share. By the same token
  the cocos conversion described above does not dilute the value
  per share but only the ownership share of existing shareholders
  who are nevertheless greatly enriched.*

- Two strategic investors, as related parties, acquired a combined equity stake of 48.5%, with a grossly unequal price of €3.34 per share paid for 19.5% of the company by its founder, Dr. Asbeck, and €8.36 per share for 29% ownership by Qatar Solar. This entity is owned by a sovereign wealth fund, the Qatar Foundation, and owns 70% of Qatar Solar Technologies, a joint venture with SolarWorld, which owns 29%. Whether these strategic investors could at least hypothetically get their money back without interest or dividends depends on whether the market price of the new shares, when issued, ends up above €3.34 or even above €8.36 after adjusting for reverse splits. Because there will only be 14.896 million new shares outstanding after the restructuring, the market cap of SolarWorld would have to be at least €124.5 million for such an outcome. A surprising new development was the November 2013 announcement of SolarWorld's acquisition of Bosch Solar Energy. The company claims that this acquisition would bolster its status as the largest crystalline silicon producer outside of China. This deal (not considered here), like the restructuring that was discussed at length, is to be completed by the end of February 2014, with details of its financing to be announced. *The funds raised from the strategic investors, €46 million, financed almost all of the estimated cash payments to debt holders of €49 million shown in Table 3. One must assume that if the debt restructuring had not had this cash component as a sweetener, the face value of the new bonds offered in exchange would have had to be higher.*

9

Reasons for Having Cocos Liabilities on the Balance Sheet

The question posed for this Part, "Why Cocos?," demands an immediate summary of the answers. Within a year after cocos first appeared in the market, this short form for contingent convertible debt securities gained currency and attracted a fair amount of derision. As we have seen in the previous chapters of Part II, however, there are in fact several good reasons for the existence of high-trigger cocos. Adding such 'recovery' cocos to the financing mix appears superior to staying only with bailinable bonds and relying simply on more equity, or to counting on voluntary restructuring or Chapter 11 (of the US Bankruptcy Code) reorganization as an expeditious and low-cost way out.

Chapter 6 explained why bailinable bonds have a problem not shared with high-trigger cocos, as the latter are designed to convert to common equity when set off automatically by a designated capital-ratio that has sunk to its trigger level. That level would be crossed well before what regulators would determine to be the point of non-viability [PONV], activating a bail-in, had been breached. Without cocos on the balance sheet, the result of deeper de-capitalization would be the partial or complete cancellation of bailinable subordinated debt outside of bankruptcy once regulators have chosen to declare that an institution has reached PONV and/or requires an injection of public funds to survive. In making these determinations in their sole discretion, regulators may consider not only the condition of the individual institution but also any adverse systemic repercussions on financial intermediation and bank funding that may result from declaring that a SIFI has reached PONV. By contrast, according to the principle of self-insurance, high-trigger cocos conversion is always based on the level of trigger data relating only to that institution. Such conversions nonetheless have a helpful and timely anti-cyclical effect because they would tend to be bunched in the lead-up to a major financial crisis. Difficulties in individual institutions can readily be amplified through network externalities and (mostly rational) contagion effects rippling through the lattice of counterparties. Hence the capital insurance obtained from issuing cocos would yield external benefits and should be encouraged by respecting the application of the issue's covenant.

Now there are severe problems with relying on government agencies—rather than self-activating built-in triggers—to set in motion remedial actions such as bail-in and write-off with or without debt-to-equity conversion. Even if the regulatory agencies would agree privately that conditions are likely to generate a major financial crisis within 1 or 2 years unless stabilizing actions are immediately initiated, they will be very careful to keep any such foreboding from the public. Government agencies are thus inclined to hushup any rumors of terrifying events, particularly if the probability of their approach is uncertain. Years are lost as leaders and their spokespersons continue to profess official optimism, justify inactivity in prudential matters, and give no cause for alarm. There are splendid exceptions to this pattern of behavior, exemplified by salt-of-the-earth public servants ahead of their time who were not afraid to publicly identify prospective risks and propose timely remedies. Names that made the 2007–2009 honor roll for such contributions to financial policy in the US are (in alphabetic order) Sheila Bair, former Chair of the FDIC, Brooksley Born, former Chair of the Commodity Futures Trading Commission, and Elisabeth Warren, who set up the Consumer Financial Protection Bureau called for in the Dodd-Frank Act of 2010 and then became the (now senior) Senator from Massachusetts.

The "Greenspan Doctrine" implies that central bankers should not even try to spot and prick supposed bubbles because they have no reliable way of measuring their inflation, let alone stopping them without risking more harm than good. They only claim to be gifted in dealing with the aftermath of breaking troubles and bubbles that burst. The relative automaticity of cocos conversion based on input data and model-based estimates reported at least quarterly, in contrast, make it hard to fudge the data over time. Pre-arranged self-help through cocos could therefore be called on to mitigate the severity and frequency of future crises. Playing fast and loose with the conversion trigger would risk penalties from regulatory agencies and lawsuits from stockholders or bondholders. The trigger refers to capital ratios that are widely publicized and followed as indicators of the solidity and resilience of a company, hence no information is added by the conversion of cocos when these trigger levels are reached. The suggestion that cocos conversion in a firm would spoil the market for its shares falsely treats cocos conversion as a cause rather than an effect of prior de-capitalization to the trigger point. It is easier to counteract such a loss of capital with high-trigger cocos on the balance sheet than without them. Equity values should correspondingly be higher than with an equal amount of non-cocos subordinated debt that must wait for regulators to trigger its being bailed in by declaring that PONV has been reached. Low-trigger cocos are second only to high-trigger cocos in this regard if they too are left to their own devices by regulators and available in an amount so large that their conversion would restore the bank to being adequately capitalized in spite of its low capital-ratio when the cocos are triggered.

Chapter 6 concluded that if one considers the alternative financing vehicles of a financial institution, with low-trigger cocos and subordinated debt on the one hand and high-trigger cocos on the other, the latter have some superior properties that earn them a place on the balance sheet jointly with these and other types of debt. It follows that the interest paid on such cocos should be treated no less favorably for the tax purposes of the issuer than discretionary bail-in triggered debt.

Chapter 7 extended these paired comparisons of high-trigger cocos and alternative financing instruments to common equity. We do not favor direct cocos mandates because they would obviate market testing of the different features of cocos and stymie their development. Instead, competition and contest between more cocos and more CET1 should be encouraged from the start. While there would be no requirement to meet any of the capital requirements with cocos, there would be a possibility that cocos—as the only acceptable alternative to CET1—could qualify as a contributor to at least one of these requirements if the issuing institution should prefer. Since financial institutions tend to target capital ratios that are several percentage points above the respective minimum, and since rating agencies as well as regulators like to see such 'excess' capital, cocos could then potentially contribute to this buffer capital as well, allowing these institutions to be rated not just *adequately*- but *well*-capitalized.

S&P (2011b) has already made room for cocos in its measure of Total Adjusted Capital [TAC]. S&P has issued guidelines (excerpted in Chapter 16 below) that would allow high-trigger cocos—defined as "going-concern hybrid capital instruments" with a "mandatory trigger linked to a regulatory ratio expressed as a specific number" (Section IV C: 70)—to qualify for inclusion, subject to certain limits, in TAC. TAC is the numerator of the risk-adjusted capital [RAC] ratio, S&P's measure of the adequacy of bank capital. The RAC ratio provides the starting point for assessing the strength of a bank's capitalization under the S&P criteria for rating banks. High-trigger cocos classified as T1 under Basel III may be credited with high equity content while low-trigger cocos classified as T2 may be credited with intermediate such content by S&P. If so, they qualify for the calculation of TAC up to an aggregate amount of equity content derived from the cocos, other qualifying subordinated debt, and preferred stock that may not exceed 33% of the bank's Adjusted Common Equity, a measure similar to Basel III's CET1. This restriction is analogous to non-common equity for AT1 being limited to no more than one third of the basic T1 capital ratio requirement under Basel III.

Cocos and common stock are generally held by quite different classes of investors and the secondary market for cocos is still very thin. It takes market testing and the gradual development of derivatives suited for arbitrage operations to discover buying opportunities, the proper size of interest spreads and risk and liquidity premiums, and how they vary over the credit cycle and by term to maturity. Some firms may well have found certain placements of cocos—such as private placements or placements in exchange for non-cumulative preferred shares—to be cheaper at times than raising common equity. Setting aside the deductibility of interest but not dividends paid from taxable corporation income, such a perception should not be based on the mere fact that the after-tax interest rate on a new issue of cocos is below the rate of return required on equity, however; instead, imperfections due to illiquidity and the high cost of incomplete hedges for cocos could be responsible for "loose" pricing and room for negotiations. Among the missing hedge instruments are CDS that treat cocos conversion as a default payout event and use replacement rates in pricing cocos that are analytically supported by the conversion prices and stock price expectations involved.

Under certain assumptions (see Miller, 1995), the marginal and average cost of capital in equilibrium are equal to the required rate of return on total assets. If these (Modigliani-Miller) premises hold, the cost of capital cannot be changed purely by changing the financing mix. That cost would change only if there is a change in the required rate of return on the firm's assets—due, for instance, to a change in the business model or in the inherent riskiness of the type of ventures in which the firm is engaged. If the required rate of return on a risk-class of business assets contains an element of compensation for the risk of bankruptcy (which in turn is a function of financial structure), the separation between the riskiness of the underlying business and of its financing is more difficult to maintain, particularly because the bank is in the risk management business. Hence there can be no prejudgment of whether and when equity is expensive relative to cocos when all the ramifications of changing leverage and risk transfer are considered. However, there is much that is yet to be discovered about the true cost of cocos and the innovations they bring to risk management in the firm; there is as yet no brief for handicapping their development by denying them any and all equity content for regulatory purposes, even though they are designed to convert to equity in adversity when equity is most needed and least available by other means.

While any systematic ability of cocos to reduce the cost of capital—except through the tax deductibility of the interest paid on them—is thus uncertain but worth testing, there are other arguments that might favor cocos over relying solely on CET1. Most of these are predicated on the ability of cocos holders to improve corporate governance. A thick equity cushion without cocos could provide management with the leeway to take excessive risks and to pursue its own interests over those of long-term shareholders. Adding cocos to the balance sheet might reduce these managerial agency problems if cocos holders have reason to expect significant losses from conversion and have access to (or representation on) the corporate board to impress their concerns on management. This in turn would encourage management to raise capital well before the trigger point is reached.

The announcement of voluntary stock issues might be interpreted as a harbinger of bad things to come. If these adverse developments are not yet sufficient material for mandatory reporting, they could still remain within the preserve of management's asymmetric information advantage. Relying on a prepositioned suite of cocos with staggered (but still high) triggers to raise the equity capital through automatic timely conversions may be preferable to doing so later through a new stock or rights issue in preparation for adversities that management may see lurking down the road. Once these reversals have materialized it could be too late and expensive for either cocos or stocks to be issued, but the prepositioned suite of cocos would still be there ready for conversion as needed. Their presence on the balance sheet thus would be reassuring rather than suspicious, and their automatic conversion into equity after a loss of capital would send no adverse signals beyond the plain facts—already begging for interpretation—that triggered them.

In Chapter 8, a third paired comparison pit cocos not against alternative financing instruments but against restructuring procedures which turned out to be very costly and time-consuming without cocos. This finding is based on a study of the voluntary (though events-driven, of course) restructuring of the German multinational SolarWorld on the brink of insolvency in 2013, both as it was and as it might have been with cocos rather than straight bonds on the balance sheet.

SolarWorld, a maker of solar panels and related equipment, was chosen as a reminder that cocos need not be solely for financial companies. Non-financial companies maintain much higher capital ratios than financial companies and credit risk cannot be assigned separately to most of their physical assets. For these reasons their cocos would require a trigger like the leverage ratio that is defined without Basel III risk-weighting of assets and set much higher, in this instance to 10%.

In just 18 months, SolarWorld's leverage ratio declined from 27.5% at the start of 2012 to just below 3% on June 30, 2013. Had two large bond issues on the balance sheet taken the form of cocos with a 10% leverage-ratio trigger, they would have been set off no later than at the end of 2012. Subject to certain conjectures about the conversion terms and market value of shares obtained in conversion, cocos holders would have recovered 55% of the value of their investment. The new shares issued in conversion would have represented a majority, accounting for 51% of the total number of shares outstanding after conversion. Pre-existing shareholders still would have held on to the remaining 49% and gained from cocos conversion what the former cocos holders lost in value, net of the value of the shares they had received.

Almost the same outcome was actually achieved under voluntary restructuring for the holders of these two issues of publicly traded bonds due in 2016 and 2017. The conversion package contained a new bond with a face value equal to about 45% of the old bond, and a cash component as well as an equity component bringing the total compensation package up to an estimated recovery of 57%. After a slow start of negotiations, several separate votes, and one failed stakeholder meeting, the restructuring, since completed in February 2014, was finally agreed to by all parties in August 2013. By that time the company's position had deteriorated to the point that, for pre-existing stockholders at least, there was little left to lose. Their ownership share was reduced from 100% of the old to 5% of the new class of shares rather than to 49% of all shares outstanding, as expected after cocos conversion. Two strategic investors acquired 48.5% of the new class of shares, and holders of two classes of bonds and a third class of other creditors together received 46.5% ownership in the restructuring of their debt claims, leaving only 5% for the original shareholders.

The upshot is that voluntary restructuring creates costly delays in resolution compared to automatic cocos conversion at the trigger point. Pervasive uncertainty about the future of a company on the brink of insolvency turns clients and suppliers away and complicates financial dealings, such as access to trade credit, that would otherwise have been routine. During the negotiation phase, the ongoing dissipation of value ultimately tends to force agreement only when there is little left to lose for existing shareholders, and their case for greater recovery may be on its way to litigation. With cocos, the entire process of debt write-off and conversion could have been completed by the end of 2012, rather than, as reported, on February 24, 2014, and pre-existing shareholders would have held on to almost half of the company. Pre-existing shareholders can thus expect to be treated much better in adversity when there are cocos on the balance sheet than if they have to undergo a so-called 'voluntary' restructuring without cocos. This is important, because existing shareholders would never allow cocos to be issued in the first place if they were convinced that they could do better in a negotiated restructuring without them. Without the regulatory cocos mandates of the kind Calomiris and Herring (2010) favor (which we have rejected as counterproductive to the development of widely marketable cocos), the conversion terms of cocos have to be solicitous to existing shareholders. Indeed, conversion should never aim to reduce book value per share or be predictably value-dilutive for existing shareholders. Otherwise they will balk at putting cocos on to the balance sheet at all.

Cocos mandates would require companies to issue high-trigger and/or low-trigger cocos amounting to no less than a specified percentage of either total assets or Basel-III risk-weighted assets. Such regulatory cocos mandates, which come on top of CET1 mandates, have been introduced only in Switzerland so far, and then only for its two largest banks, UBS and Credit Suisse. The more unpleasant regulators make cocos conversion for pre-existing shareholders—by imposing a conversion price that is a mere fraction of the market price prevailing around the time of conversion, for instance, or otherwise set so low that cocos holders would be likely to enjoy a replacement rate of over 100% in the event of conversion—the fewer cocos issues will be planned. OSFI has been one of the regulators demanding "significant dilution of pre-existing shareholders" as a condition for approving NVCC instruments (non-viability, i.e., low-trigger cocos). The often low-trigger write-down-only cocos should then be banned because they would savage cocos holders instead. In fact, choosing conversion terms so extreme as to wipe out either pre-existing shareholders or cocos holders at conversion would not yield a sustainable financing model with room for cocos.

Part III
Varieties of Cocos Design and Rationales

10

Determining Conversion Price and Risk Premium in Cocos

The most critical variables for pricing the conversion risk premium in cocos are (i) the probability of conversion [π] in each year over the term of the bond and (ii) the recovery rate [ρ] obtained from the market value of the common equity received at conversion in relation to the face value of the bond cancelled at that time. To simplify the exposition, both π and ρ are taken to be constant over the term of the bond whose face value is normalized at 1. This principal amount will be repaid if the coco has not been converted into common stock by its maturity date [T]. The probability of the debt surviving to that date is $(1 - \pi)^T$. The 'riskless' rate r * that functions as the discount rate is deemed to be free of credit risk. It is entered as either 3% or 6% in the implicit *basic* equation for R below if the term to maturity is 5 years, and as either 4% or 7% if that term is 10 years. R is the annual rate of return required on cocos under risk neutrality, meaning it does not include a premium to compensate for risk aversion but only for losses expected in the event of conversion.

$$1 = \frac{(1 - \pi)R}{(1 + r *)} + \frac{(1 - \pi)^2 R}{(1 + r *)^2} \cdots + \frac{(1 - \pi)^T R}{(1 + r *)^T} + \frac{(1 - \pi)^T}{(1 + r *)^T}$$

$$+ \frac{\pi\rho}{(1 + r *)} + \frac{\pi\rho(1 - \pi)}{(1 + r *)^2} + \frac{\pi\rho(1 - \pi)^2}{(1 + r *)^3} \cdots + \frac{\pi\rho(1 - \pi)^{T-1}}{(1 + r *)^T}$$

This equation yields an accessible basic solution for R and then the conversion risk premium, R – r *:

$$R = \frac{r * + (1 - \rho)\pi}{(1 - \pi)}$$

$$R - r * = \frac{(1 - \rho + r *)\pi}{(1 - \pi)}$$

The solution would become even simpler if payment of a full year of interest was assured in the year of cocos conversion rather than being left unpaid, as is assumed in the specification on the first line of the long implicit *basic* equation for R above. This alternative would be analogous to the "next coupon" collateralized guarantee afforded, for instance, on some Brady bonds. In principle, interest accrued up to the date of conversion is payable at conversion. This change in specification, effected by reducing the power on $(1 - \pi)$ by 1 in each term where it multiplies R on the top line of the *basic* equation, produces the alternative results for R_{alt} and the alternative conversion risk premium:

$$R_{alt} = r * + (1 - \rho)\pi$$

$$R_{alt} - r * = (1 - \rho)\pi$$

Comparing the results for R and R_{alt} shows that while the conversion risk premiums are of course 0 with both of these measures if the annual probability of conversion $[\pi]$ is zero, the same result obtains with the recovery rate $\rho = 1$ only with R_{alt}. The reason is that, in the *basic* specification leading to R, conversion by the end of a year prevents payment of the last (here annual) coupon due on cocos at the same time. Hence even if the recovery rate is 1 in that the value of the common stock received in conversion fully compensates for the principal of the cocos converted, there is a loss of interest whose size grows with r *. Under the *basic* specification which is used for the results reported in Table 4, recovery is a little less than 100% of the face value of cocos even if ρ equals 1 as long as $\pi > 0$. The exact size of this small difference is $\pi r */(1 - \pi)$, which is π percent of R because $R = r */(1 - \pi)$ when $\rho = 1$.

With values for π, ρ, r *, and T assigned to obtain results within a representative range of parameter values, the explicit equations derived above for the rate of return on cocos [R] and the conversion loss premium R − r * yield the results shown in Table 4. Much can be explained by focusing on just the last three rows of that Table. At a riskless rate [r *] of 7% (or 0.07) on 10-year Treasuries, which is far above their yield in recent years but not historically exceptional, about 4% of 0.07 (or 0.0029) would be added to r * to cover the residual conversion risk that the coupon due in the year of conversion will not be paid. Hence there is a small loss from conversion even though ρ equals 1 in the case laid out on the bottom row (20b). If ρ is reduced from 1 to 0.5 (as on row 20), R rises by almost 2 percentage points more, from 7.29% to 9.38%, and R − r * jumps from 0.29% to 2.38%. If the recovery rate is lowered further to 0%, as applies to write-off-only 'cocos' that do not convert to anything at all, both R and R − r * would rise by roughly another 2 percentage points to 11.46% and 4.46%, respectively, as shown on row 20a. In all three cases the fixed annual probability of conversion [π] is assumed to be 4% implying, that the chance of this 10-year coco surviving until maturity is only two-thirds. If everything else were the same, but π were 0.02 instead as in the case depicted on row 8, R would be back down to 9.18 and R − r * to 2.18.

For cocos offering estimated replacement rates of at least one-half, 2.4 percentage points may therefore be regarded as the most that would be needed to fully cover the loss expected in the event of conversion. Only one much larger model-deduced value for the conversion risk premium (4.46%) appears in the last column of Table 4, and that value applies to write-down-only cocos, as already described. On cocos with zero- or very low-replacement rates, the conversion risk premium required could thus be as high as 4.5 percentage points. On cocos issued in 2013 with ρ = 0, the add-on to the relevant mid-swap rate in their coupon setting formula has in fact been in the range of 325 to 450 bps. Investment in (as yet largely untested) cocos is subject to a variety of additional types of risk not here quantified, of course, such as instrument-innovation and modeling risk, illiquidity, and difficulties with diversifying and hedging cocos portfolios. All of these risks

Table 4. Risk-Neutral Required Rates of Return and Conversion Risk Premium on Cocos

Row No.	Recovery Rate [ρ]	Probab. of Conversion [π]	Riskless Interest R. [r *]	Term in Years [T]	Required Rate of Return [R]	Conversion Risk Prem. [R − r *]
1)	0	0.01	0.03	5	0.0404	0.0104
2)	0	0.01	0.04	10	0.0505	0.0105
3)	0	0.01	0.06	5	0.0707	0.0107
4)	0	0.01	0.07	10	0.0808	0.0108
5)	0	0.02	0.03	5	0.0510	0.0210
6)	0	0.02	0.04	10	0.0612	0.0212
7)	0	0.02	0.06	5	0.0816	0.0216
8)	0	0.02	0.07	10	0.0918	0.0218
9)	0.5	0.01	0.03	5	0.0354	0.0054
10)	0.5	0.01	0.04	10	0.0455	0.0055
11)	0.5	0.01	0.06	5	0.0657	0.0057
12)	0.5	0.01	0.07	10	0.0758	0.0058
13)	0.5	0.02	0.03	5	0.0408	0.0108
14)	0.5	0.02	0.04	10	0.0510	0.0110
15)	0.5	0.02	0.06	5	0.0714	0.0114
16)	0.5	0.02	0.07	10	0.0816	0.0116
17)	0.5	0.04	0.03	5	0.0521	0.0221
18)	0.5	0.04	0.04	10	0.0625	0.0225
19)	0.5	0.04	0.06	5	0.0833	0.0233
20)	0.5	0.04	0.07	10	0.0938	0.0238
20a)	0	0.04	0.07	10	0.1146	0.0446
20b)	1	0.04	0.07	10	0.0729	0.0029

Note: Under risk neutrality, the conversion risk premium is equal to the actuarial rate of compensation for the loss expected from conversion.

are to a large extent transitional, however, and likely to become less costly as the volume of cocos issuance and experience with the new instrument build.

Like the *basic* approach just before, the CDS approach to pricing the conversion risk premium—by treating conversion as if it were a default event—also requires entering a replacement or recovery rate ρ that is fixed and not at risk. A riskless rate of $r* = 2\%$ annually, i.e., $\underline{r}* = \ln(1 + r*) = 1.98\%$ in continuous time, repeatedly observed on 10-year Treasuries in 2012–2013, is reflected in both approaches. Furthermore, the survival curve generated by $\exp(-\lambda t^s)$ with $s = 1$ implies a constant exponential rate of decline $[\lambda]$ in the survival rate specified for the CDS approach. The survival curve $(1 - \pi)^t$ declines at an equally constant percentage rate of π per year in the *basic* approach. Hence if the same assumed survival rate to the point of maturity is reached under both approaches after 10 years (as in Table 5) the exponential rate $-\lambda$ is very close to the annual percentage rate $-\pi$ since $\ln(1 - \pi) \approx -\pi$.

Given these basic similarities in input functions and values, and with risk neutrality assumed under the CDS par-value approach as under the *basic* approach, results of the two approaches shown in Table 5 thus turn out to be very close under comparable conditions. However, there are also important limitations. Neither result makes any explicit reference to the extent of the CET1 capital buffer above the trigger point which the firm had maintained at the time of cocos issue. Since this ratio is a measure of the financial robustness of the firm, it should not be ignored in gauging the probability of cocos surviving without conversion until maturity or until some specified call date.

10.1 Setting the Conversion Price to Obtain a Targeted Replacement Rate

Another specification feature that is challenging for actual applications is the assumption of a fixed recovery rate *ex ante*, i.e., at the time of cocos issue. In principle, it is desirable to fix the conversion price *ex ante* so that investors can be certain of the number of shares obtained in the event of conversion. However, fixing

Table 5. Premiums for Conversion Risk from *Basic* Formula and CDS Compared

Row No.	Recovery Rate [ρ]	Probability of Conversion [π] annually	Probability of Surviving 10 Y [P_{S10}]	Riskless Interest Rate [r*]	Risk Premium from Formula [R − r*]%	Risk Premium from CDS [R − r*]%
1)	0	0.02	0.817	0.02	2.08	2.04
2)	0	0.04	0.665	0.02	4.25	4.13
3)	0.5	0.02	0.817	0.02	1.06	1.02
4)	0.5	0.04	0.665	0.02	2.17	2.06
5)	0.8	0.02	0.817	0.02	0.45	0.41
6)	0.8	0.04	0.665	0.02	0.92	0.83

Sources: Results in last column are obtained by linear interpolation of results for nearby PS10 values—for 0.8 and 0.9 surrounding 0.817, and 0.6 and 0.7 for 0.665—for s = 1 and various ρ obtained for CDS in von Furstenberg (2012a, p. 71).

the conversion price [CP] *ex ante* to be consistent with the target level chosen for ρ is a challenging proposition. The next problems therefore are (i) how CP can be set in advance so that the best estimate of interested parties is that the holders will recover the target fraction ρ of the face value of the cocos converted and (ii) how the level of CP appropriate for this purpose depends on the size of the firm's $CET1_0$ ratio at the time of cocos issue [time subscript 0 or function subscript i].

In pricing the conversion risk premium for cocos above, a fixed recovery rate was assumed; its level was treated as known and certain already from the time of cocos issue. This was done without explaining how confidence in any such pre-specified value of the recovery rate can be empirically supported. The difficulty, so far passed over, is this: given the Face Value [FV] of the cocos being converted, as well as the number of shares obtained in conversion $[N_c]$ and hence the conversion price per share [CP], the actual recovery rate cannot be determined until post-conversion market prices per common share $[MP_c]$ have been observed. Hence the only method of conversion that would hold the actual recovery rate ρ at a predetermined target level with certainty is to leave CP open until MP_c has been recorded. As the last of the three equations below shows, CP would then be set so that MP_c/CP is equal to the desired value of ρ, ρ, in the 0 to 1 range.

The lower limit of $\rho = 0$ is of little interest: it implies that no shares are received in conversion at all, as in 'cocos' providing only for write-down or write-off of the cocos debt without conversion into common shares. Full recovery, signified by $\rho = 1$ may be taken as the upper bound. It is not advisable to over-compensate cocos holders by making the targeted recovery rate even higher: doing so would strike fear of conversion into pre-existing shareholders as has sometimes been proposed. In (2011b, p. 5) I have specifically referenced ICB (2011, p. 182), Goodhart (2011, p. 117), Calomiris and Herring (2011, p. 18), Flannery and Perotti (2011, p. 4), and SFRC (2010) as having favored cocos with conversion terms that hold out the prospect of "death by dilution" or at least "severe" dilution, for pre-existing shareholders. Without a regulatory mandate for cramming down cocos, it would be counterproductive to threaten pre-existing shareholders with—for them, intentionally ruinous—terms of cocos conversion. If faced with such a threat, existing shareholders and the firm's management would make sure to keep cocos from ever being issued in the first place.

In view of this, a ρ value of around 0.8 would appear to strike the appropriate balance between cocos holders and pre-existing shareholders. Upon conversion, cocos holders should stand to lose a slice of their investment to motivate what is left of "debt discipline." At the same time they should expect to lose far less than under bankruptcy or with 0% recovery of debt write-off-only 'cocos.' Pre-existing shareholders should welcome cocos to the balance sheet because cocos could provide some debt relief under conditions so adverse that they would have triggered conversion. As long as ρ is less than 1, the combination of cancellation of the cocos debt and conversion to common shares would raise the book value of equity per share and have some positive effect on the company's stock price. Hence the result of conversion would not be dilutive of value per share, though the ownership share of pre-existing shareholders would necessarily decline.

As the following three equations lay out formally, the lower the control variable [CP], and the greater the number of shares to be issued in conversion of cocos with a given face value [FV], the higher the recovery rate for cocos holders will be and the worse the outcome for pre-existing shareholders.

$$MP_c \, N_c = \rho(FV)$$

$$CP \, N_c \equiv FV$$

$$\therefore \rho = \frac{MP_c}{CP}$$

The first equation above implicitly defines ρ as the ratio of the market value of the stock received by conversion divided by the FV of the cocos converted. The second equation is that of a rectangular hyperbola which relates CP and N_c inversely in such a way that their product always equals FV. The third equation defines ρ compactly as a ratio of prices rather than quantities. Since it results from the division of the first by the second equation, only two of the three equations are independent. The last equation links CP to the market price per share at conversion [MP_c] given the choice of ρ. However, leaving CP open until conversion, and hence the number of shares to be obtained from conversion indeterminate until then, would hurt the marketability of cocos. It is desirable for accuracy in pricing and hedging, therefore, to include CP and thus the number of shares issued in conversion in the covenant of cocos when issued.

To obtain the recovery rate $\underline{\rho}$ on cocos *ex ante*, CP must be set equal to the market price per share which is expected at issue time 0 [operator E_0] to prevail at conversion [$E_0(MP_c)$] divided by the intended target value of $\underline{\rho}$. To inform this expectation requires first to recognize that—given the $CET1_0$ ratio at the time of issue when t = 0—it would take a substantial deterioration in CET1 and in the share price for cocos conversion to be triggered at a preset CET1 trigger level of, say, 7%. In (2013b, p. 8) I previously estimated the following impact of a change in the CET1 capital ratio, expressed in percentage points, on the market price per share:

$$\ln\left(\frac{MP_c}{MP_0}\right) = 0.2067\Delta CET1$$

The standard deviation on the annualized quarterly change amounts in the CET1 capital ratios used in this equation is 0.93, or 2.94 percentage points over 10 years, assuming a random diffusion process. Now if the $CET1_0$ ratio of the financial firm were 10% (as was reported by Credit Suisse for the end of the third quarter 2013, for example) and the trigger level for cocos were 7% (as it is for the cocos issued by that firm) would have to be –3 to trigger cocos. That would mean that the z-score on a standard normal distribution would be –3/2.94 or –1.02, yielding a conversion probability of 15.39% after 10 years and thus a Probability of Survival [PR_{S10}] of 0.8461 until maturity. Since the process of de-capitalization to the trigger point is likely to be gradual rather than a jump process, conversion would be bunched in the final years of the cocos debt rather than proceeding at the constant annual percentage conversion rate of $\pi = 0.01657$ that is calculated to lead to that same PR_{S10} level, $(1 - \pi)^{10}$, after 10 years. We make use of this likely bunching near the end to telescope conversions to year T, just before the cocos debt would otherwise be repaid at maturity.

The equation above lends itself to being used counterfactually to estimate how much lower the stock price of the firm would have been if its CET1 ratio had just dropped from 10% to 7% in the same quarter, between ends of quarters. In reality such a decline in the capital ratio, net of occasional upticks, could take several quarters or even years during which the underlying tendency of the stock price to rise over time could assert itself. To crudely allow for this in estimating the stock price to expect at conversion, the MP_c inferred from the equation above is multiplied by e^{rt} where $\underline{r} = \ln(1 + r)$ and t ranges from 0 to T. This inference procedure suggests that the market price per share would be $\exp(-0.6201)$, where $-0.6201 = 0.2067(-3)$, or 53.8% of its level at the time of cocos issue times 1.219 for e^{rT} with $T = 10$ and the annual rate $r = 2\%$ implying continuously compounded $\underline{r}$ of 1.98%. Hence $E_0(MP_{cT})$ would be 0.656, and the best estimate of the stock price prevailing after the announcement of conversion would be equal to about two-thirds of the stock price numeraire, $MP_0 = 1$. Hence with ρ at, say, 0.8—and assuming that conversion occurs (if at all) toward the end of the 10-year term to maturity—CP would be set at the time of cocos issue to CP = $(0.656/0.8) = 0.82$ to yield the expected and targeted recovery rate ρ of 80%. (This result is before applying an Anti-Dilution Offset Factor [ADF] of 1.05, explained in the next section, which takes account of the fact that any rise in the conversion price also raises the expected market price per share when $\rho < 1$.)

10.2 Adjusting CP for Anti-Dilutive Effects
of Conversion when $\rho < 1$

As just shown, the CP that is to be set in the cocos covenant relative to MP_0 (the stock price at the time of cocos issue that serves as numeraire) depends on the market price of the stock that is expected to prevail around the time of cocos conversion, and on the replacement-rate target. This share price expected if and when conversion is triggered is positively related, however, to the conversion price and to the size of the entire cocos issue that is to be converted relative to the amount of pre-existing stockholders' equity outstanding. It is also positively related to the complement of ρ, $0 \leq (1 - \rho) \leq 1$, which represents the shortfall of cocos holders' recovery rate from 100%. These are the dependencies which this section will illustrate, explain, and ultimately take into account in estimating that stock price—conditional on conversion— relative to $MP_0 = 1$.

A numerical example based on the assumption that stock prices move proportionately with the book value per share of financial institutions may help explore the strength of these links when ρ is 0.8. A bank has \$200 billion [bn] in assets, that amount to \$100bn of risk-weighted assets [RWA] and CET1 of \$7bn on its balance sheet, with 350 million [m] shares initially outstanding. The cocos with a 7% trigger are all converted; their face value is taken to be \$3.5bn and cancellation of that debt raises the book value of equity by 50% from \$7bn to \$10.5bn. Book value per share would remain unchanged at \$20 if the cocos holders would obtain new shares equal to 50% of the 350m shares outstanding prior to conversion. Because the share of one-third (3.5bn/10.5bn) contributed by cocos conversion to equity is then equal to the portion (175m/525m) of the shares held by the former cocos holders through conversion, the book value of equity per share—which had been 7bn/0.35bn—is now 10.5bn/0.525bn and thus still \$20. In return for the cancellation of \$3.5bn of FV of cocos, their holders therefore obtain 175m shares worth \$20 each for a total recovery of \$3.5bn, or 100% of FV.

For a targeted recovery rate of 0.8 rather than 1, cocos holders should get shares with a book (and market) value of only \$2.8bn for their \$3.5bn contribution to the firm's equity. To achieve this, the number of shares issued in conversion must be reduced by more than 20% to less than 140 million because book value per share will rise above $20. The reason is that the number of shares outstanding post-conversion is raised by less than before, when ρ was 1 and book value per share remained unchanged by conversion. Issuing only 127.27m shares in conversion in addition to the 350m already outstanding would raise book value per share to $22 (10.5bn/0.47727bn) and provide $2.8bn ($22x127.27m) for cocos holders. It would leave existing shareholders with claims to a book value of equity of $7.7bn ($22x350m), 10% more than the $7 billion in share value they had prior to cocos conversion. The complete set of results obtained from the three-equation system laid out below consists of MP_{cT} = $22, N_c = 127.27m shares, and CP = $27.5, so that ρ = MP_{cT}/CP = 22/27.5 = 0.8, as is 2.8/3.5.

$$MP_{cT} = \frac{10.5bn}{0.350bn + N_c}$$

$$MP_{cT} N_c = 2.8bn \ (= \rho FV)$$

$$CP \ N_c \equiv 3.5bn \ (= FV)$$

The first of these results shows that conversion has raised market price per share, here assumed to rise by the same percentage as book value per share, by 10% from $20 to $22 when ρ is 0.8 rather than 1. To implement this reduction in ρ, the CP had to be raised first by 25% from $20 to $25 (= $20/0.8) for the direct effect of lowering ρ and by a further 10% from $25 to $27.50 to keep ρ on target at 0.8. The number of shares issued in conversion would fall from 175m to ($20/$27.5)175m = 127.27m. To make this happen, the conversion price would have to be increased from $20 to (175m/127.27m)$20 = $27.5, with the respective product of conversion price and number of shares issued in conversion, CP(N_c), remaining equal to 3.5bn, the FV of the cocos subject to conversion. This CP is 10% higher than it would be to yield ρ if the market price of common stock per share had not risen by 10% as a result of the anti-dilutive conversion occurring when ρ < 1.

Modifying this example helps broaden the range of results obtained which clearly depend not only on the choice of ρ but also on the amount of cocos relative to equity on the balance sheet. For the next few years it appears reasonable to assume that cocos could be just 25% as large as equity, or $1.75bn, rather than $3.5bn, half as large as before. The formulas above then would be solved with $8.75bn replacing $10.5bn, $1.4bn replacing $2.8bn, and $1.75bn replacing $3.5bn. MP_{cT} would rise by 5% from $20 to $21, and the conversion price would have to increase by the same 5% (from $25 to $26.25) on top of the rise from $20 to $25 as before, to keep ρ on its target of 0.8. The 5% increase in MP_{cT} nudges the CP up further by the Anti-Dilution Offset Factor [ADF] of 1.05. This adjustment was applied in column 4 of Table 6. Hence the conversion price depends both on the level of the targeted replacement rate and on the share of cocos relative to equity on the balance sheet. CP is lower the smaller that share, *ceteris paribus*, but higher the more ρ falls short of 1.

10.3 Summary of What to Consider in Setting the Conversion Price [CP]

A CP should be part of the cocos covenant so that the number of common shares issued at conversion is known already from the time the cocos are initially offered. To determine the yield required on cocos, both cocos issuers and investors need to know not only the probability of conversion but also what recovery rate any such CP may yield. Because the recovery rate is simply equal to the market price per share of the common stock obtained by conversion divided by CP, they need to form an estimate of what stock price to expect in the event of conversion.

To gauge how the control variable CP should be set for cocos to be expected to deliver the targeted level of the recovery rate [ρ] subject only to random misses, the following inputs are needed (these are laid out in Table 6). First the Basel III Common Equity Tier 1 capital ratio last reported before cocos are issued [$CET1_0$] has to be publicly available to assess the hybrid's quality at the point of issue. As will be discussed later in Chapter 16, the credit rating of the issuing firm or the issue rating of the cocos themselves could be used as supplementary indicators of the

Table 6. CET1 Ratios at Issuance of 10-yr. Cocos, Associated Market & Conversion Prices [MP & CP], Probability [PR] of Conversion by Maturity Date and Annually and C-Risk Premium

	Distance from 7% Trigger	MP_{e0} as Fraction Of MP_0	$E_0(MP_{cT})$ with r = 1.98 T = 10yrs.	CP with $\rho = 0.8$ ADF = 1.05	PR_{c10} of Conversion [C]	Annual C Rate π	C-Risk Premium $R - r^*$ %
	1)	2)	3)	4)	5)	6)	7)
CET10							
12%	–5%	0.3558	0.4337	0.5693	0.0446	0.00455	0.10
11%	–4%	0.4375	0.5333	0.7000	0.0869	0.00905	0.20
10%	–3%	0.5380	0.6558	0.8608	0.1539	0.01657	0.37
9%	–2%	0.6615	0.8064	1.0584	0.2483	0.02814	0.64
8%	–1%	0.8133	0.9914	1.3012	0.3669	0.04468	1.03

Source: von Furstenberg (2013b, pp. 8–9). Results in last column are derived with *basic* equation.

Notes: Entries in col. 3 would also have to be multiplied by ADF before dividing by the corresponding entries in col. 4 to show the targeted value of $\rho = 0.8$. Entries in col. 4 are 1.05(1.25) = 1.3125 times the corresponding entries in col. 3. The Anti-Dilution Offset Factor [ADF] is 1.05 if the face value of cocos outstanding is about ¼ of the book value of equity. The probability of cocos surviving to maturity [PR_{S10}] (not shown) is $(1 - PR_{c10})$.

"distance from conversion." However, the distance of $CET1_0$ from the CET1 trigger level is the most direct measure. There must then be an empirical basis for estimating the relation between observed percentage changes in CET1 and the simultaneous rate of change in the share price of a firm's common stock. For cocos to convert, the firm would have to experience a decline in its CET1 ratio (reported at least quarterly) from $CET1_0$ to 7%, assumed to be the trigger level. This decline would be associated with a fall in its expected stock price. The greater the financial strength of the firm (as measured by $CET1_0$) reflected in its stock price, the deeper is the fall in both CET1 and the share price from the time of cocos issue to conversion should the latter occur.

The second column in Table 6 thus answers the comparative-static question of how much lower the market price MP_{c0} would have been compared to the market price of $MP_0 = 1$ that actually prevailed at the time of cocos issue, if CET1 (instead of being $CET1_0$) had been down at the trigger level $[CET1_{c0}]$ at that instance. In reality, a process jumping instantly from being adequately or well capitalized to cocos conversion is not plausible; instead, the descent to the trigger level is likely to take time and be bunched near the term to maturity of the cocos if it follows a diffusion process over the assumed 10-year maturity of the cocos issue. This process implies that, given an estimate of the annualized standard deviation in $\Delta CET1$, the corresponding measure after 10 years would be $\sqrt{10}$ (or over three times) as large. To gauge what the stock market price would have been if conversion had in all cases occurred T = 10 years after issue, growth at the riskless interest rate r * in the interim is allowed for in column 3. This yields the expectation, formed at the time of issue, of what the market price MP_{cT} will be if conversion occurs just before maturity of the cocos. The conversion price per share of common stock that would yield the targeted recovery rate $\rho = 0.8$ would then be set at $ADF(MP_{cT}/0.8)$ as shown in the fourth column of Table 6. Multiplication by an Anti-Dilution Offset Factor greater than 1 is designed to raise CP so as to offset the benefit, shared by cocos holders with pre-existing shareholders, of the rise in the expected share price conditional on conversion that is produced by conversion when $\rho < 1$. This boost to the share price expected post-conversion is positively related to the relative size of the cocos issue subject to conversion and to the extent of the shortfall of ρ from the non-redistributive norm of $\rho = 1$.

Some of the numerical results in Table 6 bear further scrutiny. Column 4, for instance, shows that if $\rho = 0.8$ was intended and a firm's $CET1_0$ was 9%, its appropriate conversion price should be very close to the share price of its stock around the time of issue [MP_0]. That was the level of CP set by LBG in 2009, though the bank gave no indication of the ρ level it had intended. The examples above show how such an indication could be given and explained to potential cocos investors coherently. On the other hand, if $CET1_0$ had initially been 12% rather than 9%, CP should be only about half as large as MP_0, and the number of shares to be received in a conversion of FV consequently about twice as high to support the rational expectation of a recovery rate of 0.8. Once again, the more a firm's CET1 capital ratio exceeds its required level at the time of cocos issue, the farther that ratio—and the stock price along with it—subsequently must fall to trigger conversion. To support the intuition metaphorically, to bring down the strongest requires a much greater injury (to their CET1 capital ratio) than to bring down the weakest (to the same trigger point). This means that CP for the stronger must be lower relative to MP_0 than for the weaker issuers to yield the same prospective recovery rate (equal to ρ) for initially strong and weak cocos issuers alike.

The level of $CET1_0$ including its standard deviation and assumed diffusion process also determine the probability that the cocos will have survived to the end of their 10-year maturity. Column 5 of Table 6 shows this result, equal to $(1 - \pi)^T$, and uses it to extract the level of the corresponding fixed annual conversion rate [π] in column 6. The result is that π is eight times as high when cocos are issued by a firm whose Basel III capital ratio is $CET1_0 = 8\%$ than when issued by a firm whose $CET1_0$ is 12%. In this way an estimated relation between change in stock price and de-capitalization to the trigger point can be solved for the annualized probability of conversion [π]. That same relation, together with the initial condition and trigger level of the bank's CET1 capital ratio, determine the conversion price *ex ante* that would be most likely to yield the targeted recovery rate ρ. There is an important lesson to draw from all this. Both state variables (such as the size of the initial CET1 ratio of a bank and the size of its cocos portfolio relative to equity) and control variables (such as the level of ρ and CP) are interdependent and jointly determined with other variables such as π and hence the conversion risk premium. The solution of the *basic* equation for the conversion risk premium, $R - r^*$, under the new conditions detailed in the last columns of Table 6, show that this premium under risk neutrality and with $\rho = 0.8$ is just 0.1%, or 10 basis points, for firms with $CET1_0$ of 12%; but it is 10 times as high (1.03%) for those issuing 10-year cocos when their starting $CET1_0$ ratio is only 8%, just 1 percentage point above the stipulated trigger level.

11

Write-Down-Only Cocos

As previously deduced, the conversion risk premium on cocos can become steep when the recovery rate $[\rho]$ is zero and the annual probability of conversion $[\pi]$ is as high as 4%. Line 20a of Table 4 above shows, for instance, an expected value of that premium $[R - r \,*]$ of 4.46% for $\rho = 0$ and $\pi = 4\%$. This internally consistent inference from a pricing model must still be confronted with market data where the conversion risk premium is represented by Bloomberg estimates of G-spread and π is implied. It turns out that the average of the values of π in the last column of Table 7 that satisfy the *basic* equation with $\rho = 0$ and $r \,*$ given by the yield curve on US Treasuries for the respective G-spread is 3.96% unweighted and 3.80% when weighted by the US dollar size of each of the 10 issues. Hence the value of π implied by actual data for the cocos issues of the 10 banks featured in Table 7 is roughly the same as the 4% value set for π in the model solution described at the beginning of this paragraph. For this reason, the average of the G-spreads in Table 7 is also expected to be close to the conversion risk premium of 4.46% deduced from the *basic* equation as described before. Even though this premium is not likely to be the only contributor to the G-spread, the actual average G-spread was *lower* than the average spread deduced from the model for the conversion risk premium alone. It was 4.18% unweighted and 4.01% weighted by size of issue compared with 4.46%. Hence there is rough—but meaningful—correspondence between actual data and model-based inferences.

11.1 Inefficiently Constructed Variants of Write-Down-Only Cocos

Wipe-out cocos providing for an immediate, full, and final write-down to zero without converting to equity when a trigger event occurs have become more common since 2011. Among such non-converting cocos, paradoxically still called cocos rather than 'cocas' (contingent cancellable debt securities), there are three deviations from the standard terms just given:

1. Rabobank's 6.875% 19/03/20 10-year €1.25bn issue provided for cash equal to 25% of principal, with the remaining 75% of the principal written down, when Core Tier-1 capital [CT1] falls below its trigger level of 7%. Hence this contingent bond offers a credible (though not certain) recovery rate of 25%. The issue can also be seen as a combination product of a senior conventional bond and a standard write-off-only security for three times the face amount of the senior bond. Since investors can purchase Rabobank's senior low-risk bonds together with any of the types of cocos being offered in any combination they care to choose, it is highly doubtful that value can be created by offering a fixed bundle.

2. Rabobank's 8.375% perpetual contingent capital bond issued 01/26/2011 may be written down in steps by just enough to cure successive (non-)viability events if necessary until the instrument has been written down to zero. It may, however, never be written back up. Hence this contingent capital bond may have a recovery rate that would be greater than zero if the regulators approve one or more partial write-downs and the bank, thereafter, remains adequately capitalized. That would mean that a complete write-down is not needed before what is left of the security is paid in full by being called after 5 or more years or redeemed and replaced after 30 years. Because this perpetual issue has a CT1 < 8% trigger, it would be junior to the 10-year issue described just before that has a CTI < 7% trigger. Anything but a complete write-off at the first trigger event would probably not be large enough to restore the company to full health given that this $2bn issue was equal to only 0.7% of the dollar value of Rabobank's risk weighted assets in mid-2013. Administering recapitalization help that is at best moderate in total—in what may

Table 7. Write-Down-Only Cocos and their Implied Annual Conversion Rate π

Name	Coupon	Maturity [M]	Tier	Amount	Settle	First Call [FC] Date	Price Par = 100	Yield [R]	G-Spread	r*	Rating	Trigger	Nearest T	Implied π
RABOBK	8.375%	07/29/49	T1	$2bn	01/26/11	FC07/26/16	109.65	4.53%	4.01%	0.53%	BBB+	CT1 < 8%	3Y 0.62%	3.83%
CS	7.875%	02/24/41	T2	$2bn	02/24/11	FC08/24/16	108.6	4.54%	3.99%	0.55%	BBB-	CET1<7%	3Y 0.62%	3.82%
RABOBK	8.4%	11/29/49	T1	$2bn	11/09/11	FC06/29/17	111.5	4.90%	4.03%	0.87%	BBB+	CT1 < 8%	3Y 0.62%	3.84%
UBS	7.625%	08/17/22	T2	$2bn	08/17/12	M08/17/22	115.75	5.35%	2.82%	2.52%	BBB	CET1<5%	10Y 2.77%	2.68%
BARCLAYS	7.625%	11/21/22	T2	$3bn	11/21/12	M11/21/22	105.375	6.82%	4.23%	2.58%	BB+	CT1 < 7%	10Y 2.77%	3.96%
KBC	8%	01/25/23	T2	$1bn	01/25/13	FC01/25/18	107.75	5.89%	4.78%	1.10%	BB+	CT1 < 7%	5Y 1.42%	4.52%
BARCLAYS	7.75%	04/10/23	T2	$1bn	04/10/13	FC04/10/18	105.5	6.30%	5.11%	1.19%	BBB-	CT1 < 7%	5Y 1.42%	4.81%
UBS	4.75%	05/22/23	T2	$1.5bn	05/22/13	FC05/22/18	98.25	5.12%	3.95%	1.18%	BBB	CT1 < 5%	5Y 1.42%	3.75%
CS	6.5%	08/08/13	T2	$2.5bn	08/08/13	M08/08/23	105.5	5.75%	3.11%	2.64%	BBB	CET1<5%	10Y 2.77%	2.94%
SOCGEN	8.25%	11/29/49	T1	$1.25bn	09/06/13	FC11/29/18	104.25	7.23%	5.79%	1.44%	BB	CET1<5%	5Y 1.42%	5.40%

Source: Bloomberg, quotations for 11/08/13 (close) and 11/11/13–11/14/13 (intraday).

For π: Basic equation with ρ set to 0 solved for $\pi = (R - r^*)/(1 + R)$, with $R - r^* =$ G-Spread.

Notes: Ratings are composite if more than one credit agency rated the security. Core Tier-1 [CT1] ratios with RWA may include cocos issued before mid-2012. They are being replaced in 2014 with CET1 triggers with only common equity in the numerator. The 11/08/13 yield of the UST. The 11/08/13 yield of the UST. security with a constant maturity, from the Fed's H.15 release, is nearest to the remaining M of the cocos shown but not used directly for G-spread which Bloomberg defines as "interpolated bond spread to Government curve matching currency bond yield [here all in USD] minus interpolated [US] government bond yield."

turn out to be a number of sips—would apply a drawn-out low-dosage conversion regimen to cocos that is likely to be ineffective in removing doubts about the health of the bank after the initial conversion.

3. The Perpetual Contingent Bond issued by Société Générale on 09/06/2013 has a write-down, write-up structure. However, to qualify as Tier-1 regulatory capital under European Banking Authority [EBA] rules, write-up must be entirely at the issuer's discretion. A contractual undertaking to write up would render these bonds ineligible to qualify as regulatory capital. It is unclear what could motivate management to agree to a write-up—presumably over the objections of shareholders in this environment. Any funding advantage gained from including the write-up feature in the cocos covenant is unlikely to materialize, or to fall victim to time-inconsistency, under these conditions. If the voluntary write-up feature were nonetheless taken seriously by investors, the cocos would be non-cumulative Preferred Equity by another name as only interest payments could be cancelled. In Table 7 these SOCGEN securities have one of the highest coupons (8.25%) right after those of Rabobank. Their implied annual probability of conversion is the highest, however, 5.4% compared to 3.8% for the two RABOBK issues shown in Table 7. Offering voluntary write-up does not appear to be a selling point. In December 2013, Société Générale again issued full or partial write-down cocos, with write-up at the option of the company, thereby continuing to combine two of the three worst features of the write-down-only deviants here considered.

With the deviations noted, all of the 10 cocos issues listed in chronological order in Table 7 are *bona fide* write-off-only cocos except for the second one: the February 2011 Credit Suisse [CS] issue with a coupon of 7.875%. There is nothing that makes that issue stand out from the surrounding Rabobank cocos issued in the same year. The November 8, 2013 yields on these three cocos were all between 4.5% and 5%, the G-spreads all just about 4%

and the implied values of π, 3.8%. The G-spread should have been much less on the 2011 CS issue, however, because this is in fact a regular cocos that converts into equity when triggered. Hence the assumption of a zero recovery rate would be incorrect unless CS stock is expected to be worthless when the company's fortunes have deteriorated to the point where cocos are triggered.

Reasoning about the recovery rate to be expected on this issue is complicated because its conversion price [CP] is set equal to the share price at conversion [MP_c] provided MP_c turns out not to be less than the minimum price per share set in the cocos covenant. The minimum actually set on this issue, a CP_{min} of \$20, was a little less than half the MP_0 of \$46.75 (NYSE) prevailing at the close of the 02/17/2011 announcement date. The recovery rate from the stock issued in conversion would thus be 1 (i.e., 100%), if MP_c is no less than \$20, and otherwise a fraction given by $MP_c/CP_{min} = MP_c/20 < 1$. In view of the price history of CS shares from the time of cocos issue (\$46.75) until November 8, 2013 (\$29.07) to be described below, it is almost certain that the market price prevailing if conversion should occur at some future date T [MP_{cT}] would be less than \$20: then the minimum conversion price of \$20 would be binding. MP fell from \$46.75 to \$22.86 already by 09/09/2011, and closing prices then remained below \$20 from June 11, 2012 through September 5, 2012, reaching lows of \$16.20 in both July and August. If such low market prices can persist even in moderately good times, stock prices would surely be much lower in times of stress leading to cocos conversion. If one assumes that MP_{cT} would be a mere 20% of CP_{min} or about 25% of the minimum closing price actually recorded since the time of cocos issue, the expected recovery rate $\rho = MP_{cT}/CP_{min} = 4/20$ would be 0.2 rather than zero.

If investors gave credit for this recovery rate, the G-spread should be correspondingly lower. However, since it was not below that for the surrounding Rabobank issues, the only way to explain this lack of differentiation is to solve the *basic* equation for $\pi = (R - r\,*)/(1 - \rho + R) = 0.03992/0.8454 = 4.72\%$ with the new value of $\rho = 0.2$. This would push the estimate of the annual probability of conversion for CS implausibly high up into the same 4.5% to 4.8% range shown for the KBC and Barclays Bank 2013 cocos issues, though not up to the 5.40% level estimated for Société Générale. This leaves two possibilities: either the recovery value available from the CS common shares issued in conversion is ignored or severely 'discounted' by investors in CS cocos, or the probability of conversion is in fact rated higher on CS cocos with a 7% trigger that convert into common stock than on 5% trigger cocos that are just written off when triggered. Comparing the implied values of π on Table 7—3.82% for the 7% trigger issue of CS (entry 2) and 2.94% for the 5 percent trigger cocos (entry 9)—provides some empirical support for the latter proposition.

Logically, the probability of conversion must be higher for the going-concern than the gone-concern cocos, if both types of cocos have been issued by the bank, simply because a capital ratio of 7% must be passed and raised by conversion of going-concern cocos, before a capital ratio as low as 5% can possibly be breached in a renewed down-sweep. If the high-trigger conversion is enough to save the bank and keep it at least adequately capitalized until the low-trigger cocos mature, low-trigger conversion would not follow and hence be rarer than the conversion of high-trigger cocos.

Looking again at the data assembled in Table 7, it is clear that by November 18, 2013 the prices of all but one of the 10 cocos shown had risen well above their par and issue value of 100. Part of this premium is due to the required rate of return on cocos falling as the distance to their first call date within these windows—generally 5 years after the initial settle and first interest-accrual date, or alternatively to maturity of 10 years—diminishes over time. Normal backwardation in the term structure of interest rates produces this effect when the coupon rate is fixed for the entire term and the security slides down the term structure of interest rates as its remaining term-to-effective-maturity diminishes. More importantly, as experience with cocos has accumulated, their characteristics may have been reassessed and viewed more favorably than at the time of issue. Furthermore, 7 out of the 10 cocos in Table 7 were investment-grade, rated BBB- or higher. The average yield required on these 7 cocos was 5.21%, and their average annual π was 3.67%. The yield was 6.65% on average, and average π was 4.63% on the three cocos that were below investment grade. Hence there was evident coherence between the yield and conversion-risk data and the credit ratings of cocos.

12

Actual or Prospective Recovery Rates from Converting Cocos

The recovery rate was previously treated as a control variable. Given the expected stock price in the event of conversion, the replacement or recovery rate could be set by choosing a conversion price that would yield it. For instance, if the estimated market price in the event of conversion [MP_c] is projected to be $8 per share, setting a conversion price of $10 would imply an 80% recovery rate provided the estimate of MP_c had already taken this target value of ρ—and what it implies for the number of shares outstanding after conversion—into account. It was argued that such a recovery rate would provide the right incentives for both cocos holders and pre-existing shareholders to be vigilant. The latter would be hurt by the de-capitalization that led to conversion and any associated stock price decline, but not by conversion itself so long as the recovery rate for cocos holders is less than 100%.There are indications from the first of the two cases that follow that the actual recovery rate to be expected has not gotten even close to 80%. This means that of all the bad consequences pre-existing shareholders may face when the capital ratio of their bank has declined to the trigger point, conversion of minimal-replacement cocos may be by far the sweetest for them while being unduly harmful to (usually institutional) cocos holders and their institutional counterparties. If there is a tendency in the finance sector to build up tail risk by favoring investment strategies that promise to generate high yields much of the time while courting a low risk of incurring disastrous losses on rare occasions, here is a good example of this destructive tendency.

12.1 The Downs and Ups of Lloyds Banking Group

The pioneering LBG Enhanced Capital Note [ECN] issues totaling almost £9 billion, announced on November 3, 2009, all had a
conversion price that was defined in pence [Gbp]. Because that
fixed amount would be applied at cocos conversion in the currency—such as USD, EUR, or JPY—in which the different cocos issues were denominated, it can be compared to stock prices quoted
in pence for LLOY.L on the London Stock Exchange [LSE].

Picking up some of the many detailed terms of issue described
in my discussion paper (2011a, pp. 10–12) for LBG alone and in
(2011b, pp. 32–33) for all the early cocos issuers, including Bank
of Cyprus discussed below, the initial LBG conversion price of
89.7246 GBp was set at the volume-weighted average price of
Ordinary Shares on the LSE for five consecutive trading dates in
the period of November 11–17, 2009. This price was adjusted to
59.2093 GBp to compensate for dilution from a massive rights
issue processed later that month. The closing price of LLOY.L
soon started to fall and remained below 59.2093 GBp for over two
years, from May 3, 2011 through May 14, 2013. The low during
this time, set on December 19, 2011 was 23.47 GBp, equal to
a mere 40% of the conversion price. Had decapitalization to the
trigger point (and hence conversion) in fact been imminent, the
market price would undoubtedly have been much lower, perhaps
equal to only 10% of the conversion price, or around 6 GBp. This
would have meant a market price conditional on conversion equal
to 25% of the lowest stock price recorded since the time of cocos
issue, as assumed for Credit Suisse before, but the recovery rate
would have been only 0.1, far from the optimal ρ-level of 0.8 previously deduced.

The first step to raise the expected recovery rate is to lower the
conversion price from 100% to (no more than) 50% of its level at
the time of cocos issue, i.e., from 59.2093 to 29.6047 GBp. This is
roughly how Credit Suisse set the minimum conversion price on
some of its cocos issues. The second step is to give all investors
in a cocos issue an option embedded in the instrument to convert
their individual holdings to common shares when the stock price

of the issuer is down to 80% or less of the conversion price, being at or below 23.6838 GBp. Although slightly lower prices (down to 23.47 GBp) were in fact recorded for LBG since the time of cocos issue, stock prices obviously could have behaved differently if those low market prices had been approaching an option trigger. In addition, some individual investors may regard the low stock prices as fleeting and maintain their position in cocos knowing that if other investors opt to convert their cocos this will supplement equity in the firm and benefit those who hold out.

The closing price of LLOY.L was 75.16 GBp per share on November 8, 2013, our common reference date, and the yield of Lloyds 7⅜% 11/01/2020 LBG Capital No. 1 USD issue was R = 6.43%. On November 8, 2013, this 10-year issue was almost exactly 7 years from maturity and the yield on the US Treasury constant-maturity 7-year benchmark was 2.12%, leaving the G-spread [R – r *] at 4.31%. With ρ of 0.1, the *basic* equation then implies that π = (R – r *)/(1 – ρ + R) = 0.0447, or 4.47%. Hence a low recovery rate and an elevated annual probability of conversion go hand in hand.

Any exercise of the option to convert cocos if the market price of the common stock is at least 20% below the conversion price stipulated in the cocos covenant for mandatory conversion can serve as an early warning signal for regulators and cocos holders to press for a credible recapitalization plan. Such an option would not supersede mandatory conversion geared to the designated trigger level of a Basel III CET1 capital ratio. Instead, if mandatory conversion is triggered before the stock price of the cocos issuer has fallen to the level at which the conversion option can be exercised, that option would be void, and *vice versa*. Nevertheless at least two of the softest—and in some cases implicitly waived—current requirements for issuing cocos that may be counted as AT1 or T2 regulatory capital could be violated by adding an option whose exercise is voluntary: (i) that all cocos of a given trigger class must be converted or written off fully at the same time, and (ii) that they must have a minimum maturity, usually of five years, unless converted earlier on account of a contingency or other "event" under Basel III rules. Nevertheless, the spirit of the additional requirement—that undated cocos must be replaced by capital with equivalent or greater loss-absorption capacity before or at the moment they may be called—would presumably be satisfied by allowing holders under certain downside conditions to convert their cocos ahead of any mandatory conversion.

12.2 The Bank of Cyprus Conversion Saga

The struggle for survival that ended in a near-death experience and restructuring of the Bank of Cyprus (ticker symbol BOC.AT on the Athens Stock Exchange) may teach additional lessons because it contained the first notable conversion of cocos. By May 18, 2011, BOC had issued €890 million of the €1,342 million offered in April with an initial coupon rate of 6.5% to existing shareholders whose pre-emption rights were respected. Because conversion proceeded in several steps, each of which was uncertain, prospective replacement rates were highly unstable and almost impossible to forecast. BOC's T1 cocos were named Convertible Enhanced Capital Securities [CECS] with a 5% CET1 trigger. The number of ordinary shares outstanding jumped from 900 million at year-end 2011 to 4,698 million at the end of November 2013 as a result of a rights issue and the conversion of convertible debt and even of large deposits into common stock. Most of these measures were worked out by the Central Bank and Government of Cyprus with the troika of European Union, IMF, and European Central Bank when BOC was recapitalized and restructured. The bank was under resolution from March 25, 2013 to July 30 of the same year before being restored to private management. Our chief concern, however, is not with the extraordinary bailout measures *per se* but with cocos design and functioning under stress.

Because determination of the conversion price of cocos was needlessly complicated, relevant provisions from Bank of Cyprus (2011) are reproduced below and then interpreted.

Mandatory Conversion Price. The CECS will be converted into a number of Ordinary Shares determined by dividing the principal amount of each CECS by the higher of the Floor Price and the Mandatory Conversion Price in effect on the relevant Mandatory Conversion Date.

Mandatory Conversion Price means at any time when the Ordinary Shares are admitted to trading on a recognized Stock Exchange in respect of a mandatory Conversion Date the lowest of (a) a ceiling price of €3.30 (subject to customary adjustment for corporate action events) and (b) 80% of the volume-weighted average of the reference Market price of an Ordinary Share on the 5 Business Days prior to the Contingency Event or Viability Event notice. [This share price will be referred to as 80% of MP_c, the market price at conversion.]

[A Contingency Event occurs when the CET1 capital ratio falls below its trigger level of 5%. A Viability Event is deemed to occur if BOC determines that the conversion of CECS is necessary to ensure the bank's viability or the bank requires extraordinary public-sector support to prevent non-viability.]

The Floor Price means the nominal value of each ordinary share (being at the Issue Date €1.00).

As BOC itself finally summarized the complicated language about the conversion price, that price is simply equal to 80% of the market price (ascertained as above) but no more than €3.30 and no less than €1.00.

This 'enhanced' cocos issue provided for voluntary upside conversion which would be profitable if MP_c were greater than €3.30 so that conversion would result in $\rho > 1$. The two-week conversion periods—scheduled four times a year starting with September 1–15, 2011—never saw the price of BOC common shares rise above €3.30, although that price had been exceeded as recently as February 2011.

While of little practical consequence in this case, it is important to note that inserting an upside conversion option for holders into the cocos contract had apparently not prevented CECS from being regarded as Basel III compliant. They were counted as Tier 1 equity-like regulatory capital with true loss-absorbing characteristics.

When the conversion price [CP] is between €3.30 and €1.00, it is 80% of MP_c. Hence the recovery rate MP_c/CP would be $\rho = 1.25$ in that range where $CP = 0.8MP_c$. For cocos holders, any such recovery rate above 1 constitutes a conversion pusher. The recovery rate can be less than 1 only if MP_c is less than €1.00 while CP is constrained to be at its minimum level of €1.00. The latter will happen only if $0.8MPC < 1$ or $MP_c < 1.25$. Hence ρ would decline from 1.25 to 1 as MP_c shrinks from € = 1.25 to € = 1 while CP stays at its minimum of €1. If MP_c continues to decline to some fraction of 1, the replacement rate would be equal to that fraction. BOC's common stock started to fall within months of issue and remained below €1 from November 1, 2011 on. On March 27, 2012,when CECS were converted into ordinary shares by a circuitous route, the share price at the close was down to €0.47 yielding $\rho = 0.47/0.75 = 0.63$ after dividing by a CP of € = 0.75 rather than € = 1.00. The reduction in the minimum level of CP is explained by the addition of one share for every 3 obtained by conversion of cocos to MCNs.

Although the CECS were technically perpetual, they did not last very long. In November 2011, BOC found a way to convert cocos at a higher trigger level and a lower conversion price than specified in their covenant. This happened after CET1 had dropped to 5.8% of RWA after an initial 50%, €1 billion write-down of its holdings of Greek government bonds. Short of capital and seeing conversion coming, the bank's management accelerated the process by sweetening the terms for converting cocos first into short-fused Mandatory Convertible Notes [MCNs] of equal par value and then into common shares. Terms were reset from one share per €1 euro of principal amount of cocos—the maximum share amount per euro specified in the cocos contract—to 1 and ⅓ share (i.e., one bonus share for every 3 new shares) per euro of MCN as if the conversion price had been lowered from €1.00 to €0.75. This was done to incentivize cocos holders to participate in the exchange and subsequent conversion before the company's prospects and the price of its shares could deteriorate further.

Here are the details of the timetable of steps leading up to issuance of new shares to the former cocos holders which were needed to select MP_{ct}, the stock market price at conversion at time t.

- The acceptance period of the voluntary tender exchange offer extended from February 23 through March 19, 2012. The stock price on the latter day's close was €0.53.

- The issue date of the MCNs was March 20, 2012 when the BOC.AT common stock closed at €0.50.

- The date of redemption of MCNs with new shares and of the issue of bonus shares was March 27, 2012. The stock closed at €0.47 that day and at €0.46 the following business day, March 30, with no sign of panic.

By July 25, 2012, the stock price was down to €0.21 which was also the last trade on March 15, 2013, before trading in BOC.AT shares was suspended indefinitely. The suspension likely will be kept in force at least until year-end 2014 to allow time for restructuring and a return to profitability. The low for the period from July 13, 2012 until the date of suspension was €0.11 on September 3, 2012.

Things went from bad to worse in 2012. In spite of €2.3 billion provisions for impairment, the non-performing loan ratio reached 23.7% by the end of the year, and provisions in percent of non-performing loans were still a mere 55% of expected losses. Converting the cocos, which according to BOC's Annual Report 2011 (pp. 6 and 23) had strengthened core capital by €592 million, could achieve little against mounting losses from loan impairments and Greek Government Bonds whose impairment had grown to €1,682 trillion. Looked at by itself, €592 million of T1 capital would not be inconsiderable. It would amount to 2% of BOC's total assets (€31.032 billion) and 2.5% of its RWA at the end of 2012. Faced with a massive 'tail-risk' event, however, the CECS proved entirely insufficient to deal with the damage internally, or to head off a bailout principally led by unsecured Cypriot depositors, the government of Cyprus, and the troika (of EU, ECB, and IMF). BOC's CT1 capital ratio by the end of 2012 had sunk to −1.9% compared with a minimum requirement of 8.7% CT1 imposed by the Central Bank of Cyprus (Bank of Cyprus, 2013, p. 10).

One final insight to be gained is that, in a massive de-capitalization and liquidity crisis, cocos holders, management, and regulators may all have an interest in precipitating conversion. Regulators can force conversion by declaring that a viability event has occurred. But management can do so as well by inducing cocos to be exchanged for an asset such as MCNs which are scheduled to convert within a matter of days on better set terms than are expected to prevail if conversion is triggered by a contingency event down the road. BOC's cocos holders were richly rewarded in the rush to convert. Had they been willing and able to sell at the market prices reported for the day the common shares were issued to them, they would have obtained a replacement (i.e., recovery) rate of 63%. This actual recovery rate of $\rho = 0.63$ is vastly in excess of the 0.2 rate inferred for Credit Suisse and the 0.1 believed to be in prospect for LBG; it is also much nearer to the $\rho = 0.8$ previously found to be commendable. Yet whoever held shares in the bank as it entered bankruptcy had far less as it emerged from reorganization and recapitalization at their expense. As much as 81.4% of the shares outstanding in November 2013 had come from the involuntary conversion into equity of unsecured deposits, and 18.1% were held by Cyprus Popular Bank (Laiki Bank) that is being resolved. This left only 0.5% for all other claimants on BOC. Because the book value of BOC amounted to €4.7 billion at the time as reported by the Bank of Cyprus (2013, p.4), only €94 million thereof was allocable to the 0.5% who had owned the bank before it went into reorganization.

This is a humbling lesson that cocos surely cannot cure all, or prevent all failures. Another lesson is that, just as vaccines do not work against diseases already in progress, cocos are best injected when the issuer is robustly capitalized and fit to get 'immunized' and develop 'antibodies.' Cocos are also bound to be least costly to issue under such conditions. Both LBG and Bank of Cyprus violated this principle of issuing cocos in good times. Now that LBG is on much firmer footing than in 2009 when its most expensive cocos were issued, these cocos—whose first optional redemption date is 2020—look very much like candidates for exchange offers or replacements that have a high prospective recovery rate and are more reasonably priced.

13

Government Capital Injections and Bailout Cocos

So far we have considered write-down-only cocos and cocos which convert into common shares when triggered. The former type of cocos provide for an extreme form of private-sector debt-holder involvement in loss absorption outside bankruptcy known as bail-in. Writing off the cocos debt of a concern that remains in operation subordinates the claims of cocos holders to those of existing shareholders when a contingency event has occurred. Upon conversion, cocos holders lose their entire investment while shareholders gain from the debt relief. The same debt cancellation is also provided by cocos that convert into common stock, but cocos holders do not lose everything because the recovery rate from the common shares cannot (yet) be down to zero outside of bankruptcy when the cocos are accurately triggered. What cocos holders do not lose from conversion, pre-existing share-holders cannot gain. Whether cocos convert into common shares or not does not affect how much the book value of equity is raised by conversion, but only how that elevated book value—and hence ownership and control—are shared between pre-existing shareholders and new shareholders from conversion.

The bail-out cocos to be considered next are antithetical to bail-in cocos. Instead of increasing private-sector involvement in loss absorption and shielding tax payers from having to bail out SIFIs and groups of banks that are collectively "too big" or "too many" to fail, these cocos are the first step in a bail-out process. In some countries caught up in the worst of the euro crisis they have been issued by failing banks to government agencies authorized to act as lender (or on-lender of EU stability mechanism funds) of last resort to individual private institutions in an emergency. In

Chapter 17, Article 31 of Document 6 lists the conditions under which "capital instruments subscribed by public authorities in emergency situations" may be included in CET1 capital instruments by the assisted financial institutions. Interest rates in the range of 8% to 10% per annum were typically applied to these cocos in 2009–13 in order to achieve both political and economic objectives. These steep interest rates were to show that the government was setting tough (perhaps even punitive) terms on its rescue funds. Economically, the recipient of cocos funds was to be pressured by high interest rates to repurchase the cocos from the government as soon as improved cash flow from operations or a successful return to the capital market should permit. Failing that, the government itself could attempt to sell these high-yield cocos in the market before the date set in the cocos covenant by which it otherwise would have to convert its holdings into shares of common stock—usually after 3 to 5 years from issue.

It appears therefore, that these bail-out cocos are designed to buy time to restructure and stabilize a financial institution so that the last step in the bail-out process—a partial or complete government takeover of a financial institution—can be avoided or at least kept brief.

13.1 Capital Injections under Fed and US Treasury Programs

Cocos have not been issued by US-based financial institutions so far. Still, the government's emergency investments in cumulative preferred shares—which could be repurchased by the originally distressed financial institutions that issued them, and that could otherwise turn non-cumulative before being exchanged for common shares to conserve cash—bears a close resemblance to arrangements made for state-aid in some European countries. These countries (notably Ireland, Spain, and Portugal) used cocos with a mandatory terminal trigger for conversion into common stock added to the regular Basel-III-based trigger to convey some of the government's capital injections.

In the United States, the Department of the Treasury's Office of Financial Stability and the Board of Governors of the Federal

Reserve System are the government agencies most directly involved in exceptional and emergency lending to individual financial institutions in difficulties. Section 13(3) of the Federal Reserve Act requires "unusual and exigent circumstances" for the Board to determine that "discounts for individuals, partnerships, and corporations" may be justified. The Dodd-Frank Wall Street Reform and Consumer Protection Act of 2010 in paragraph (3)(B)(i) added that

> the Board shall establish, by regulation, in consultation with the Secretary of the Treasury, the policies and procedures governing emergency lending... Such policies and procedures shall be designed to ensure that any emergency lending program or facility is for the purpose of providing liquidity to the financial system, and not to aid a failing financial company, and that the security for emergency loans is sufficient to protect taxpayers from losses and that any such program is terminated in a timely and orderly fashion.

While these strictures do not square with being too big to fail, they show a political concern with appearing tough on failing financial institutions while providing systemic (but strictly temporary) help on an emergency basis. Such direct and politically costly aid will end up costing the government very little, at least not in terms of net disbursements which have political salience; administration of the Troubled Asset Relief Program [TARP] followed this pattern. This program was created by the Emergency Economic Stabilization Act of 2008 [EESA] which was enacted into law on October 3, 2008, less than three weeks after the Lehman disaster. At first the Treasury had been as eager as the Federal Reserve to act tough and then bury the big stick: it charged AIG a cumulative dividend of 10% for TARP funds in October 2008, but that dividend was made non-cumulative and promptly suspended in March 2009. In the case of Citigroup, on February 27, 2009, the Treasury did not stop the successive negotiated (rather than automatic) exchanges of financial instruments at that stage but allowed them to become even more favorable to the client. It required the ultimate conversion of the liquidation value of the $25 billion of cumulative preferred with a 5% initial dividend—invested in Citi under its Capital Purchase Program [CPP], devolved from the TARP—not just to non-cumulative preferred but to common stock. In addition, the conversion price was far above the depressed market value at the time, meaning that the Treasury chose to receive fewer shares of common stock than it could have claimed. Nevertheless the Treasury had sold the last of its Citigroup shares by the end of 2010 at a "profit" of $12 billion (on an investment of $45 billion), unadjusted as before, and not counting the billions of tax revenue lost on ccount of a special tax ruling on retaining Citi's loss carry-forward in spite of an ownership change. That ruling was exceptionally favorable to Citigroup and to its new US govern-ment majority owner eager to minimize the overt budget costs of its assistance, which should have included the costs from the forgiveness of taxes otherwise normally due.

EESA did not provide much guidance on how private parties could repurchase the senior preferred equity sold to the Treasury and the warrant which had to be issued to the Treasury at the same time with an exercise value equal to 15% of that of preferred equity. The CPP term sheet specified that the warrant was to be for 10 years and that the exercise price for determining the number of shares of common stock subject to the warrant was to be the market price of the common stock on the date of the senior preferred investment calculated as a 20-trading day trailing average. The unseemly haggling over the repurchase price of these warrants that erupted soon after they were first issued and their uneven degrees of underpricing by the Treasury are detailed in my article (2009, p. 70). The requirement of demonstrating the ability to raise qualified equity before CPP preferred shares could be redeemed by their issuers was waived in the American Recovery and Reinvestment Act of 2009 [ARRA]. Instead, the Treasury, upon being notified of an institution's intention to repay, would refer that request to its primary regulator for a recommen-dation under its new Supervisory Capital Assessment Program.

The conversion of debt-like cumulative preferred to common stock that is ultimately sold by the Treasury to private investors achieves an outcome similar to cocos conversion: the bank's debt-like liabilities go down and equity goes up. Nevertheless, compared with the automaticity of cocos conversion that is set off by objectively ascertainable triggers, in the United States this other path to conversion occurred in a negotiation-intensive, uncertain, and forever "evolving" regulatory process. If the government instead sells the debt-like claim to a third party in the private sector and not back to the issuing institution, as has happened with cocos in some European countries, it acts as an underwriter and market-maker for that institution and also as a dealer in cocos. The issuing bank then ends up with more cocos debt owed to private parties, and hence more AT1 or T2 capital and less CET1 on its balance sheet because cocos liabilities had received CET1 credit as long as they were held by the government. The outcome is the opposite of what would happen in a regular cocos conversion although the only "conversion" involved is the ownership change of the cocos and the resulting loss of their CET1 classification.

13.2 Ireland's Bailout Cocos

As in the United States, the Government of Ireland conducted its capital injections mainly by acquiring preferred shares in the banks receiving its support. The National Asset Management Agency [NAMA] established in December 2009 was charged with acquiring, administering and eventually redeeming these assets within a maximum of 10 years. Starting in 2010, NAMA shared in the external support provided to Ireland by the European Financial Stability Mechanism [EFSM], the European Financial Stability Fund [EFSF], and the International Monetary Fund [IMF] as major sources of funding. According to its website, "NAMA's statutory commercial objective is to obtain, in so far as possible, the best achievable financial return for the State having regard to the cost to the Exchequer of acquiring and dealing with bank assets, NAMA's cost of capital and other costs" and to do so "over the shortest possible time span, having regard to market conditions and to optimizing the realized value of its assets." There is a partial match here with the Least Cost Principle of Resolution prescribed for the FDIC in the United States, though with exceptions for mitigating systemic risk. One difference with the United States is that the preference shares obtained by the government were not converted to common shares before being put up for sale to private investors.

In 2011, Ireland's two biggest banks, Allied Irish Banks [AIB] and Bank of Ireland [BOI], sold respectively €1.6 billion and €1 billion cocos to the Government of Ireland, but the combined amount accounted for only 4% of the €64 billion of taxpayers' money pumped into the banks during the crisis. At the start of 2014, AIB still remained 99.8% owned by the government (pension) fund. But with AIB having received almost one third of the €64 billion government bailout funding, the Irish government was reported to be eager to start selling its stock in AIB hopefully at a price that would again bring a "profit" to advertise politically. Early in 2013 the government of Ireland had already managed to sell the State's entire holding of €1 billion in cocos (i.e., Contingent Convertible Notes [CCNs]) in BOI. This marked the first time that a European bailout instrument has been marketed to private investors. "Remarketed" at a price of 101% of their par value plus accrued interest compared with the original issue price of par, the government thus made a €10 million "profit" as the Minister of Finance, Michael Noonan, proudly pointed out. Sold by the government with a coupon of 10% per annum in mid-January of 2013, the 5-year, re-marketed cocos maturing on 07/13/2016 appreciated to almost 105 from par of 100 within a few days from reissue. On November 11, 2013, this price had risen to 108.676 to afford a yield of 6.382% over the remaining term of less than 3 years. Although these cocos have a comparatively high CT1 trigger of 8.25%, a contingency trigger event is unlikely to occur before the remaining years of their tenor.

The BOI prospectus for the cocos issued on 07/29/2011 contains a number of authorizations and restrictions, some of which are specific to bailout cocos. The most interesting of these are quoted below (along with my analysis) from the sections, "Description of the CCNs," and "T&C, Terms and Conditions of the Contingent Capital Tier 2 Notes."

- The "Remarketing Option" (item 3.12) with authority for the initial holder of cocos to change their terms upon sale is specific to bailout cocos being resold by the government. It gives the initial holder of 100% of the CCNs the right to raise the interest rate under certain conditions, for instance, and confers "absolute discretion as to whether to sell CCNs, to whom it may sell the CCNs outside bankruptcy and the terms of any such sale."

- Conversion (3.13) must be "in whole and not in part. CCNs so converted shall be automatically cancelled by the Issuer and may not be held, reissued or resold." Hence repeated fractional conversions in successive slices—designed to keep the regulatory capital ratios just adequate to eliminate the capital deficiency until the entire cocos issue has been written off if necessary—are ruled out. Furthermore, the "CCNs are not convertible into Ordinary Stock at the option of Holders at any time and are not redeemable in cash as a result of a Conversion Event." Hence my suggestion to add a stop-loss-type conversion option for cocos investors that may be exercised if the stock's price falls some moderate percentage (such as 20%) below the conversion price intended to achieve ρ would not fly here. Indeed, Article 63(i) (excerpted as Document 6 in Chapter 17) is explicit in that where the relevant instruments include one or more call options or repayment options, "the options are exercisable at the sole discretion of the issuer or debtor." The wording in Article 52(h) of that same CRR document is only slightly different, stating in regard to AT1 that "where the provisions governing the instrument include one or more call options, the option to call may be exercised at the sole discretion of the issuer." An EBA document (excerpted as Document 4 in Chapter 17), however, contains an unfortunately rather stenographic section entitled, "Holders' right for

Conversion Open option—to be determined on a case by case basis: possibility to include a right for holders to convert the BCCS (i.e., cocos) into shares." Hence the prohibition on including holders' options may not be settled doctrine and may perhaps be negotiable.

- "Upon conversion, accrued interest shall become due and payable on the conversion date." This was the "alternative" possibility considered when modeling the conversion risk premium in Chapter 10 above.

- Redemption, Purchase, or Buy Back (T&C.6(b)) are not allowed. Specifically, "none of the Issuers nor any of its Subsidiaries nor any other Group Company shall purchase, redeem, buy back or otherwise acquire any of the CCNs prior to the maturity date." This provision is intended to ensure that loss absorption outside of bankruptcy from cocos conversion occurs outside the bank that issued them, and outside the banking sector as a whole so as to strengthen the bank holding companies in a crisis.

In addition, there are two essential definitions which appear with further references on p. 55 of the prospectus.

1. The first of these is particularly relevant for bailout cocos as it makes clear that "Core Tier 1 Amount includes any capital instruments injected at any time by the Initial Holder or any other State Entity to strengthen the capital base of the Group and deemed by the Competent Authority to be eligible to count towards Core Tier 1 Amount." The CT1 capital ratio that calibrates the trigger then is the Core Tier 1 Amount divided by the RWA Amount.

2. Although the cocos in question are not likely to be converted during the short time remaining to maturity, the determination of the conversion price and the relation of its chosen minimum to the stock market price prevailing at the time of issue are of interest more generally as a matter of design.

"Conversion Price" means at any time when the Ordinary
Stock are admitted to trading on a Recognized Stock
Exchange [such as the Irish Stock Exchange], in respect of
any Conversion Date, the greater of:

(a) The Volume-Weighted-Average Price of a unit of
Ordinary Stock of the Issuer over the 30 Business Days
prior to the date of the relevant Conversion Event, and

(b) the Floor Price of a unit of Ordinary Stock on the
date of the relevant Conversion Event (being, at the Issue
Date, €0.05 (five cents)).

The Floor Price applies also when the Ordinary [Shares]
are not admitted to trading on a Recognized Stock Exchange.

Counting back 30 trading days from the July 29, 2011 issue date,
the average closing price from June 17 to July 28, 2011 was €0.11.
Hence the minimum was set at 45% of the stock's price at the time
of issue. This market price would have to fall by at least 55% to
less than €0.05 before the replacement rate would be less than 1
(i.e., below 100%) when the conversion price is at its floor. BOI
was in dire straits when it was being recapitalized in small part
with the help of the July 29, 2011 €1 billion cocos issue. Hence
to reach a desirable level of the replacement rate expected in the
event of conversion, the minimum conversion price should not
have to be set far below the stock market price then prevailing,
which had already been depressed by all the bad news on BOI
at the time. It is worth noting that in the first week of December
2013, BIR.IR was quoted at more than 5 times the floor price, so
that the bailout program appears to have succeeded in its immediate objective, at least so far.

14

Misuses of Cocos in Government-Led Recapitalizations of Banks

Some of the most questionable uses of cocos have been made in the recapitalization programs of leading banks in the Iberian Peninsula.

14.1 Cocos as Government Bailout Tool for Spanish and Portuguese Banks

Several factors drove the purchases of cocos from banks headquartered in Spain and Portugal by their respective governments. First came the desire for governments to use the acquisition of cocos—rather than preferred or common stock—from troubled banks in their jurisdiction to put off official recognition of the budgetary costs of the government's capital injections into these banks. Secondly, although the conversion price sets the amount by which the face value of cocos is reduced per share issued $[FV/N_c]$ and thus includes a rate of exchange which the government is willing to accept, the consequences of agreeing to such a rate are not as transparent and controversial as setting the price which the government would be willing to pay for outright purchases of shares of banks in the private sector. An agreement on acquiring cocos might thus be easier and quicker to achieve than an agreement on acquiring shares directly. Politically, this strategy helped disguise government ownership as long as possible even if acquisition of the majority of a bank's outstanding shares could not ultimately be avoided: that would hopefully happen at a time by which the government's budget constraints had eased. In the meantime the government could represent its purchase of cocos as an investment of greater value than its costs, given that the interest rate on cocos was generally set administratively well above the government's own borrowing rate. As a result, the reported effect on the fisc would be zero or even deficit-reducing as long as these high-interest bullet cocos were fully serviced prior to maturity and not converted into common stock paying no dividends.

To scale back the government's exposure to the assisted banks— which had grown as the sovereign debt crisis and the banking crisis became fiscally and economically intertwined—the issuing banks were encouraged to repurchase and cancel the cocos as soon as alternative ways of shoring up their capital ratios without relying on further government assistance had opened up. To protect its interests, the government needed to be prepared for the contingency that repurchase might not be feasible for the issuers within a few years after issue and that the cocos would then have to be converted into Special Shares after all. For that event the conversion price was set so low as to promise a recovery rate of over 100% of the funds which the government had injected into the banks via cocos. The Special Shares that can only be held by the State would need to be converted into common shares at a 1:1 rate before being disposed of through the exercise of the Bank's Buyback Option, the Shareholder's Statutory Right of Acquisition, or through direct sale to other investors. Should the government become the interim majority shareholder at any point, it would decline to exercise the full rights of ownership and operational control. Instead it would continue to treat the institutions involved as still essentially private and sell the shares at the earliest opportunity in the market to recover its outlays on cocos.

One of the principal agencies involved in Spain is the Fondo de Reestructuración Ordenada Bancaria (Fund for Orderly Bank Restructuring, [FROB]). It had received a total of €41.3 billion in December 2012 and February 2013 from the troika of EU, ECB, and IMF for the reorganization and recapitalization of banks headquartered in Spain. FROB is a public, 100% state-owned entity whose Governing Committee is chaired by the Deputy Governor of the Bank of Spain. A "Summary Table on Restructuring of the Spanish Banking Sector" contained in its April 2013 report, simply titled by the Fund's English name, showed cash assistance either committed or already provided totaling €61.2 billion, of which cocos were 63% (€38.8 billion). The remainder consisted mostly of contributions to "capital" (acquisition of ordinary shares by the Fund from the conversion of convertible preference shares already owned and from share purchases from the assisted banks). The cocos had to be issued by "Group 3" banks planning a significant capital increase equal to 2% or more of risk-weighted assets under the recapitalization scheme to meet their capital needs by the end of December 2012 at the latest. The cocos were subscribed by the FROB using program resources. They could be redeemed until 30 June 2013 if the issuing banks succeeded in raising the necessary capital from private sources. Otherwise FROB would convert some or all of the cocos it held into ordinary shares.

A similar Fund for bank restructuring, resolution, and asset management, the Fundo de Resolução, was established at the central Banco de Portugal with €12 billion made available to assist its banks. The eagerness of the government to unload all Government Subscribed Instruments [GSIs] within about 5 years was shared by their issuers in the case of cocos because they faced a coupon rate that, while high from the start at 8.5%, was scheduled to step up to 8.75% in the second year, 9% in the third, and 9.5% in the fourth, and 10% in fifth. These step-ups would provide precisely the redemption incentive that would make cocos ineligible for inclusion in regulatory capital if the government could not exempt itself from its own rules. Document 2 from the BCBS (excerpted in Chapter 16) states, for instance, that to be included in AT1 capital it is required that "there are no step-ups or other incentives to redeem." GSIs were still treated as Core Tier 1 [CT1] capital regardless. Hence they could help meet capital needs when Portuguese banks were directed by the Bank of Portugal to maintain a minimum CT1 ratio of 10% from the end of 2012. This minimum had been raised in part to prepare for the impending phase-in of Basel III rules starting in January 2014 that would shift the focus of regulatory capital requirements from CT1 to CET1. In addition, CET1 itself would be defined more narrowly by phasing in deductions over five years, starting in 2014, for amounts exceeding limits for Deferred Tax Assets and Mortgage Servicing Rights among others. The European Banking Authority [EBA] also added to the planned capital requirements by proposing a minimum CT1 ratio of 9% for all European banks, including a temporary 1% buffer to cover sovereign risk in their portfolio of government debt. These requirements were made less onerous because the liabilities created in banks by government capital injections, including through the acquisition of cocos, were still regarded as adding to T1 capital for regulatory purposes. The capital injections were financed by drawing on EU-financed and monitored support funds.

Although keeping cocos on their books might have been helpful to confront any future crisis, on the whole the cocos that were issued to government agencies in both Portugal and Spain during the recovery from the most recent crisis made only a short-lived appearance on banks' books. Table 8 for example shows that prominent banks in Portugal—Banco Comercial Português [BCP], a strategic shareholder of Bank Millennium and Portugal's largest commercial bank, and Banco Português de Investimento [BPI], the third largest bank—intended to start repaying the €3 billion and €1.5 billion they respectively received from the sale of cocos to their government soon after the funds were received. BCP, with estimated capital needs of €3.5 billion started repaying in 2014 thanks to the help of a €0.5 billion rights issue with an exercise price of €0.04 per share that caused the number of its ordinary shares outstanding to rise by 12.5 billion, or 173%. Following the capitalization exercise conducted by the EBA, BPI's capital needs had been assessed as €1.4 billion, or €1.2 billion with credit for impairment of Greek debt already recognized in reported results. BPI started its cocos buyback literally within two months of the June 2012 issue date of its cocos, repaying €0.2 billion still in 2012 with the help of a rights issue that raised the number of ordinary shares by 40%. For comparison, the earliest any TARP funds were repaid by any bank in the United States [ONB] was 4 months after they had been received. In the cases of BCP and BPI, repayment of the undated securities that were sold to the government was to be achieved in full within 5 years from issue, i.e., by 2017.

Table 8. Cocos Amortization Proposed by or for Management of Two Portuguese Banks, 2012–17 (outstanding balances in billions of euro)

	Issued	Year-end:	2012	2013	2014	2015	2016	2017
BCP	3.0		3.0	3.0	2.5	1.5	0	
BPI	1.5		1.3	1.15	0.88	0.57	0.275	0
BPI Alternative			1.3	1.1	0.8	0.3	0	

Sources: Millennium BCP Institutional Presentation, 2013, "BCP: New Business Plan for 2013–15," presented September 11. http://ind.millenniumbcp.pt/en/Institucional/investidores/Documents/Inst_Presentation.pdf and Millenium Investment Banking, Financials, Portugal, 2012, "BPI Recapitalization Plan: Snapshot," June 12, pp. 2–3. http://ind.millenniumbcp.pt/pt/Particulares/Investimentos/Documents/Snapshots_RaioX/junho2012/BPI_06junho2012.pdf

With official encouragement, both banks are aiming to complete the repurchase process a year earlier than required, as shown by BPI's alternative repayment plan in Table 8.

Altogether these Iberian cocos were designed very differently from those that would qualify in the future for AT1 treatment in regulatory capital. Under Basel III, qualifying cocos would have to be perpetuals that may be called after 5 years at the earliest subject to their replacement by regulatory capital of equal or higher quality, and there must be no coupon-rate step-ups or other incentives to redeem. The short-lived appearance of high-yield cocos on the balance sheet of Iberian banks was thus motivated by political and economic considerations of government budget management and deficit-dressing. It was intended to pressure banks and their shareholders into loss absorption by raising equity—apparently no matter how value- and ownership-dilutive it might be—to avoid having to see these cocos converted by a preset date.

Such pressure tactics, as well as the high coupon rate with step-ups set on the bailout cocos, were clearly meant to be punitive. The conversion price on the BPI cocos for instance applies a 35% discount to the ordinary share price, reflecting the traded market value of the shares at the time conversion is announced and taking into account the effect of dilution. Assuming the ordinary share price already reflects the effects of the imminent dilution, this means that the value of the shares issued in conversion is 54% higher than the face value of the cocos converted. Giving the state agency a recovery rate of $1/0.65 = 1.54$ at conversion after a few years of high interest would be usury indeed if conversion were in fact intended. The alternative of avoiding state aid by issuing more stock to both existing and outside investors in unreceptive markets—well below its prior market price—to cover the capital shortfall was also quite punishing for Iberian banks during the euro crisis. For instance, Bloomberg news carried a report on October 11, 2012 that a core group of BPE (discussed below) shareholders represented on its board would end up owning about 23% of the company after the sale of stock, compared with 31% before, after contributing €421 million. This stock sale was thus highly dilutive.

When the cocos sold to government agencies are treated as no more than a hoped-for bridge loan—supposed to pave the way for a speedy return to equity finance, the proceeds of which are then applied to repurchase the cocos—they will no longer be outstanding when the next crisis hits, and thus cannot serve the prudential purpose of providing a mobile defense of capital positions. The principal function of pre-positioning contingent convertibles is to inject equity capital through debt cancellation outside of bankruptcy when such equity is most needed but otherwise least available to capital-short banks. That function is not well served when cocos are used to provide temporary government financing for bank restructuring.

In 2013, two Spanish bank groups, Banco Bilbao Vizcaya Argentaria [BBVA] and Banco Popular Español [BPE], neither of which had issued cocos to FROB, helped restore the original purpose of cocos. BBVA issued €1.5 billion of perpetual securities with a 9% coupon until the first call date of 05/09/2018. Fitch Ratings rated this issue as BB-, three steps below investment grade. BPE, a weaker bank whose cocos were not rated, also issued a perpetual type of cocos with a coupon of 11.5% per annum and with a first call and reset date of 10/10/2018, five years after the "interest accrual and settle" date of the issue. Both issues qualified as AT1 regulatory capital under the new rules adopted in 2013 since they were non-step-up, non-cumulative Contingent Convertible Perpetual Preferred Tier 1 Securities. They were first callable after five years but only with replacement by capital instruments of equal or higher quality and conformed to the newly adopted EU Capital Requirements Regulation [CRR-IV] for qualification as AT1 capital in all other respects. BBVA's cocos had a 7% CT1 trigger which will be replaced by a 5.125% CET1 trigger once the sovereign charge has been lifted. The minimum conversion price of €5.00 per share was about half of the market price of €9.87 at the close on the issue date of 05/09/2013. BPE had the same trigger measure as BBVA except that it would start out with CT1 of 6% rather than 7% before transitioning to the CET1 trigger of 5.125%.

There was, however, one interesting additional trigger: it would kick in if the Bank or Group reports losses, in respect of each of its four most recent quarterly financial reporting periods, with the result that the capital and reserves of the Bank or Group have been reduced by one-third or more from the beginning of the first of such quarterly financial reporting periods. Hence if the bank had a CET1 ratio of 12% after 2013 and then had a series of losses over four successive quarters that would cause that ratio to fall monotonically to 8% indicating progressive deterioration, the cocos would be triggered at an 8% rather than a 5.125% CET1 capital ratio: timely help instead of waiting for the bitter end of such a downslide.

The BPE floor price, subject of course to all customary anti-dilution adjustments, was initially set at €2.015 per common share. This was about half of POP.MC's average closing price of €4.074 over the five trading days of October 3–9, 2013. If the floor price was not binding, the conversion price on the date of the conversion event would be equal to the current market price of a common share, calculated as the volume-weighted average price of a common share on each of the 5 consecutive trading days ending on the dealing day immediately preceding the date of that event. Such a specification is compatible with the terms required for AT1 classification in the European Union's latest Capital Requirements Directive [CRD IV] that went into effect in July 2013. If cocos have a conversion price that is equal to the market price of the stock around the time of cocos conversion or any fixed fraction thereof, they have no upside: the replacement rate will be the same regardless of the price of the stock received by conversion. For the same reason they also have no downside if that market price has the depth and resilience to bounce back when large blocks of stock have been offered. When the floor price is binding, however, the replacement rate fluctuates with the stock price since it is the ratio of that stock price at conversion to the CP, which is then constant.

There is just one other matter requiring comment. As BPE's offering circular dated October 4, 2013, states on p. 72, "The Bank or any member of the Group, may purchase or otherwise acquire any of the outstanding Preferred Securities [here cocos] at any price in the open market ... subject to the prior consent of the Regulator" who may require replacement. The currently required yield on both the BBVA and the BPE high-yield cocos is below their coupon rate, and the price of their cocos on November 8, 2013 was 105 and 103.7, respectively. Since they are callable at par on certain anniversary dates, there would normally be no reason to repurchase them at a premium. Paying large premiums on cocos may also be particularly risky because both tax and regulatory events may entitle issuers to initiate a call at par. Exercising the first call that becomes available may well be the best option since the high interest costs cannot be reduced substantially at the reset dates, starting with the first call date; at that time the fixed coupon rate is converted into a variable rate that may very well be higher after the Federal Reserve's stimulus program has ended. For BBVA that variable rate is USSW5 + 826.2 bps, compared with the fixed coupon rate of 9%. For BPE it is 1074.3 bps plus the same 5-year US mid-swap rate, compared with 11.5%. Because the swap rate has been abnormally low for years and is heading up, there is a high likelihood of a coupon rate increase resulting from this arrangement that would provide an incentive to exercise a call at the earliest opportunity. Building in such a predictable redemption incentive is generally in violation of AT1 requirements, although regulators will decline to challenge it because the incentive derives from interest-rate forecasts, and the configuration of the variable coupon rate is conventional.

14.2 Struggling Greek Banks Passing Up Bailout Cocos

Compared with FROB, which is entrusted with similar functions of promoting the stability of the banking system and the capital adequacy of its banks, the Hellenic Financial Stability Fund [HFSF] is a curious chameleon. It claims to be a purely private entity—presumably to facilitate off-budget financing—whose status as such is called into question neither by its entire capital being subscribed by the Greek government nor by the issuance of the relevant decisions by the Minister of Finance. The HFSF invested €27.5 billion of the proceeds from the Floating Rate Notes [EFSF FRNs] received from the European Financial Stability Fund to support the recapitalization of the four Greek banks that were judged to be viable. These were National Bank of Greece [NBG], Piraeus Bank, Alpha Bank, and Eurobank, the latter having since become a candidate for merger. Focusing on NBG alone, the HFSF thus issued commitments that grew to €9.756 billion to meet that bank's new capital requirements. These funds were to be released following an agreement on the share capital increase or the convertible bond issuance according to the rules of the European Commission on state aid. Both HFSF and EFSF thus regarded funds received through new stock issues and cocos issues within limits as equally effective in raising Tier 1 capital in the proposed recapitalization. However, to remain under private management and control, Greek banks had to raise at least 10% of the recapitalization funds from the market. When NBG had raised the minimum required amount of €9.756 billion through the sale of 2,274,125,874 common registered voting shares at an offer price of €4.29 per share the previously announced companion issue of €1.9 billion cocos as buffer capital was scrapped. In May 2013, NBG conducted a reverse split of its shares in the ratio of 10:1; on June 14 the bank then issued a perfunctory statement that, in view of the amount raised, contingent convertible bonds (cocos) need not be issued. Piraeus Bank had a new capital requirement of €7.3 billion to meet, and at first sought shareholder approval of a €2 billion cocos issue in January 2013, but later demurred, making the issuance of cocos dependent on the actual amount of equity raised in the market. Both banks thus clearly treated the issuance of bailout cocos as the least desirable measure of last resort.

Perhaps they had good reason to do so. Even though the coupon rate on the cocos would have started at 7% rather than 8.5%, as on the Portuguese bailout issues, cocos financing would have reduced cash flow and retained earnings compared to issuing new equity that would not pay dividends, at least not right away. The payment of interest on cocos issued to the government, unlike on cocos held by private parties, cannot normally be cancelled outside of bankruptcy or without creating a conversion event. Because the troika was in charge no matter how 'private' the HFSF, raising equity capital (regardless of how dilutive) rather than issuing cocos to meet capital and capital-buffer needs would clearly conserve the resources of the banks and of those who might have to support them. If the interest could not be paid to the government in full and when due, the competent government agency would have to convert the cocos it had bought from banks into common shares. The attempt to keep the bank in private hands with official assistance would have come to naught. This strengthens the initial impression that the government's use of cocos as a bailout instrument is a dubious practice, even if Irish banks and their government agencies appear to have made creative use of them.

Part IV
Policy Choices and Essentials for Cocos' Success

15

The Tax Treatment of the Interest Paid on Cocos

For their treatment under the corporation and business income tax, it matters in several ways whether hybrids, such as cocos, are classified as predominantly debt-like or equity-like. Dividends and capital gains are taxed at preferential rates in some countries, and some countries do not tax capital gains at all. In the United States, for instance, the federal tax rate on qualified dividends and realized long-term capital gains that are paid to fully taxable recipients is capped at 20%. This rate is only about half as large as the maximum individual income tax rate of 39.6% for 2013.

Preferential treatment of some sort is justified by the double taxation that arises when dividends are paid out of after-tax income and again taxed to their recipients without credit for the corporation income tax already paid on the funds paid out to shareholders. To the extent retained earnings ultimately show up in long-term capital gains realized by fully taxable entities, they too are subject to a double taxation that is ameliorated by the low tax on capital gains. By contrast, interest paid on most debt instruments issued by businesses and corporations is deductible from their taxable income. For these reasons it has been argued that countries with tax systems that are in these respects similar to that of the United States discriminate against equity financing in favor of debt financing, thereby contributing to excessive leverage and financial fragility.

One (inevitably imperfect) way of dealing with this issue—without violating the principles of horizontal equity and progressivity in the individual income tax—is to include dividends and capital gains in ordinary taxable income without any special rates, while dispensing with the corporation income tax entirely.

However, as things stand in the United States and several other countries, a tax administration agency like the IRS must provide interpretative guidance on the Internal Revenue Code—and ultimately give a ruling in concrete cases of hybrids like cocos on what is more like debt or more like equity, and what therefore is deductible (interest) and what is not (dividends).

Following Allen & Overy's (2013, p. 13) reissue of "Tax Treatment of Additional Tier 1 Capital under Basel III," The United States and Australia appear to be the outliers least disposed to treat cocos that satisfy the Basel III criteria for AT1 capital as debt and the interest paid on them as tax deductible. The publication characterizes the "Impact of Basel III" on tax deductibility in ten countries, eight of them European, roughly as follows:

1. *(Tax Deductibility is) Readily Available*: France, Italy, Luxembourg, Spain

2. *Difficult but Not Impossible* (main difficulties for deductibility are in parentheses): Belgium (issuer may cancel distributions), Germany and Netherlands (perpetual feature), United Kingdom (certain financial constructs supporting deductibility are no longer available)

3. *Not Generally Available*: Australia (T1 capital is treated as equity for accounting and tax purposes), United States (lack of fixed or ascertainable maturity)

Moody's (2014, p. 2) reported in 2013 that, "banks also started to issue AT1 securities as their tax treatment became clearer. A number of European jurisdictions, including the United Kingdom, Spain, Sweden and Italy have already granted tax deductibility to AT1 securities... German banks are still waiting for clarification from the authorities" since received in April 2014.

Cocos that qualify only for inclusion in T2 do not share some of the most equity-like features of T1 cocos, such as being perpetual and allowing cancellation of interest payments by the issuer. Hence there is less of a question about interest payments on T2 cocos being tax deductible everywhere.

15.1 Likely US IRS Conditions for Interest Deductibility on Cocos

Because of the outlier status of the United States, it is perhaps most instructive to delve in some detail into those provisions of its Internal Revenue Code [I.R.C.] that appear at odds with interest deductibility and to consider how these conflicts may be resolved.

The IRS has not provided definitive guidance on the types of cocos it would consider qualified for the deductibility of interest paid. If cocos are sufficiently debt-like to be viewed as a substitute for comparable non-contingent debt on the balance sheet of financial institutions, the deductibility of some or all of the interest paid on them raises no new tax neutrality issues with respect to the tax treatment of dividends. Provision of the privately and socially valuable insurance services cocos can yield should not be discouraged by biasing the tax system against cocos debt. Yet the question of whether to encourage or discourage cocos issuance by financial institutions through the US tax system ultimately is a policy matter that the US Treasury must decide. OCC (2003) may still contain currently valid baseline guidance on the qualifications required for subordinated debt, including mandatory convertibles with a maturity of 12 years or less, to be approved as T2 capital.

Section 385 of the I.R.C. grants authority to the Treasury to prescribe regulations necessary to determine whether a type of security is debt or equity, and Section 385(b) contains a set of (no longer very helpful) factors that the Treasury may use in constructing its regulations. Section 163(l)(a)—which is reproduced below—was added in 1997 on instruments that are disqualified from tax treatment as debt. However, this disqualification does not appear to apply to cocos insofar as their conversion into equity, while conditional, is not "reasonably expected." There is also no "substantial certainty" that the issuer's put of shares in return for the cocos to be cancelled will be triggered and hence exercised.

Section 163(l)(a) defines "Disqualified Debt Instruments." I.R.C. § 163(l) was adopted in 1997 and disallows any interest deduction on "disqualified debt instruments" that are issued by a corporation. Generally, "disqualified debt instruments" are debt instruments that are payable in equity of the issuing corporation or a related party. More specifically, they are debt instruments for which (i) a "substantial amount" of the principal or interest is payable in or convertible into equity (or determined by reference to such equity) or is part of an arrangement that is "reasonably expected" to result in such a transaction or (ii) the holder of that instrument may require that it be paid in such manner (i.e., in equity or other consideration that is based on equity) and there is "substantial certainty" that the option will be exercised. It would appear, therefore, that cocos that are issued by a well-capitalized firm should qualify for deductibility of interest paid since the chance of conversion is sufficiently small.

Under US law there may be a question, however, of whether all the interest is deductible or only that part which would be paid on an otherwise comparable bond without the adverse conversion feature. In other words, there is a question of whether the non-contingent bond method, described in § 1.1275-4(b) of the IRS Tax Regulations, applies to cocos. The comparable yield for the contingent debt instrument is the yield at which the issuer would be able to issue a fixed-rate non-contingent debt instrument with terms and conditions similar to those of the contingent debt payment instrument. Among these terms are the level of subordination, term-to-maturity, timing of payments, and general market conditions. However, "no adjustments are made for the riskiness of the contingencies or the liquidity of the debt instrument" (§ 1.1275-4(b)(4)(i)(B)) so that the instruments compared may differ in these regards.

The entire amount of interest paid would in fact be deductible on debt that is convertible at the holders' option into equity, as long as the conversion price per share was initially above the stock price prevailing at the time the debt was issued. Now the interest rate required on debt that was sweetened by the holder's call option to convert is of course lower than that on comparable straight debt. By contrast, the interest rate on cocos must be higher because exposure to the issuer's contingent "put" right and obligation comes with them.

Title 26 of the Internal Revenue Code, Subtitle A, Chapter 1, Sec. 163(k)(1) (1)-(3)(A)-(C) first denies the interest deduction for a *disqualified* debt instrument defined as "indebtedness of a corporation which is payable in equity of the issuer or a related party or equity held by the issuer." However, Revenue Ruling 2002-31 then reminds that under §163(l) indebtedness shall be treated as payable in equity only if "a substantial amount of the principal or interest is required to be paid or converted, or at the option of the issuer or a related party is payable in, or convertible into, such equity" *and* "the indebtedness is part of an arrangement which is reasonably expected to result in a transaction described [above]"and there is "substantial certainty" that any conversion options involved will be exercised. Since cocos conversion is contingent upon being triggered on its terms, but mandatory when triggered, it is neither unconditionally required nor optional for cocos issuers. Furthermore, since the triggering of conversion is a low-probability event, cocos are not disqualified debt instruments as defined in the above Section.

15.2 Tax Aspects of Debt Write-Off

Tax aspects arising from debt write-off (cancellation of indebtedness) either by itself or in conjunction with conversion to common equity have not received adequate attention. When cocos are converted, the difference between their face value—or actual acquisition-cost basis if bought in the secondary market—and the (normally appreciably lower) fair market value of the common equity issued in return could be regarded as a tax-effective capital loss for cocos holders. Conversely, cocos debt cancellation associated with cocos conversion could give rise to taxable income, or more pertinently for the corporate issuer in difficulties, reduced loss carry-forward.

However, PricewaterhouseCoopers (2009, p. 1) advised clients that "[u]pon conversion, the issuer will generally reclassify the carrying value of the convertible debt instrument to equity with no gain or loss recorded." If that is so, and the net income from debt-cancellation is not taxable to the firm, the costs associated with generating potential income from write-off by paying a higher interest rate beforehand should also not be deductible for consistency. Application of the non-contingent bond method would achieve this and appears to that extent justified. Hammer, Chen and Carman (2011, p. 97) further state that "[a] holder of a convertible debt instrument generally does not recognize gain or loss when the holder exchanges the debt for stock in the corporation that issued the debt security. Instead, the holder will receive a carry-over basis in the stock received upon conversion." A deductible capital loss could then be realized when the stock is sold. All these matters are far from settled: they call for much further guidance from the US tax authorities and the Office of Domestic Finance of the US Treasury, as KPMG (2011, pp. 10–11) has pointed out in its treatment of tax issues surrounding cocos.

The conversion terms on cocos may also have a bearing on whether they are characterized as debt for US tax purposes. Hammer and Bush (2011, p. 142) find that if the conversion price is set equal to book value per share, or, more precisely, to the amount of the issuer's tangible common equity per share, the probability of those cocos being classified as debt could be improved. They note that in a panicked market, the prices at which shares of common stock trade are arguably not a reflection of true Fair Market Values, and tangible common equity may then be viewed as a better measure of value (satisfying the requirements of Revenue Ruling 85-119). Setting a fixed conversion price [CP] which lies far below the share price of the bank's common stock at the time of cocos issue [MP_0] might also signal that the bank believes it has great "distance from conversion," thereby strengthening the claim that its cocos deserve to be treated as debt for tax purposes.

On the basis of these past IRS rulings, cocos would very likely have to be endowed with all of the following debt-like features for most or all of the interest payments on them to be deductible for corporation income tax purposes:

1. A finite maturity—barring perpetuals and requirements to replace at maturity

2. Mandatory and non-deferrable payments of interest on the scheduled coupon dates—barring non-payment and cancellation of interest in the absence of cocos conversion

3. Conversion that occurs when either their built-in trigger or the point of non-viability is reached—precluding discretionary activation by regulators except pursuant to a finding of non-viability or due to 'contingency-trigger' activation based on the regulator's (and/or issuer's) appraisal that the built-in trigger event has occurred, with confirmation expected from forthcoming (quarterly or special-audit) accounting data

4. Conversion that is unlikely to occur, being tied to a low-probability, objectively ascertainable trigger event rather than being unconditionally mandatory or expected with a 'substantial' degree of certainty at the initiative of regulator, issuer or investor. Issuing cocos when the firm's regulatory capital ratio is several percentage points above the high-trigger of going-concern cocos may reduce the likelihood of conversion to a level so low that it no longer jeopardizes the tax deductibility of interest paid

5. A recovery rate of over 50% from the common shares issued in conversion to underline partial-loss features similar to those of subordinated debt

Assuming these conditions for tax deductibility of interest paid on cocos are correctly captured and stay in place, IRS-compliant cocos could be issued voluntarily, have a final maturity of 5 to 50 years, and would not have to be replaced when called or reaching maturity. They would pay mandatory and non-deferrable interest at a fixed or variable (money-market or swap + fixed number of bps) rate without step-ups on schedule unless conversion has been triggered.

Next, the likelihood of cocos surviving to maturity would be enhanced by avoiding very long effective maturities and adopting a target level that is well above the trigger level of the capital ratio referenced at the time of cocos issue. For the high-trigger level of its going-concern cocos, the bank could choose either the minimum

CET1 requirement plus the fully loaded Capital Conservation Buffer requirement (i.e., 7% combined) or this plus the final prospective level of the progressive charge on G-SIBS, if applicable, which could bring the appropriate going-concern trigger level up to 9.5%. Transitory buffers like the Countercyclical Buffer requirement that may be imposed by national regulators need not be considered for this purpose. Cocos covenants should include provisions for mandatory and automatic updating when the relevant percentages prescribed by regulators change, with due notice, for the industry as a whole or for an individual bank. This would avoid such an action from constituting a "regulatory event" that would allow cocos to be called immediately and without replacement. Cocos subject to these trigger levels should be issued when the actual capital ratio of the respective bank is at least 2.5 percentage points higher to make conversion of cocos sufficiently far from 'substantially' certain. As will be seen in the next Chapter, combined capital ratios 4 percentage points above the required level at the time of issue, which would range from 11% to 13.5% in this example, would normally ensure an investment-grade rating for cocos from S&P, provided that the Stand-Alone Credit Profile [SACP] rating of their issuer is no less than a–. S&P uses lower-case letters for SACP ratings.

How often these cocos, whose maturity may range from 5 to 50 years, will be subject to conversion is still anyone's guess. So far only one out of a handful of cocos issued to private investors between 2009 and 2013 (by Bank of Cyprus) has been converted. Because high-trigger conversion of debt to equity is intended to ward off bankruptcy, conversion rates are likely to be a multiple of the bankruptcy rates of investment-grade corporates. Average cumulative issuer-weighted default rates between 1970–2010, reported by Moody's (2011, p. 32; see also S&P, 2011a) for investment-grade issues, are 1.0% after 5 years, 2.6% after 10 years, 4.5% after 15 years and 6.7% after 20 years. It may be reasonable to assume that cumulative conversion rates of investment-grade cocos will be found to be between 2 and 4 times greater than these reported default rates. Then they would be 2% to 4% after 5 years; 5% to 10% after 10; 9% to 18% after 15; and 13% to 27% after 20 years.

15.3 Setting the Conversion Price for a Recovery-Rate Target

If firms have managed to build up their capital ratio to a level well above the respective trigger point so as to make near-term conversion unlikely, the conversion terms still have to be set that would help assure that there is substantial recovery value should conversion occur nonetheless. Setting the conversion price—roughly like the floor price on two 2011 cocos issues set by Credit Suisse, equal to half the stock market price prevailing around the time of issue—would provide for an expected recovery rate of about 80% according to my previous estimate (2012a, pp. 61, 68–69).

Proceeding step by step, the current example again involves an eighty percent recovery rate for cocos holders. This recovery or replacement rate is to be achieved by setting the conversion price equal to 125% of the market price per share [MP_c] which forms after the announcement of conversion.

Step 1: The initial value of the firm is $1,600. There are 100 shares outstanding worth $10 per share so that equity is $1,000. The only debt consists of cocos with a total face value of $600.

Step 2: The value of the firm falls to $800, equity drops to $200, and the price per share to $2.

Step 3: Cocos are triggered and all are converted to common equity, with the number of shares newly issued in conversion being ($600/1.25MP_c$), where $1.25MP_c$ is the conversion price and $MP_c/(1.25MP_c) = 0.8$ is the targeted recovery rate. The act of conversion by itself should not affect the value of the firm that is based on the earnings power of its assets. It will however affect the distribution of that value between pre-existing shareholders and the holders of the newly issued shares obtained by conversion of the cocos. The expected value of MP_c can be found by solving the equation $100MP_c + (600/1.25MP_c)MP_c = 800$ for $MP_c = \$(800-480)/100$ which is $3.20. Equity, which would have fallen from $1,000 to $200 in the absence of cocos, falls 'only' to $320. The $120 added to the value of pre-existing shareholders' holdings of common stock is taken away from cocos holders who recover $480 of the $600 principal balance owed to them for a recovery rate of 80%. Since the conversion price is $4, cocos holders get 150 newly issued shares at cancellation of their original cocos debt claim and hold a majority of the 250 shares then outstanding.

Had this been a real-world case, it would be used both for and against debt-like treatment of cocos, most likely in a self-contradictory way. Having a recovery rate at least equal to that normally expected on senior unsecured debt has been used as an argument in favor of such treatment. Substantial recovery, however, can be derived only from conversion into equity. Nevertheless, this conversion feature has at the same time been used as an argument *against* debt-like treatment of genuine cocos, as opposed to write-down-only instruments that have no recovery value at all. Critics of debt-like treatment also point out that if cocos conversion leads to the former cocos holders ending up with a majority of the shares outstanding after conversion, such as 150 of 250 in the example above, strategic investors seeking control might regard cocos as equity just waiting for a market opportunity to be achieved. If a sovereign-wealth fund, private equity, or hedge fund had such an eventual takeover in mind, it might choose to defer investing in cocos until the issuer is weakly capitalized and its cocos have come closer to the trigger point. Such a development might justify reclassifying cocos from debt to equity for tax purposes. How and for what purpose instruments are used by issuers and investors is one of the factors taken into account for classification by the IRS.

For comparison with the 80% recovery rate used in the example above, Moody's (2011, p. 5) reported that the 1982–2010 issuer-weighted average corporate debt recovery rate—measured by trading prices 30 days after the default date of the debt—was 51% for senior secured bonds and 25% for junior subordinated bonds. An expected recovery rate of 80% for cocos is thus far greater than the average for junior subordinated bonds which would approximate the status of cocos prior to conversion. This further strengthens the case for deductibility of the interest paid because cocos would provide substantial recovery value even if their conversion was triggered before they can be paid off in full at maturity. The applicable principle here is that a transfer with a reasonable expectation of repayment has a good chance to be treated as debt. Moody's points out that actual default and recovery rates are negatively correlated, so that higher default rates must be associated with lower recovery rates, and default and recovery rates vary jointly over time. In the example above, however, the recovery rate is a 'design' variable that is controlled by setting the conversion price a chosen percentage (e.g., 25%) above the market price per share after the announcement of conversion so as to obtain the recovery rate intended.

16

Major Credit Rating Agencies' Approaches to Rating Cocos

Cocos can enter into credit ratings in at least two ways. They can be rated essentially like other subordinated debt on the likelihood that they will survive until their first call date (if undated) or maturity (if dated), that interest will be paid in full in a timely manner, and taking into consideration what the recovery rate would be should they be converted into equity rather than just written off. Secondly, as FitchRatings noted in a brief report on "Bank Contingent Capital to Rise," dated May 28, 2013:

> Cocos with a high capital ratio trigger are particularly relevant in stress tests and recovery planning as their write-off or equity conversion, once a pre-determined trigger is breached, is designed to absorb losses on a "going concern" basis before fundamental viability is threatened. In recognition of this, we assign such instruments either 50% or 100% equity credit in our bank capital analysis [that feeds into the firm's rating], broadly depending on coupon flexibility.

If coupons that are mandatory and cumulative are 'inflexible,' while discretionary coupon payments that are non-cumulative are 'flexible,' there is an obvious conflict between having a high equity content and a high issue rating for cocos. S&P in particular has dealt with these conflicts and arrived at a transparent rating scheme which can be presented through excerpts from official CRA documents with only small changes to preserve continuity. Fitch's commendable approach to rating cocos (see FitchRatings, 2009; 2011a; 2011b; 2012) appears in many ways similar to that of S&P: hence separate coverage would be duplicative. By contrast, Moody's, at least until February 2014, did not rate high-trigger cocos at all, a decision that will be explained in Moody's words and then subsequently questioned. This chapter focuses on what S&P appears to require for Cocos to be rated investment-grade, i.e., no less than BBB–. In the excerpts included below, the format and layout were preserved, as were most subheadings, paragraphs, section headings, and numbering from the underlying documents. This was done to facilitate locating these excerpts in the respective documents by those who are interested not just in the conceptual overview intended here, but also in the many fine practices of rating.

16.1 Requirements for Cocos to be Rated Investment-Grade by S&P

The previous chapter outlined what it may take for interest paid on cocos to be deductible from taxable corporate income in the United States. The next question is whether these requirements can be met and still allow cocos to achieve an investment-grade rating from S&P. The Dodd-Frank Wall Street Reform and Consumer Protection Act of 2010 requires Nationally Recognized Statistical Rating Organizations [NRSROs] to disclose their methodologies. With regard to explaining their rating of cocos, S&P, followed by Fitch Ratings, have done so to the greatest degree so far.

According to excerpts from S&P (2011b) that are gathered in the next section of this chapter, S&P regards certain types of hybrid-capital securities as eligible for inclusion in a bank's Total Adjusted Capital [TAC]. Cocos can qualify for TAC under the "intermediate" equity-content category under several combinations of conditions. Some of these mirror those that must be met by regulatory capital to be recognized under Basel III. The most central here are:

1. automatic conversion into common equity on a going-concern basis, characterized by a trigger set for mandatory conversion at a capital ratio of at least 7% without causing default,
2. a capital ratio whose definition, rules for calculating it, and level are publicly available—being reported at

least twice yearly within three months of the calculation date—together with the bank's minimum target for the regulatory ratio,

3. a residual life of the cocos debt security of at least 15 years if the Stand-Alone Credit Profile [SACP] of the bank is investment grade (bbb– or higher) and there are no incentives to redeem the security sooner than the residual life, such as coupon step-ups on earlier call dates, and

4. documentation stipulating that the cocos instrument will be replaced by common equity or by an equivalent or stronger instrument before any redemption prior to maturity.

TAC is the numerator of S&P's Risk-Adjusted Capital [RAC] ratio for banks (the denominator is S&P's version of RWA). To qualify for inclusion in TAC with an "intermediate" degree of equity content—subject to a limit of amounting to no more than 33% of the bank's Adjusted Common Equity—cocos must be able to absorb losses upon satisfaction of their contingency clause while the bank is a going concern. They must also qualify for inclusion in the bank's regulatory capital, thus making inclusion in TAC depend on national recognition of cocos in regulatory capital; such recognition of cocos as AT1 is granted by regulatory agencies in Europe but not in the United States, as the next chapter will show. Discrepancies with Basel III in national standards in this regard undermine global comparability of issue and issuer ratings because cocos that are not qualified as regulatory capital in any particular jurisdiction cannot contribute to TAC there. Except in those jurisdictions, and not just in the unlikely event of conversion, the RAC ratio may be immediately raised by issuing going-concern cocos. This can benefit the bank's rating under S&P's criteria for rating banks.

Still guided by S&P (2011b), the methodology for assigning an issue rating to cocos is to notch down from the SACP rating of the issuing institution in most cases. The minimum notching for cocos that convert to common equity when triggered is two notches below the SACP if the bank's SACP is assessed bbb– or higher. A bank's proximity to a quantitatively-defined CET1/RWA contingency trigger determines the additional notching on a going-concern cocos, as shown in Table 9. If the bank's SACP is at least investment-grade (bbb– or higher), the minimum notching for a bank's cocos is two notches below the SACP. The bank's projected proximity to a mandatory contingency trigger determines the additional notching on a going-concern contingent capital instrument. Table 9 shows that only banks with an SACP rating of a– or higher would be able to issue investment-grade cocos provided their voluntary buffer capital is so strong that their CET1/RWA ratio is more than 4 percentage points above the trigger level. If cocos with an issue rating below investment grade were not marketable, banks rated below a– would have to find other means to bolster their capital ratios until their ratings improve. However, as shown in Table 7, in 2013, a cocos with a composite rating as low as BB has been issued, five notches down from the a– SACP rating of the bank in question, Société Générale. As a rule, even banks whose SACP is rated aa– or higher would need their regulatory capital ratios (projected for 18–24 months) to remain at least 201–300 bps above the cocos' contingency trigger if those instruments are to be rated investment grade, i.e., at least BBB–.

The S&P cocos ratings in all but the last (CCC) row in Table 9 would be one notch higher than shown in two cases: (i) Setting off the going-concern capital-ratio trigger leads only to mandatory coupon non-payment for as long as the trigger condition persists. (ii) The payment of interest on cocos is non-deferrable but cocos can absorb losses by write-off and conversion before the bank's liquidation and without causing a default on senior obligations. Assuming conservatively that it takes an SACP rating of at least a–, what percentage of big banks could be qualified to issue investment-grade cocos rated at least BBB–, three notches down from a– ? Issuer credit profiles published by S&P (2012) for the top 100 banks globally show that 51 of them were rated at least a– (3 were aa, 12 a+, 18 a, and 18 a–) on a stand-alone basis. S&P (2011b, p. 3) reports that an average bank in developed economies would place in the SACP categories bbb and a, with the lowercase letters designed to differentiate this stand-alone credit profile from

Table 9. Rating Caps for Going-Concern Cocos as a Function of the Stand-Alone Credit Profile [SACP] Rating of the Issuing Bank and the Size of its Projected Capital Buffer

	SACP of Bank				
Projected buffer over (CET1/RWA)% trigger (bps)	aa– or higher	a+	a	a-	bbb+
401 or more	**BBB+**	**BBB+**	**BBB**	**BBB–**	BB+
301–400	**BBB**	**BBB**	**BBB–**	BB+	BB
201–300	**BBB–**	BB+	BB+	BB	BB-
101–200	BB	B	B	B	B–
0–100	CCC*	CCC	CCC	CCC	CCC

Source: S&P (2011b, p. 17)

*This combination is unlikely because the SACP assessment of the issuer would have been lowered to the lowest buffer level to reflect the deterioration of the bank's capital position.

Note: Combinations rated BB+ above would be rated BBB– when 2 notches off SACP, rather than 3 notches off SACP, is the preliminary rating rule that is applied.

the Issuer Credit Rating, ICR. Hence the set of banks that could qualify for issuing cocos, provided they are well capitalized with a voluntary buffer of more than 300 bps above the trigger level, is far from empty.

Any high-trigger T2 cocos here envisaged would be less loss-absorbing than T1 cocos, in that they would be dated securities that pay non-deferrable and presumably tax-deductible interest up to the date of conversion after which such payments and redemptions would be no longer due. They would have a built-in going-concern trigger which—when activated under its contingency clause—automatically leads to irreversible debt write-off through conversion to common equity. The trigger levels of CET1/RWA for going-concern cocos would be set at 7% or more, with the target level of that ratio over 3 percentage points higher than the trigger level. Such a substantial voluntary buffer would make conversion sufficiently unlikely and thereby help maintain tax deductibility of interest paid and an investment-grade rating for the instrument. If regulators nevertheless regarded such cocos as ineligible for regulatory capital, S&P would have to rate them CCC under its current criteria. Such a rating, which carries the warning of a security being "currently vulnerable," would likely doom these T2 cocos: it would make issuing them prohibitively expensive for lack of support and "accreditation" from regulators.

These are the fatal features of design enumerated by S&P (2011b, p. 18) that would also cap its issue rating of cocos at CCC:

1. A contingent capital trigger linked to a specific rating.

2. A contingent capital instrument with an exceptionally sensitive or vulnerable trigger that can be activated although the SACP has not deteriorated significantly. Examples of such triggers include those linked to market capitalization or share price bcause these factors do not always correlate with changes in credit-worthiness.

3. Other triggers based on regulators' concerns about financial stability in the broader market or to events or situations that are not observable using public information. This includes situations in which a regulator has full discretion to activate the trigger on a going-concern basis. However, if the regulator's discretion only extends to deciding whether a bank is about to breach a defined and observable regulatory ratio and the capital-based trigger clearly states this ratio as a specific number, then Tables 3a and 3b in S&P (2011b) apply if the trigger is a going-concern trigger. [S&P's Table 3a shows the rating for cocos with mandatory write-down or conversion to common equity features. These ratings are reproduced as Table 9 here. Table 3b of the underlying document presents the ratings assigned when a trigger event leads only to mandatory coupon nonpayment. Both tables from S&P will be referred to again later in this chapter.]

It appears therefore that going-concern cocos which S&P would judge to be eligible for investment-grade rating must be rated on the merits of the issuing institution and the specific trigger and conversion terms of the instrument, and not on conditions in the economy or its financial sector at large. In addition, these triggers must operate automatically and not be subject to suspension or activation by regulators, except when the regulators judge the contingency event specified in the instrument to be imminent or to have already occurred without as yet showing up in trailing accounting data. For triggering the going-concern cocos here considered, non-viability or insolvency would rarely come into play: the high trigger level of going-concern cocos is well above that associated with the non-viability or insolvency of a financial institution whose eventual failure the conversion of going-concern cocos is meant to prevent. S&P is also not particularly concerned with the residual maturity of going-concern cocos which would be rated as long-term hybrid capital instruments whether dated or undated. Hence cocos can be designed with all the features regarded as required for tax deductibility of interest in the United States without jeopardizing an investment-grade rating by S&P if the issuer has an SACP rating of at least a–.

Indeed several design features required for tax deductibility also help assure such a rating: the non-deferral of interest payments, the severely limited amount of discretion granted to bank supervisors, the high level of the voluntary buffer capital accumulated above the trigger level that reduces the probability of conversion, and the high expected recovery rate from the equity issued upon conversion. These features provide a basis on which a match may be found between issuers—interested in reducing their cost of capital and strengthening their defenses against failure in a crisis—and investors who want cocos with calculable conversion, excused interest-nonpayment, and recovery risks based on preset terms.

16.2 Documentation of S&P's Methodology for Rating Cocos

The following contains partial and condensed excerpts from a key document issued by S&P:

S&P (2011b), Criteria / Financial Institutions / Banks: "Bank Hybrid Capital Methodology and Assumptions," *Global Credit Portal Ratings Direct*, Nov. 1

http://img.en25.com/Web/StandardandPoors/BankHybrid-Capital_Methodology_11_1_11_4216.pdf

See also S&P (2011c) for a description of its rating methodology not only for hybrids. Of particular relevance in that publication are Chapters VI and VII, which deal with the methodology of "Setting the Issuer Credit Rating" and "Stand-Alone Credit Profile," respectively.

Overview of criteria for including cocos in the total adjusted capital of a financial institution. The criteria comprise standards for: (i) determining whether a hybrid capital instrument is eligible for inclusion in the calculation of a bank's total adjusted capital [TAC], (ii) classifying a bank's hybrid capital instrument based on its degree of equity content, and (iii) assigning a rating to a bank's hybrid capital instrument. TAC is the numerator of S&P's risk-adjusted capital [RAC] ratio for banks. The RAC ratio provides the starting point for assessing the strength of a bank's capitalization under the criteria for rating banks. Bank hybrid capital instruments that can qualify for inclusion in TAC include "contingent capital" instruments and those with write-down features.

II. Summary of the Criteria

8. Hybrid capital instruments include—but are not limited to—preferred stock, deferrable subordinated notes, trust preferred securities, and mandatory convertible securities. The equity content of a hybrid capital instrument (or hybrid) can affect the rating on a bank by influencing the measurement of the bank's capitalization. Equity content refers to the extent to which a bank hybrid capital instrument can function as equity and therefore—via features such as

coupon nonpayment or deferral, a principal write-down, or conversion into common equity—absorb a portion of a bank's losses. The criteria classify the equity content of bank hybrids into one of three categories: (i) high, (ii) intermediate, or (iii) minimal.

9. To qualify for inclusion in Total Adjusted Capital (TAC), subject to certain limits, a bank hybrid capital instrument must qualify for inclusion in regulatory capital and contain features consistent with the criteria for classification in either the high equity content category or the intermediate equity content category...

10. Qualifying for inclusion in a bank's regulatory capital is a necessary condition, but does not automatically qualify a bank hybrid capital instrument for inclusion in TAC... Inclusion in the calculation of TAC also depends on an instrument's specific features.

13. To qualify for the intermediate equity content category, a hybrid capital instrument must be able to absorb losses while the bank is a going concern. A so-called "going-concern contingent capital" instrument can qualify for the intermediate equity content category if it can absorb losses upon satisfaction of its contingency clause while the bank is a going concern. The method of absorbing losses may be conversion into common equity or a write-down of principal (see Methodology, Section B.4 below)...

14. A hybrid capital instrument with minimal equity content, such as one that can absorb losses only in a "non-viability" situation, is ineligible for inclusion in TAC. Non-viability refers to when a bank is in breach of, or about to breach, regulatory requirements for its license. Such instruments include Non-Viability Contingent Capital (NVCC). The market sometimes refers to NVCC instruments as "bail-in" capital if these instruments share the cost of a government's rescue of a bank.

17. The methodology for assigning an issue rating to a bank hybrid capital instrument is to notch down from the bank's Stand-Alone Credit Profile (SACP), except in the situations

such as an issuer credit rating (ICR) on the bank that is lower than its SACP. For these exceptions, the notching is from the ICR. The minimum notching for a bank hybrid capital instrument ranges from two notches below the SACP (if the bank's SACP is assessed at 'bbb–' or higher) to three notches below the SACP (if the bank's SACP is 'bb+' or lower). An issue rating is a forward-looking opinion that reflects the risk of non-timely or partial payment on a bank hybrid capital instrument and the subordination of the instrument. If an instrument shows a higher risk of non-timely or partial payment than the SACP assessment indicates, additional notching from the SACP applies. [S&P uses lower-case letters for SACP ratings but upper-case letters for all other credit ratings.]

19. The rating on an NVCC instrument would be one notch lower than that on an equivalent hybrid capital instrument that does not contain a contingency clause.

20. A bank's proximity to a mandatory contingency trigger determines the additional notching on a going-concern contingent capital instrument. A rating cap applies when a trigger relates to maintenance of a specific regulatory capital ratio, depending on both the bank's SACP and its proximity to the trigger. The rating cap is 'CCC' if the trigger is exceptionally sensitive or linked to rating transitions, or if its activation is independent of a deterioration of the SACP (see paragraph 72 below for examples).

21. The methodology for rating a bank's *non-deferrable* subordinated debt instrument that qualifies as a hybrid capital instrument is to notch down from the SACP: one notch, if the bank's SACP is 'bbb–' or higher; or two notches if the SACP is 'bb+' or lower. The criteria treat non-deferrable subordinated bank debt as hybrid capital if the relevant legal or regulatory framework insulates senior debt from defaults on the subordinated debt. An example of such a framework is a resolution regime that allows a bank's subordinated debt to absorb losses (such as via the write-down of principal) without causing the bank's liquidation.

VI. Methodology

26. The methodology for bank hybrid capital instruments (hybrids) incorporates thee Subparts:

27. Subpart A describes the features that identify bank capital instruments as hybrid capital.

28. Subpart B describes the criteria for classifying the equity content of bank hybrid capital instruments into one of three categories, "high", "intermediate", and "minimal". Hybrid capital instruments classified in the high equity content category or the intermediate equity content category count toward the calculation of total adjusted capital (TAC).

29. Subpart C describes the criteria for assigning ratings to all bank hybrid capital instruments, even those classified in the minimal equity content category and therefore not included in the TAC calculation.

A. Identifying Hybrid Capital

31. A hybrid capital instrument displays features of both debt and equity and can absorb losses via nonpayment of the coupon, a write-down of principal, or conversion into common equity, without causing a legal default or wind-up of the issuer.

32. Hybrid capital instruments include—but are not limited to—preferred stock, preference shares, deferrable subordinated notes, trust preferred securities, and mandatory convertible securities (mandatory convertibles). A mandatory convertible is a hybrid capital instrument, irrespective of whether it is senior or subordinated before conversion into common equity. The criteria treat noncumulative and cumulative deferrable subordinated debt securities as hybrid capital instruments.

33. Non-deferrable subordinated debt securities are not usually hybrid capital instruments, except in certain jurisdictions. The reason for this is that they cannot absorb losses before the bank's liquidation, or without causing a default on senior obligations. However, such instruments qualify as hybrid capital instruments if the regulatory and legal frameworks

insulate senior debt from a default on subordinated debt. An example of such a framework is a bank resolution regime that allows a bank's subordinated debt to absorb losses without causing the bank's liquidation.

34. A non-viability hybrid capital instrument has features that allow it to absorb losses only when the bank is at or close to the point of "non-viability". The criteria define a non-viability situation as one in which a bank is in breach of or about to breach regulatory requirements for its license, and regulatory intervention may therefore be imminent. An example of a non-viability feature is a clause that requires coupon payments or prevents a principal write-down if a bank meets minimum regulatory capital requirements. Another example is a feature that allows coupon nonpayment or a principal write-down only after a bank has breached the minimum regulatory capital requirements. Other non-viability features may limit a bank's ability to suspend coupons or write down principal, even though it is in distress. A non-viability hybrid capital instrument typically absorbs losses no sooner than when a bank's SACP is at 'ccc' or lower.

36. A "going-concern" hybrid capital instrument contains features that allow it to absorb losses when a bank is not at, or close to, the point of non-viability; in other words, when the bank is still a going concern. If the bank's SACP were 'bbb–' or higher at the time of issuance, these hybrid capital instruments would absorb losses early enough for the bank to maintain an SACP of at least 'b+'.

37. A contingent-capital trigger activates the mandatory conversion of contingent capital into common equity or a mandatory write-down of principal. A bank can set these triggers to activate while it is still a going concern, that is, on a "going-concern basis". An instrument with such a trigger is a going-concern contingent capital instrument. If a trigger activates in a non-viability situation, the instrument is a non-viability contingent capital (NVCC) instrument.

B. *Equity Content Classification*

39. The criteria for classifying bank hybrid capital instruments in either the high, intermediate, or minimal equity content categories differ from the criteria for hybrid capital instruments in other sectors. This is because banks are highly sensitive to market and investor confidence and often need ongoing access to wholesale debt markets. The equity content classifications reflect the relative likelihood that a bank hybrid capital instrument can absorb losses when required.

B.1. Equity content categories

41. This section shows how hybrid capital instruments count toward bank capital, depending on the classification of equity content into one of three categories: (i) high, (ii) intermediate, or (iii) minimal. The classification determines the degree to which a hybrid capital instrument is eligible for inclusion in TAC, depending on the features of the instrument...

b) Intermediate equity content: Qualifying subordinated instruments, preferred stock, or contingent capital instruments that allow nonpayment of coupon, principal write-downs, or conversion into equity on a going-concern basis, without causing a default may have intermediate equity content. A hybrid capital instrument with such content is eligible for the TAC calculation until the aggregate amount is equivalent to 33% of the bank's Adjusted Common Equity (ACE).

A sublimit applies for hybrid capital instruments with intermediate equity content, in that the aggregate amount of hybrid capital instruments with high and intermediate equity content cannot exceed 50% of ACE. This means that if hybrid capital instruments with high equity content are equivalent to 50% of ACE, then the overall limit is exhausted and hybrid capital instruments with intermediate equity content are not included in the calculation of TAC.

B.4. Contingent capital structures and hybrids with write-down features that can be credited with intermediate equity content

52. A contingent capital instrument with features that could lead to mandatory conversion into common equity or a write-down of principal does not have high equity content if issued by a bank or finance company. This is because the activation of the loss-absorption trigger could cause a loss of investor confidence, restricting the bank's funding . flexibility. Such an instrument can count as a hybrid with intermediate equity content if it satisfies the other relevant conditions for that category.

53. A contingent capital instrument qualifies for the intermediate equity content category—regardless of its initial form—if it can absorb losses on a going-concern basis. The criteria treat such instruments as "going-concern contingent capital". An eligible instrument has:

- A residual life of at least 10 years, if the bank's SACP is at 'bb+' or lower, or at least 15 years if the SACP is at 'bbb–' or higher. These residual periods are shorter than the residual life standards for all other hybrid capital instruments with intermediate equity content;

- Documentation stipulating that it may only be replaced by common equity or by an equivalent or stronger instrument (such a replacement would take place before the redemption of the instrument); and conversion feature that transforms it into common equity or a feature allowing a permanent write-down of at least 25% of the principal. The triggers for these features would kick in mandatorily and on a going-concern basis.

C. Assigning Issue Ratings to Bank Hybrid Capital Instruments

57. The gap between the issue ratings on senior bank debt and those on bank hybrid capital instruments widens if more government support [that is not extended to hybrid capital, particularly if it forms part of a bank's regulatory capital that is intended to absorb losses] is included in the issuer

credit rating (ICR) and the senior debt ratings.

69. If activation of a capital-based trigger—expressed as a specific number—leads to mandatory loss absorption on a going-concern basis, the issue rating depends on the bank's proximity to the trigger. If a mandatory capital trigger relates to compliance with a respective national regulator's minimum total capital requirement to maintain a banking license, it is a non-viability trigger.

70. If a going-concern hybrid capital instrument has a mandatory trigger linked to a regulatory ratio expressed as a specific number, then it receives an issue rating based on: (i) the bank's SACP, (ii) S&P's projections of the specified regulatory ratio, and (iii) an estimate of the regulatory ratio that the bank can maintain if it uses its financial flexibility. The projected regulatory ratios look forward 18–24 months, in line with the time frame for the rating outlook, and can differ from the bank's forecasts. The rating outcomes are one notch lower for cocos with a going-concern trigger leading to a mandatory write-down or conversion into equity than for going-concern cocos with mandatory coupon nonpayment when triggered.

71. If a bank's data do not facilitate the monitoring of the specific regulatory ratio referenced in a mandatory trigger, the hybrid capital instrument receives an issue rating of 'CCC'. To monitor a regulatory ratio included in a trigger and expressed as a specific number: (i) the definition of the ratio must be publicly available, (ii) the rules for calculating the ratio are publicly available, (iii) the bank publishes the ratio at least twice yearly and within three months of the calculation date, and (iv) the bank publishes a minimum target for the regulatory ratio.

72. The criteria cap the issue rating on a bank hybrid capital instrument with a contingent capital trigger linked to a specific rating at 'CCC'. Likewise, the highest issue rating is 'CCC' if a contingent capital instrument has an

exceptionally sensitive or vulnerable trigger that can be activated although the SACP has not deteriorated significantly. Examples of such triggers include those linked to market capitalization or share price because these factors do not always correlate with changes in creditworthiness. Other triggers may relate to regulators' concerns about financial stability in the broader market and to events or situations that are not observable using public information. This includes situations in which a regulator has full discretion to activate the trigger on a going-concern basis.

If the regulator's discretion only extends to deciding whether a bank is about to breach a defined and observable regulatory ratio and the capital-based trigger clearly states this ratio as a specific number, then Table 3a or 3b (identified before) applies if the trigger is a going-concern trigger. If the regulator's discretion only extends to deciding whether a bank is nonviable, then the instrument is an NVCC instrument and paragraph 69 applies.

C.3. Non-deferrable subordinated bank debt

73. The issue ratings on a bank's conventional non-deferrable subordinated debt are one notch below the Issuer Credit Rating (ICR) on investment-grade issuers (i.e., banks rated 'BBB–' or higher). The issue ratings are two notches below the ICR if the ICR is 'BB+' or lower.

74. The criteria take a different approach if a non-deferrable subordinated debt instrument constitutes part of a bank's regulatory capital and represents higher default risk than the senior debt. This occurs in countries where the regulatory and legal frameworks, including bank resolution regimes, could lead to the conversion of non-deferrable subordinated debt into bail-in capital or to untimely or partial payment of coupon or principal, without provoking a legal default or the bank's liquidation.

16.3 Moody's Continued Reluctance to Rate Going-Concern Cocos

Moody's (2013), "Moody's Proposed Approach for Rating Certain Bank Contingent Capital Securities and Update to Approach for Rating Bank Subordinated Debt: A Proposed Update to Moody's Consolidated Global Bank Rating Methodology," Global Credit Research—10 April. Excerpts from Press Release and Request for Comments

http://www.moodys.com/research/Moodys-Proposed-Approach-for-Rating-Certain-Bank-Contingent-Capital-Securities-PBC_150964

Moody's Investors Service is requesting comments on its proposed approach for rating contractual non-viability securities, one type of contingent capital (CoCo) issued by regulated banking institutions. Contractual non-viability securities are typically junior securities, with or without coupon suspension mechanisms, which absorb losses either through conversion to equity or a principal write-down that is triggered at or close to the point of non-viability when a bank is deeply distressed. In February 2010, Moody's issued a Special Comment titled "Rating Considerations for Contingent Capital Securities" that established a moratorium on rating contingent capital securities where loss absorption is subject to regulatory discretion and/or the breach of regulatory capital triggers. Moody's hesitation to rate was based on the difficulty in predicting when loss absorption would be triggered due to rapidly changing regulatory and political environments.

Since that time, the regulatory and political willingness to impose losses on creditors, particularly subordinated creditors, as a pre-condition for an ailing bank to receive public-sector support has become evident. Basel III has also made it clear that regulatory capital needs to absorb losses either contractually or through the use of regulatory powers to "bail in" subordinated securities. In addition to sharing this view, local regulators have increasingly become comfortable with the issuance of "high trigger" contingent capital securities that absorb losses for banks as a going concern.

These developments have made clear the regulatory intent of burden sharing with subordinated creditors and have improved Moody's visibility around determining when loss absorption will be triggered, particularly if it is at the point of non-viability.

The Basel Committee defines the point of non-viability as the earlier of: (1) a decision that a write-off, without which the firm would become non-viable, is necessary, as determined by the relevant authority; and (2) the decision to make a public-sector injection of capital or equivalent support, without which the firm would have become non-viable, as determined by the relevant authority. See "Minimum requirements to ensure loss absorbency at the point of non-viability," Basel Committee, 13 January 2011 [excerpted as Document 1 in Chapter 17 below].

The additional visibility around the trigger points for loss absorption allows the rating agency to consider assigning ratings to certain types of contingent capital securities. Moody's proposal is to evaluate contractual non-viability securities within the framework of Moody's proprietary Baseline Credit Assessment (BCA), which expresses an opinion on the standalone financial strength of a bank, absent any extraordinary support from an affiliate or government. As such, BCAs capture the likelihood that the issuer will reach the point of non-viability, which is generally the time when a failing bank needs to be recapitalized, without which it would not be able to continue to operate. BCAs are indicators of the likelihood that a bank will reach the point at which it requires extraordinary support to avoid default, typically when there is burden sharing among creditors in order to justify a government stepping up to provide support. To the BCA, Moody's adds consideration of parental support, if applicable, to arrive at Adjusted BCA. Similar to the anchor point for hybrid securities and, in many jurisdictions, subordinated debt, Moody's Adjusted BCA is the starting point for rating bank contractual non-viability securities.

The BCA can be used as a proxy to determine the point of non-viability, which is generally the time when a failing bank needs to be recapitalized, without which it would not be able to continue as a going concern. The issuance of bank contingent capital or cocos with triggers linked to the point of non-viability when a bank is in deep distress, as well as the global regulatory push toward burden sharing by creditors, now allow these instruments to be rated. If this proposal is implemented, Moody's would rate both contractual non-viability securities and junior securities at risk of burden sharing connected with regulatory intervention if a bank is in severe financial distress. The proposed framework takes into consideration the relative expected loss potential for non-viability securities either on a contractual or statutory bail-in basis.

Specifically excluded from this proposal are "high trigger" contingent capital securities where loss absorption may be triggered well ahead of the point of non-viability. These securities remain subject to Moody's moratorium, given the continued difficulty in predicting when the trigger will be breached because it may occur in advance of the point of non-viability and is not directly captured by the risks addressed through our BCAs. In addition, "high trigger" securities do not respect the priority of claim hierarchy, potentially subordinating them to equity. However, should our visibility improve around predicting when high triggers could be breached, we may in the future decide to rate these securities.

To date, almost all contingent capital securities have been issued by banks, Swiss Re(insurance) Co. high-trigger cocos being one of the exceptions. For non-bank institutions, Moody's would use an analytic thought process similar to the one proposed for banks.

The regulatory and political willingness to impose losses on "plain vanilla" subordinated creditors has also led Moody's to re-examine its systemic support assumptions for bank subordinated debt. The agency is proposing a revised methodology that does not assume systemic support for bank subordinated debt and instead uses judgment on a country-by-country basis to identify those instances where there may continue to be a willingness and ability to support subordinated debt. "Plain vanilla" subordinated debt is typically dated subordinated debt and has no coupon skip mechanism. Tier 2 cocos share some of these characteristics. They may be dated for maturity and have coupons that are mandatory and cumulative, and not discretionary and non-cumulative, unless regulators order coupon skipping at the point of non-viability or ahead of a government capital-injection event.

17

Regulatory Requirements at Cross-Purposes

This chapter will document the development of the capital and instrument requirements proposed under Basel III and how they have affected design, volume of issuance, and regulatory uses of cocos. To deduce the outlook for cocos from their regulatory treatment to date, it will present excerpts from key documents released by the Basel Committee on Banking Supervision [BCBS] and the European Banking Authority [EBA]. These documents in turn provided the foundation for the Capital Requirements Regulation [CRR-IV] issued in Europe in 2013 and the "final rule" adopted by bank regulators in the United States in the same year. Both of these regulations, also excerpted here, aim to implement Basel III in their respective countries or zones. Starting with the global regulatory framework first proposed in BCBS (2010 and 2011c) "for more resilient banks and banking systems," the Chapter will focus on how regulations pertaining to the role of cocos in meeting capital requirements have evolved from the time they were first proposed to when they were adopted with variations by both the European Union and the United States.

The substance of what was originally envisioned in 2010–2011 did not always survive unchanged in EU and US regulations. For example, the third document excerpted below, BCBS (2011d), subsumes the following specification for going-concern contingent capital instruments: "[They] *fully* convert to CET1 through a *permanent* write-off or conversion to common shares when the CET1 of the banking group falls below at least 7% of risk-weighted assets" (emphasis added). Document 6, however, containing excerpts from the European Commission's CRR (EC, 2013), no longer requires the entire principal amount of the instrument to be written off or converted if a lower amount would be sufficient to restore the CET1 ratio of the institution to at least

5.125%. Furthermore, the write-down of debt may be temporary. Document 5, EBA (2013b), thus contains a lengthy Article of Regulatory Technical Standards [RTS] on "[the] nature of the write-up of the principal amount following a write-down."

As already touched on in Chapter 2, the BCBS, also known simply as "the Basel Committee," can propose what the senior representatives of bank supervisory authorities and central banks of currently 26 countries plus Hong Kong SAR have agreed to put forward for consideration and eventual adoption by their respective national authorities. Just as the Basel Committee can only advise and promote the adoption of new global standards, and aim for adoption of a single rule book by the competent authorities of its member countries, the European Union and the European Parliament cannot legislate for its members in the many areas involved. Any "directives" proposed must be processed and passed by them into law, often with tolerated, if limited, national deviations. Regulations also undergo a multistage process leading to the adoption of most or all Basel III rules. First these rules must be translated into a proposed Capital Requirements Regulation [CRR-IV]. The European Commission published its consultative proposals for the CRR first in July 2011, which were then amended in a process that took about two years until acceptable to EU members collectively. The CRR-IV was finally adopted by the Council of the EU and the European Parliament on June 20, 2013. Guided by the latest CRR that went into effect on June 28, 2013, EU supervisory agencies—and ultimately the banks and investment houses in their jurisdiction—must then implement the rules, standards and criteria in the CRR as adopted "to the satisfaction of the competent authority," often in consultation with the EBA.

The regulatory approach to ending up with a single rule book for EU members does not shy away from imposing on the legislative process required for the adoption of the Capital Requirements Directive [CRD IV]. The excerpt from the preamble (item 45) to the CRR shows that if the legislative process does not act, there is the implicit threat that the regulatory process will. The important principle that is to be advanced with such urgency is that all additional T1 and T2 non-common-stock ("non-common") instruments of an institution should constitute bail-in ("bailinable") debt. For this purpose item 45 declares that "if by 31 December 2015, Union law governing the requirement that capital instruments should be capable of being fully and permanently written down to zero or converted into Common Equity Tier 1 instruments in the event that an institution is no longer considered viable has not been adopted, the Commission should review and report on whether such a provision should be included in this Regulation and, in light of that review, submit appropriate legislative proposals." Item 75 of the preamble adds, "This regulation should not affect the ability of competent authorities to maintain pre-approval processes regarding the contracts governing Additional Tier 1 and Tier 2 capital instruments. In those cases, such capital instruments should only be computed [unusual phrasing in original] towards the Institution's Additional Tier 1 capital or Tier 2 capital once [the competent authorities] have successfully completed these approval processes."

In the United States, there is another multistage process which takes the form of primarily internal—rather than mostly international—dispute resolution. Because there are three federal agencies involved in bank supervision and regulation, the FDIC, OCC, and Fed, this US troika must first come to agree on what to propose for the banks. To actually move forward, they must then continue to agree on transition rules and schedules for implementation and satisfy Congressional demands and the demands of legislators elsewhere as needed. As recapitulated in Document 7 excerpted in this Chapter (78 FR 62017 October 11, 2013, p. 14), on August 30, 2012, the three US agencies published three joint notices of proposed rule-making, seeking public comment on revisions to the risk-based and leverage requirements, and on methodologies for calculating risk-weighted assets under the standardized and advanced approaches. The proposed rules, in part, reflected agreements reached by the BCBS in "Basel III: A Global Regulatory Framework for More Resilient Banks and Banking Systems," including subsequent changes to the BCBS's capital standards and recent BCBS consultative papers. The proposal also included changes consistent with federal law such as the Dodd-Frank Reform and Consumer Protection Act of 2010.

When the *final rule* was published on October 11, 2013, in the name of the Comptroller of the Currency [OCC] and the Federal Reserve System—without approval from the Federal Deposit Insurance Corporation [FDIC]—the wrestling over this rule obviously was not over yet (see the last document excerpted in this chapter). The Fed too could hold things up at a later stage. Thus Bloomberg reported on December 18, 2013, that the Fed had decided to delay imposing limits on leverage at eight of the biggest US financial institutions until a global agreement is completed by the BCBS that could shape up as weaker than the US plan. The FDIC and OCC, however, had favored finishing a US rule by the end of 2013.

While the road from first proposal at the level of the BCBS to ratification by national agencies is long and sinuous, it remains true that the rules that are finally adopted nationally are generally consistent with the Basel III rules. Indeed, national rules stricter than Basel III (within limits) are commonly anticipated and pre-authorized in the Basel III rules, as well as in the CRR. The BCBS monitors the implementation of Basel III regulatory reforms on a continuing basis, with past and forthcoming semi-annual reports available at www.bis.org/bcbs/implementation/bprl1.htm.

To provide at least partial documentation for cocos requirements that merit comment, the seven excerpts that follow are taken from the BCBS (1–3), EBA (4–5), EU-CRR (6) and US-OCC-FED (7) agency publications with some changes in arrangement, headings, and punctuation to make the excerpts intelligible by themselves. The purpose of this selection is to show that the wide discretion regulators demand over the interest payments and conversion of cocos and the equity-like features they already impose on them from the time they are issued are not compatible with an invest-ment-grade issue rating by S&P. In addition, the type of cocos which regulators may find acceptable to satisfy all or part of AT1 and T2 regulatory capital requirements are not likely to qualify for tax deductibility of interest payments in the United States, which is an outlier in this regard. Hence the three desiderata for the success of cocos are brought into conflict, rather than synergy, with each other: (1) being qualified for meeting some part of regulatory capital requirements, (2) being rated investment-grade rather than high-yield ("junk") debt by S&P, the major rating agency of cocos, and (3) paying interest that is also tax-deductible in the United States and not just in most other countries. Because satisfying one of the three conditions may very well be at the expense of violating another under present conditions, cocos issuance has been made unnecessarily expensive and correspondingly held back.

Chapter 15 above has already shown that cocos would very likely have to be endowed with all of the following debt-like features for interest payments on them to be deductible for corporation income tax purposes: (i) a fixed final maturity, (ii) mandatory and non-deferrable payments of interest on the scheduled coupon dates, (iii) mandatory conversion only when either their built-in trigger—which is to be based on a regulatory capital ratio and not a stock price variable—or the point of non-viability is reached, (iv) conversion that is unlikely to occur, being tied to a low-probability, objectively ascertainable trigger event rather than being unconditionally mandatory or expected with a "substantial" degree of certainty.

Issuing cocos when the firm's regulatory capital ratio is three or more percentage points greater than the high trigger of going-concern cocos could reduce this degree of certainty to a level low enough not to jeopardize the tax deductibility of interest paid. Some top-tier banks like UBS have already indicated that they expect to raise their CET1 much faster and much farther than currently required for their own reasons. Concretely, against the background of a "fully loaded" CET1 requirement of 9.5%—as it might be for a G-SIB when Basel III is fully applied at the end of the phase-in period in 2019—the announced aim of UBS is already to bring the actual CET1 ratio up to 13% in 2014 and to raise it further in later years. Other G-SIBs have also already gone beyond "early delivery" of the Basel III capital requirements only applicable from the start of 2019.

Assuming these conditions for tax deductibility of interest paid on cocos stay in place, there are several contradictions between what the BCBS has proposed for adoption by national regulators after 2013 on and what the EBA requires from internationally active banks in Europe, on the one hand, and what the capital market requires for cocos to become a success. Among the latter conditions are (1) an investment-grade rating from S&P that would allow their interest costs to be well below the required rate of return on common equity to which, in an emergency, they would convert, and (2) tax deductibility of interest paid to prevent them from being severely handicapped against otherwise comparable unsecured long-term (but non-contingent and non-convertible) debt. The basic conflict is between regulators who want the cocos to be very equity-like from the beginning and not just upon conversion, tax authorities which want them to be very debt-like, and rating agencies which prefer cocos issuers to be so well-capitalized as to have a margin over the trigger-level of the capital ratio that is initially ample enough to make even high-trigger conversions unlikely.

Regulators—including those favoring cocos in theory—appear unaware or unconcerned with the damage they do to market acceptance of cocos when they expand their discretionary powers while also imposing crippling design features on cocos. As already mentioned in Chapter 6, in Canada, for instance, OSFI has insisted that "Canadian authorities will retain full discretion to choose not to trigger [cocos] notwithstanding a determination by the Superintendent that a [Deposit Taking Institution] has ceased, or is about to cease, to be viable…" Exercising this veto right over conversion could mean no further accrual of interest and a lock-in of cocos holders who could see the value of the (much more liquid) common stock otherwise received in a high-trigger conversion shrink to the point of zero recovery. It is useless for a firm to buy a form of capital insurance by issuing cocos if the pay-out on that insurance can be denied by regulators disengaging the trigger whenever its suits their macroeconomic objectives. If such an unreliable coco should prove to be marketable nonetheless, the tax authorities in the United States would not allow interest deductibility on an instrument with discretionary enhancement of loss-absorption. Furthermore, S&P would not rate it investment-grade but CCC or not rate it at all, because the recovery value of this coco could be subject to expropriation if regulators block the conversion promised by its internal trigger.

Finally, OSFI's declaration of unqualified power to override any cocos trigger would run counter to the EBA's (2013b) language in Document 5: "Where the institution has established that the CET1 ratio has fallen below the level that activates conversion or write-down of the instrument, the management body or any other relevant body of the institution shall without delay determine that a trigger event has occurred and there shall be an irrevocable obligation to write-down or convert the instrument. The amount to be written down or converted shall be determined as soon as possible and within a maximum period of one month from the time it is determined that a trigger event has occurred." While the EBA obviously holds no sway over Canada, Canadian banks are likely to find it difficult to issue high-trigger cocos whose trigger operation and controls can be seized by OSFI. All the same, two of the big Canadian banks, whose working relations with OSFI are likely to be excellent, successfully issued AT1 cocos shortly after the beginning of 2014. Potential investors in cocos would needlessly be exposed to regulatory uncertainty nonetheless, and would presumably charge for it.

Elsewhere, in Document 4 under "mandatory conversion," the EBA considers as an "open option—to be determined on a case-by-case basis: the possibility to include a mandatory conversion at a fixed date" in the cocos contract. Adding such a feature would make a mockery of the "perpetual" life they are supposed to have if they are to qualify as regulatory capital. Adding a mandatory conversion feature could also increase the cost of issuing cocos because raising the probability of conversion within a few years after issue to 100% increases the expected loss not only from conversion in some cases but also from the denial of tax deductibility of interest paid by the issuers when the equity characteristics of cocos are reinforced in this way. Document 3 from the BCBS also "does not exclude the possibility that national jurisdictions could impose additional requirements [on going-concern cocos], for example inclusion of a market-based trigger alongside the other trigger." Such an addition would make cocos un-ratable by S&P, i.e., of grade CCC.

17.1 Differences between European and US Approaches to Cocos

The reliance placed on cocos differs strikingly between Europe and the United States.

17.1.1 The European Approach

Document 4 clearly states that in the view of the EBA "since buffers are intended to absorb potential (contingent) losses, newly issued private contingent convertibles are eligible to be considered as a part of the buffer if consistent with the EBA's common term sheet." The Common Term Sheet adds for good measure that, "For the avoidance of doubt, the BCCS will be treated for regulatory purposes as hybrid instruments which qualify as Tier 1 capital." Issues by BBVA, Société Générale, Barclays, and 9 other banks listed in Moody's (2014, pp. 5–6) of AT1 cocos in 2013 prove that the EBA's common term sheet did not raise insurmountable barriers against issuing cocos that could help meet T1 capital requirements. In Barclays' case, cocos are to contribute up to 1.5% of RWA to AT1 with an additional 0.5% of RWA from these same cocos proposed for use as T2.

To facilitate the use of bailout cocos and investment in govern-ment bonds issued to fund bad banks, European regulators have also made clear in Document 4 that "[g]overnment support mea-sures are included in the definition of Core Tier 1 which comprises CET1 plus hybrid instruments provided by governments." "The in-clusion of government support measures in this definition reflects the expectation of supervisors that these instruments will be fully available to absorb losses and shelter banks in case of difficul-ties." In the pre-amble items (107) and (108) of the CRR (see EC, 2013), the European Commission is instructed to take into account that institutions calculating the liquidity coverage requirements [LCR] in accordance with the CRR should be permitted to include senior bonds issued by Ireland's National Asset Management Agency [NAMA] and by the Spanish Asset Management Company as assets of extremely high liquidity and credit quality at least until December 2019 and 2023, respectively. Naturally no comparable instructions were found in OCC & Fed (2013b).

17.1.2 The US Approach

In Document 7 issued by the OCC and Fed, cocos are treated very differently and summarily dismissed from contributing to AT1 on account of their treatment as debt under US Generally Accepted Accounting Principles [GAAP]. The document reads, "To the extent that a contingent capital instrument is considered a liability under GAAP, a banking organization may not include the instrument in its Tier 1 capital under the final rule." In addition to barring cocos from AT1, the US has banished cocos categorically from meeting any part of the regulatory buffer capital requirements and reserved for CET1 the exclusive distinction of being a capital instrument of the highest quality. "[H]owever, the (three US) agencies believe that it is appropriate to retain the flexibility necessary to consider new instruments on a case-by-case basis as they are developed over time to satisfy different market needs." Furthermore as a result of the proposed new minimum CET1 capital requirement, and higher T1 capital requirement, OCC & Fed (2013b) proposed lifting the existing 2% of RWA limitation on T2 capital that could be recognized in total capital, as well as the existing limitations on the amount of certain capital instruments (that is, term subordinated debt) that could be included in T2 capital. Hence T2 cocos could contribute to raising the total capital ratio above the required minimum of 8%, but not substitute for CET1 and AT1 under the rules proposed by the US agencies.

17.2 Outline by Source Documents

The documentation below starts out with the BCBS structures first proposed in 2011 for gone-concern cocos. These are low-trigger cocos whose conversion is set off by the authorities when they judge a financial institution to have reached the point of non-viability. Conversion of cocos may open the way to official injections of capital or assist with resolution in the event of bankruptcy reorganization. Knowing gone-concern cocos makes it easier to appreciate how going-concern, high-trigger cocos—the main subject of this monograph—function differently to protect and enhance the continued viability of a firm.

The second document lists the principal original BCBS criteria for inclusion in Additional Tier 1 [AT1] or Tier 2 [T2] capital and how the definition of these non-common parts of regulatory capital is scheduled to evolve. The treatment of minority interest and a long list of regulatory adjustments are omitted here, though some of the latter are mentioned in the disclosure requirements and transitional arrangements which are included.

The third and last of the BCBS selections contains a crisp summary of the proposed minimum requirements for going-concern contingent capital. Going-concern cocos must trigger no later than when the ratio of Common Equity Tier 1 [CET1] to Risk-Weighted Assets [RWA] has declined below 7% while gone-concern cocos may have triggers as low as 5% or 5.125%. Gone-concern cocos also have much greater exposure to activation of the non-viability trigger than going-concern cocos: the latter should have been triggered on their own terms well before the firm reaches the point of non-viability.

The fourth document excerpts two Annexes and a Common Term Sheet published by the EBA. Annex II specifies the size and content of regulatory capital buffers and Annex III proposes regulations for cocos, there called buffer convertible capital securities, specifically. Only material that serves as a lead-in from Annex II to III is reproduced here, but Annex III is presented in full. The document highlights measures that are meant to strengthen banks' capital positions which may include cocos. The fifth document adds some Regulatory Technical Standards [RTS] drafted by the EBA to clarify the meaning of certain terms or references used in the proposed regulations.

The sixth document contains excerpts from the Capital

Requirements Regulation [CRR-IV] adopted in 2013 for AT1 and T2 capital in the European Union [EU]. Finally, the seventh document offers excerpts from US regulations, also from 2013, implementing much of Basel III but disqualifying cocos from AT1. Here again, the textual divisions into Parts, Titles, Chapters, and the numbering, spacing, and other identification of paragraphs contained therein is generally retained for ease of reference to the original documents, and only a few link words and explanations have been inserted for continuity.

17.3 Document 1: Excerpts from BCBS

Basel Committee on Banking Supervision [BCBS] (2011b), "Annex: Minimum requirements to ensure loss absorbency at the point of non-viability," Bank for International Settlements, BIS Press Release on "Final elements of the reforms to raise the quality of regulatory capital issued by the Basel Committee," January 13, pp. 3–4.

http://www.bis.org/press/p110113.htm

Annex: Minimum requirements to ensure loss absorbency at the point of non-viability

Qualification requirements for non-common Tier 1 and Tier 2 instruments

1. The terms and conditions of all non-common Tier 1 and Tier 2 instruments issued by an internationally active bank must have a provision that requires such instruments, at the option of the relevant authority, to either be written off or converted into common equity upon the occurrence of the trigger event unless:
    (a) the governing jurisdiction of the bank has in place laws that (i) require such Tier 1 and Tier 2 instruments to be written off upon such event, or (ii) otherwise require such instruments to fully absorb losses before taxpayers are exposed to loss;

(b) and it is disclosed by the relevant regulator and by the issuing bank, in issuance documents going forward, that such instruments are subject to loss under clause (a) in this paragraph.

2. Any compensation paid to the instrument holders as a result of the write-off must be paid immediately in the form of common stock (or its equivalent in the case of non-joint stock companies).

3. The issuing bank must maintain at all times all prior authorization necessary to immediately issue the relevant number of shares specified in the instrument's terms and conditions should the trigger event occur.

Non-viability trigger event invoked by regulator

4. The trigger event is the earlier of: (1) a decision that a write-off, without which the firm would become non-viable, is necessary, as determined by the relevant authority; and (2) the decision to make a public sector injection of capital, or equivalent support, without which the firm would have become non-viable, as determined by the relevant authority.

5. The issuance of any new shares as a result of the trigger event must occur prior to any public sector injection of capital so that the capital provided by the public sector is not diluted.

Treatment of banks in financial groups

6. The relevant jurisdiction in determining the trigger event is the jurisdiction in which the capital is being given recognition for regulatory purposes. Therefore, where an issuing bank is part of a wider banking group and if the issuing bank wishes the instrument to be included in the consolidated group's capital in addition to its solo capital, the terms and conditions must specify an additional trigger event [i.e., public-sector injection of capital in the jurisdiction of the consolidated supervisor]....

7. Any common stock paid as compensation to the holders of the instrument must be common stock of either the issuing bank or of the parent company of the consolidated group (including any successor in resolution).

Transitional arrangements (some details here omitted)

Instruments issued on or after 1 January 2013 must meet the criteria set out above to be included in regulatory capital. Instruments issued prior to 1 January 2013 that do not meet the criteria set out above, but that meet all of the entry criteria for Additional Tier 1 or Tier 2 capital set out in *Basel III: A global regulatory framework for more resilient banks and banking systems*, will be phased out from 1 January 2013.

17.4 Document 2: Excerpts from BCBS

BCBS (2011c), "Criteria for inclusion in Additional Tier 1 (AT1) capital [or: Tier 2 capital]," in *Basel III: A Global Regulatory Framework for More Resilient Banks and Banking Systems*, December 2010, rev. June 2011.

http://www.bis.org/publ/bcbs189.pdf

1. Common Equity Tier 1 (CET1) (for its accounting definition see pp. 13–15 of source document)

2. Additional Tier 1 (AT1) capital

Criteria for inclusion in AT1 capital:

1. (The instruments must have been) issued and paid-in.
2. Subordinated to depositors, general creditors and subordinated debt of the bank.
3. Are neither secured nor covered by a guarantee of the issuer or related entity or by any other arrangement that legally or economically enhances the seniority of the claim vis-à-vis bank creditors.

4. Are perpetual, i.e., there is no maturity date and there are no step-ups or other incentives to redeem.

5. May be callable at the initiative of the issuer only after a minimum of five years:

    a. To exercise a call option a bank must receive prior supervisory approval; and

    b. A bank must not do anything which creates an expectation that the call will be exercised; and

    c. Banks must not exercise a call unless:

    They replace the called instrument with capital of the same or better quality and the replacement of this capital is done at conditions which are sustainable for the income capacity of the bank; or

    The bank demonstrates that its capital position is well above the minimum capital requirements after the call option is exercised.

6. Any repayment of principal (e.g., through repurchase or redemption) must be with prior supervisory approval and banks should not assume or create market expectations that supervisory approval will be given.

7. Dividend/coupon discretion:

    a. the bank must have full discretion at all times to cancel distributions/payments

    b. cancellation of discretionary payments must not be an event of default

    c. banks must have full access to cancelled payments to meet obligations as they fall due.

    d. cancellation of distributions/payments must not impose restrictions on the bank except in relation to distributions to common stockholders.

    [Clarification: A consequence of full discretion at all times to cancel distributions/payments is that "dividend pushers" are prohibited. An instrument with a dividend pusher obliges the issuing bank to make a dividend/coupon payment on the instrument if it has made a payment on another (typically more junior) capital instrument or share. This obligation is inconsistent with the requirement for full discretion at all times. Furthermore, the term "cancel distributions/payments" means extinguish these payments. It does not permit features that require the bank to make distributions/payments in kind.]

8. Dividends/coupons must be paid out of distributable items.

9. The instrument cannot have a credit sensitive dividend feature, that is a dividend/coupon that is reset periodically based in whole or in part on the banking organization's credit standing.

11. Instruments classified as liabilities for accounting purposes must have principal loss absorption through either (i) conversion to common shares at an objective pre-specified trigger point or (ii) a write-down mechanism which allocates losses to the instrument at a pre-specified trigger point. The write-down will have the following effects:
a. Reduce the claim of the instrument in liquidation;
b. Reduce the amount re-paid when a call is exercised; and
c. Partially or fully reduce coupon/dividend payments on the instrument.

12. Neither the bank nor a related party over which the bank exercises control or significant influence can have purchased the instrument, nor can the bank directly or indirectly have funded the purchase of the instrument.

13. The instrument cannot have any features that hinder recapitalization such as provisions that require the issuer to compensate investors if a new instrument is issued at a lower price during a specified time frame.

14. If the instrument is not issued out of an operating entity or the holding company in the consolidated group (e.g., a special purpose vehicle—"SPV"), proceeds must be immediately available without limitation to an operating entity or the holding company in the consolidated group in a form

which meets or exceeds all of the other criteria for inclusion in Additional Tier 1 capital.

Stock surplus (share premium) resulting from the issue of instruments included in Additional Tier 1 capital;

56. Stock surplus (i.e., share premium from stock issued at a price over par) that is not eligible for inclusion in Common Equity Tier 1, will only be permitted to be included in Additional Tier 1 capital if the shares giving rise to the stock surplus are permitted to be included in Additional Tier 1 capital.

Tier 2 (T2) capital

57. Tier 2 capital consists of the sum of the following elements:

• Instruments issued by the bank that meet the criteria for inclusion in Tier 2 capital (and are not included in Tier 1 capital);

• Stock surplus (share premium) resulting from the issue of instruments included in Tier 2 capital;

• Instruments issued by consolidated subsidiaries of the bank and held by third parties that meet the criteria for inclusion in Tier 2 capital and are not included in Tier 1 capital. See section 4 (not included in the present compilation) for the relevant criteria;

• Certain loan loss provisions as specified in paragraphs 60 and 61 (see below); and

• Regulatory adjustments applied in the calculation of Tier 2 Capital. The treatment of instruments issued out of consolidated subsidiaries of the bank and the regulatory adjustments applied in the calculation of Tier 2 Capital are addressed in separate sections.

Instruments issued by the bank that meet the Tier 2 criteria

58. The objective of Tier 2 is to provide loss absorption on a gone-concern basis. Based on this objective, the following box sets out the minimum requirements for an instrument to be included in Tier 2 capital.

Criteria for inclusion in T2 Capital

1. Issued and paid-in.

2. Subordinated to depositors and general creditors of the bank.

3. Same as for AT1, 3.

4. Maturity:
   a. minimum original maturity of at least five years
   b. recognition in regulatory capital in the remaining five years before maturity will be amortized on a straight line basis
   c. there are no step-ups or other incentives to redeem

5. Same as for AT1, 5.

6. The investor must have no rights to accelerate the repayment of future scheduled payments (coupon or principal), except in bankruptcy and liquidation.

7. Same as AT1, 9.

8. Neither the bank nor a related party over which the bank exercises control or significant influence can have purchased the instrument, nor can the bank directly or indirectly have funded the purchase of the instrument.

9. Same as AT1, 14 (except here for T2 capital).

Stock surplus (share premium) resulting from the issue of instruments included in Tier 2 capital;

59. Same as for AT1, 56 (except here for T2 capital).

General provisions/general loan-loss reserves (for banks using the Standardized Approach for credit risk)

60. Provisions or loan-loss reserves held against future, presently unidentified, losses are freely available to meet losses which subsequently materialize and therefore qualify for inclusion within Tier 2. Provisions ascribed to an identified deterioration of particular assets or known liabilities, whether individual or grouped, should be excluded.

Furthermore, general provisions/general loan-loss reserves eligible for inclusion in Tier 2 will be limited to a maximum of 1.25 percentage points of credit-risk-weighted assets calculated under the standardized approach.

Excess of total eligible provisions under the Internal Ratings-Based (IRB) Approach

61. Where the total expected loss amount is less than total eligible provisions, as explained in paragraphs 380 to 383 of the June 2006 Comprehensive version of Basel II, banks may recognize the difference in Tier 2 capital up to a maximum of 0.6% of credit-risk-weighted assets calculated under the IRB approach. At national discretion, a limit lower than 0.6% may be applied.

4. Minority interest (i.e., non-controlling interest) and other capital issued out of consolidated subsidiaries that is held by third parties (omitted from this compilation)

5. Regulatory adjustments (see pp. 21–27 of source document)

66. This section sets out the regulatory adjustments to be applied to regulatory capital. In most cases these adjustments are applied in the calculation of CET1.

6. Disclosure requirements

91. To help improve transparency of regulatory capital and improve market discipline, banks are required to disclose the following:

• a full reconciliation of all regulatory capital elements back to the balance sheet in the audited financial statements;

• separate disclosure of all regulatory adjustments and the items not deducted from Common Equity Tier 1 according to paragraphs 87 and 88 (not included in present compilation);

• a description of all limits and minima, identifying the positive and negative elements of capital to which the limits and minima apply;

- a description of the main features of capital instruments issued;
- banks which disclose ratios involving components of regulatory capital (e.g., "Equity Tier 1", "Core Tier 1" or "Tangible Common Equity" ratios) must accompany such disclosures with a comprehensive explanation of how these ratios are calculated.

92. Banks are also required to make available on their websites the full terms and conditions of all instruments included in regulatory capital.

93. During the transition phase banks are required to disclose the specific components of capital, including capital instruments and regulatory adjustments that are benefitting from the transitional provisions.

17.5 Document 3: Excerpts from BCBS

BCBS (2011d), "Annex 3: Proposed minimum requirements for going-concern contingent capital," *Global Systemically Important Banks: Assessment Methodology and the Additional Loss Absorbency Requirement: Rules text*, November, p. 26.

http://www.bis.org/publ/bcbs207.pdf

Annex 3: Proposed minimum requirements for going-concern contingent capital

An analysis of the pros and cons of contingent capital is made difficult by the fact that it is a largely untested instrument that could come in many different forms. For example, in addition to the level of the trigger for conversion, the trigger itself could be based on any combination of regulatory ratios, market based ratios, accounting ratios, bank discretion, supervisory discretion, and more. Other characteristics of the instrument could also vary, such as the features of the instrument prior to conversion, the mechanism through which common equity is created and the number of shares issued on conversion.

The Basel Committee considered the various potential features of contingent capital and developed a proposed set of minimum criteria that contingent capital should meet if it is to merit consideration to meet the additional loss absorbency requirement for G-SIBs. This proposal was designed to help anchor the Basel Committee's consideration of the pros and cons of contingent capital. It does not exclude the possibility that national jurisdictions could impose additional requirements, for example inclusion of a market-based trigger alongside the minimum trigger.

Specifications subsumed to consider the pros and cons of contingent capital

1. Fully convert to CET1 through a permanent write-off or conversion to common shares when the CET1 of the banking group subject to the additional loss absorbency requirement falls below at least 7% of risk-weighted assets;

2. Include in its contractual terms and conditions a cap on the number of new shares that can be issued when the trigger is breached. The issuing bank or banking group must maintain, at all times, all prior authorization necessary to immediately issue the relevant number of shares specified in its contractual terms and conditions should the trigger be breached; and

3. Meet or exceed all of the T2 entry criteria (incl. the point of non-viability trigger). See press release of 01/13/11 at http://www.bis.org/press/p110113.htm reproduced as (1) BCBS before).

Treatment of a bank in a financial group

4. Irrespective of the group entity that issues the contingent capital instrument, the mechanism of permanent write-off or conversion to common shares must create common equity in a form that will be fully recognized as CET1 of the banking group subject to the additional loss absorbency requirement.

Capital treatment for issuer and investor

5. Contingent capital used to meet the additional loss absorbency requirement will not be eligible to meet any of the other regulatory capital requirements to which the bank is subject. Banks that invest in contingent capital are required to deduct such investments from their CET1 in accordance with the treatment of common stock investments under Basel III.

17.6 Document 4: Excerpts from EBA

EBA (2011a), Excerpts from "Annex II: Capital Buffers for Addressing Market Concerns over Sovereign Exposures" (pp. 8–10), and "Annex III. Buffer Convertible Capital Securities: Common Term Sheet," *EBA Recommendation on the Creation and Supervisory Oversight of Temporary Capital Buffers to Restore Market Confidence* (EBA/REC/2011/1), Dec. 8, pp. 16–21.

http://www.eba.europa.eu/documents/10180/16460/
EBA+BS+2011+173+Recommendation+FINAL.pdf/
b533b82c-2621-42ff-b90e-96c081e1b598

Annex II: Capital buffers for addressing market concerns over sovereign exposures:

Methodological note

This note summarizes the methodology adopted for identifying capital buffers according to the new targets at the bank level.

Key dates *(details here omitted)*

Definition of Core Tier 1

The definition of Core Tier 1 is the same used in the 2011 EU-wide stress test (including existing capital instruments subscribed by governments). This definition of capital comprises the highest quality capital instruments (common equity) and hybrid instruments provided by governments as announced by the EBA for the 2011 EU-wide stress test...

This means, in particular, that the commercial instruments included in Core Tier 1 have to be simple, issued directly by the institution itself and able, both immediately and without any doubt, to meet the criteria of permanence, flexibility of payments and loss absorption in going concern situations. The inclusion of government support measures in this definition reflects the expectation of supervisors that those instruments will be fully available to absorb losses and shelter banks in case of difficulties. Government support measures need to be consistent with the European State aid rules and approved by the European Commission.

Eligible capital instruments for meeting the buffers

As a general rule, the capital buffers are to be covered with Core Tier 1 as defined in the EBA's 2011 EU-wide stress test. In particular, only commercial instruments of the highest quality are included in this Core Tier 1 definition—ordinary shares or similar instruments in line with the principles detailed in CEBS/EBA guidelines on core capital. However, since buffers are intended to absorb potential (contingent) losses, newly issued private contingent convertibles are eligible to be considered as a part of the buffer if consistent with the EBA's common term sheet set out at Annex III. Only new issuances of very strong convertible capital will be accepted if in line with strict and standardized criteria further to be defined by the EBA. The EBA has since issued several of these clarifying Regulatory Technical Standards (RTS). They are listed as a sequel to Annex III. Existing convertible capital instruments were not to remain eligible unless they were converted into Core Tier 1 according to the above definition by the end of October 2012. [The Committee of European Banking Supervisors, CEBS, is the predecessor of the EBA, which came into being on January 1, 2011.]

Annex III: Buffer Convertible Capital Securities

Common Term Sheet

All these provisions will have to be agreed by the relevant national supervisor (who may ask for stricter requirements than the minimum requirements or ask for specific requirements when none is mentioned in this term sheet).

Issuer, Securities Offered

Buffer Convertible Capital Securities ("BCCS")

Total Issue Size, Nominal Value, and Issue Price and Date

Status and Subordination

The BCCS constitute direct, unsecured, undated and subordinated securities of the Issuer and rank pari passu without any preference among themselves. They are fully issued and paid-in.

The rights and claims of the holders of BCCS of this issue:

- are subordinated to the claims of the creditors of
  the Bank, who are:
  · depositors or other unsubordinated creditors of the Bank
  · subordinated creditors, except those creditors whose claims rank
  or are expressed to rank *pari passu* with the claims of the holders
  of the BCCS
  · holders of subordinated bonds of the Bank.

- rank *pari passu* with the rights and claims of holders of other junior capital subordinated issues qualifying as Tier 1 capital

- have priority over the ordinary shareholders of the Bank.

For the avoidance of doubt, the BCCS will be treated for regulatory purposes as hybrid instruments and will qualify as Tier 1 capital.

The amount BCCS holders may claim in the event of a winding-up or administration of the Bank is an amount equal to the principal amount plus accrued interest but no amount of cancelled coupon payments will be payable.

Cancellation of any payment does not constitute an event of default and does not entitle holders to petition for the insolvency of the Bank.

In the event of Conversion of the BCCS to shares, the holders of BCCS will be shareholders of the Bank and their claim will rank pari passu with the rights and claims of the Bank's ordinary shareholders.

Maturity date

Unless previously called and redeemed or converted, the BCCS are perpetual without a maturity date.

Coupon

To be determined on a case by case basis—minimum requirement: no incentive to redeem to be included.

Interest payment and interest date

To be determined on a case by case basis—minimum requirement: dates to be aligned with dividend payment dates.

Conversion rate

To be determined on a case by case basis—minimum requirement: either i) specification of a predetermined range within which the instruments will convert into ordinary shares or ii) a rate of conversion and a limit on the permitted amount of conversion.

Conversion period

To be determined on a case by case basis. The provisions to be included shall not undermine the conversion features of the instrument and shall not in particular restrict the automaticity of the conversion.

Issuer's Call option:

The Bank may, on its own initiative, elect to redeem all but not some of the BCCS, at their principal amount together with accrued interest, on fifth anniversary or any other Interest Payment Date thereafter, subject to the prior approval of the [name of the national supervisor] and provided that:

(a) the BCCS have been or will be replaced by regulatory capital of equal or better quality; or

(b) the Bank has demonstrated to the satisfaction of the [name of the national supervisor] that its own funds would, following the call, exceed by a margin that the [name of the national supervisor] considers to be significant and appropriate, (i) a Core Tier 1 Ratio of at least 9% by reference to the EBA(2011b) Recommendation, EBA/REC/2011/1, published on December 8, 2011 or (ii) in case the Recommendation referred to under (i) has been repealed or cancelled, the minimum capital requirements in accordance with the final provisions for a Regulation on prudential requirements for credit institutions and investment firms to be adopted by the European Union.

Optional coupon cancellation

The Bank may, at its sole discretion at all times, elect to cancel any interest payment on a non-cumulative basis. Any coupon not paid is no longer due and payable by the Bank. Cancellation of a coupon payment does not constitute an event of default of interest payment and does not entitle holders to petition for the insolvency of the Bank.

Mandatory coupon cancellation

Upon breach of applicable minimum solvency requirements, or insufficient Distributable Items, the Bank will be required to cancel interest payments on the BCCS.

The Bank has full discretion at all times to cancel interest payments on the BCCS.

The [name of the national supervisor] may require, in its sole discretion, at all times, the Bank to cancel interest payments on the BCCS.

"Distributable Items" means the net profit of the Bank for the financial year ending immediately prior to the relevant coupon payment date together with any net profits and retained earnings carried forward from any previous financial years and any net transfers from any reserve accounts in each case available for the payment of distributions to ordinary shareholders of the Bank [formulation to be amended as far as necessary according to applicable national law].

Any coupon payment cancelled will be fully and irrevocably cancelled and forfeited and will no longer be payable by the Bank. Cancellation of a coupon payment does not constitute an event of default of interest payment and does not entitle holders to petition for the insolvency of the Bank.

Mandatory conversion

1. If a Contingency Event or Viability Event occurs, the BCCS shall be mandatorily fully converted into Ordinary Shares.

2. Open option—to be determined on a case by case basis: possibility to include a mandatory conversion at a fixed date.

The Issuer will arrange for the authorized share capital of the Bank to be sufficient for the Mandatory Conversion of all of the BCCS. All necessary authorizations are to be obtained at the date of issuance of the BCCS.

Contingency event(s)

"Common Equity Tier 1 Capital Ratio Contingency Event" means that, after January 1, 2013, the Bank has given notice that its "Common Equity Tier 1 Capital Ratio", in accordance with the final provisions for a Regulation on prudential requirements for credit institutions and investment firms to be adopted by the European Union and taking into account the transitional arrangements, is below 5.125% [or a level higher than 5.125% as determined by the institution—to be determined on a case by case basis]. The Bank shall give notice as soon as it has established that its CET1 Capital Ratio is below 5.125% [or a level higher than 5.125% as determined by the institution—to be determined on a case by case basis].

The CET1 Capital Ratio Contingency Event is applicable as of January 1, 2013. It shall remain applicable after January 1, 2013 as long as the EBA Recommendation EBA/REC/2011/1 has not been repealed or cancelled.[In case a statutory approach is claimed, the clause will have to make clear that the jurisdiction has an equivalent regime in place].

Holders' right for Conversion Open option—to be determined on a case by case basis: possibility to include a right for holders to convert the BCCS into shares.

Substitution, variation, redemption for regulator/legal purposes

In case of changes in the laws or the relevant regulations of the European Union or of a country or national regulator which would lead in particular to the situation where the proceeds of the BCCS do not qualify after January 2013 as AT1 capital in accordance with the final provisions for a Regulation on prudential requirements for credit institutions and investment firms to be adopted by the European Union, the Bank may, with the prior consent of the [name of the national regulator], redeem all the BCCS together with any accrued interest outstanding.

Alternatively, the BCCS, with the consent of the [name of the national supervisor], may be exchanged or their terms may be varied so that they continue to qualify as AT1 or T2 capital in accordance with the final provisions for a Regulation on prudential requirements for credit institutions and investment firms to be adopted by the European Union, or qualify as senior debt of the Bank. Substitution/Variation should not lead to terms materially less favorable to the investors except where these changes are required by reference to the final provisions above.

Use of proceeds:

The net proceeds of the Issue will be used to maintain a Core Tier 1 (CT1) Ratio of at least 9% by reference to the EBA Recommendation EBA/REC/2011/1. For the avoidance of doubt, the BCCS features do not prejudge the future regulatory framework to be applicable in accordance with the final provisions referenced above.

17.7 Document 5: Excerpts from EBA

EBA (2013b), "EBA draft Regulatory Standards-Near Final Version on Own Funds [Part 1] under the draft Capital Requirements Regulation (CRR), EBA-RTS-2013-01 (near final)," 5 June, pp. 23–28.

http://www.eba.europa.eu/documents/10180/16058/EBA-RTS-2013-01(Near-final+Draft+RTS+on+OF+Part+1).pdf

Chapter 2: Additional Tier 1 Capital

Section 1: Form and nature of incentives to redeem

Article 12: Form and nature of incentives to redeem under Article 49(1)(g)of the CRR

1. Incentives to redeem shall mean all features that provide, at the date of issuance, an expectation that the capital instrument is likely to be redeemed.

2. The incentives referred to in paragraph 1 shall include the following forms:
    (a) a call option combined with an increase in the credit spread of the instrument if the call is not exercised.
    (b) a call option combined with a requirement or an investor option to convert the instrument into a Common Equity Tier 1 instrument where the call is not exercised;
    (c) a call option combined with a change in reference rate where the credit spread over the second reference rate is greater than the initial payment rate minus the swap rate;
    (d) a call option combined with an increase of the redemption amount in the future;
    (e) a remarketing option combined with an increase in the credit spread of the instrument or a change in reference rate where the credit spread over the second reference rate is greater than the initial payment rate minus the swap rate where the instrument is not remarketed;

(f) a marketing of the instrument in a way which suggests to investors that the instrument will be called.

Section 2: Conversion or write-down of the principal amount

Article 13: Nature of the write-up of the principal amount following a write-down under Article 49(1)(n) of the CRR

1. The write-down of the principal amount shall apply on a pro rata basis to all holders of Additional Tier 1 instruments that include a similar write-down mechanism and an identical trigger level.
2. For the write-down to be considered temporary, the following conditions shall all be met:
   a. any distributions payable after a write-down shall be based on the reduced amount of the principal;
   b. write-ups shall be based on profits after the institution has taken a formal decision confirming the final profits;
   c. any write-up of the instrument or payment of coupons on the reduced amount of the principal shall be operated at the full discretion of the institution subject to the constraints arising from points (d) to (f) and there shall be no obligation for the institution to operate or accelerate a write-up under specific circumstances;
   d. a write-up shall be operated on a pro rata basis among similar Additional Tier 1 instruments that have been subject to a write-down;
   e. the maximum amount to be attributed to the sum of the write-up of the instrument together with the payment of coupons on the reduced amount of the principal shall be equal to the profit of the institution multiplied by the amount obtained by dividing the amount determined in point (i) by the amount determined in point (ii):
   (i) the sum of the nominal amount of all Additional Tier 1 instruments of the institution before write-down that have been subject to a write-down;

(ii) the total Tier 1 capital of the institution.

f. the sum of any write-up amounts and payments of coupons on the reduced amount of the principal shall be treated as a payment that results in a reduction of Common Equity Tier 1 and shall be subject, together with other distributions on Common Equity Tier 1 instruments, to the restrictions relating to the Maximum Distributable Amount as laid down in Article 131 of Directive xx/xxx [CRD], as transposed in national law or regulation.

Article 14: Procedures and timing for determining that a trigger event has occurred under Article 49(1)(n) of the CRR

The following procedures and timing shall apply for determining that a trigger event has occurred:

(a) Where the institution has established that the Common Equity Tier 1 ratio has fallen below the level that activates conversion or write-down of the instrument at the level of application of the requirements as defined under Title II of Regulation xx/xxx [CRR], the management body or any other relevant body of the institution shall without delay determine that a trigger event has occurred and there shall be an irrevocable obligation to write-down or convert the instrument.

(b) The amount to be written-down or converted shall be determined as soon as possible and within a maximum period of one month from the time it is determined that the trigger event has occurred;

(c) The competent authority may require that the maximum period of one month referred to in point (b) is reduced in cases where it assesses that sufficient certainty on the amount to be converted or written down is established or in cases where it assesses that an immediate conversion or write-down is needed.

Section 3: Features of instruments that could hinder recapitalization

Article 15: Features of instruments that could hinder recapitalization under Article 49(1)(o) of the CRR

Features that could hinder the recapitalization of an institution shall include, in particular provisions that require the institution to compensate existing holders of capital instruments where a new capital instrument is issued.

Section 4: Use of special purposes entities for indirect issuance of own funds instruments

Article 16: Use of special purposes entities for indirect issuance of own funds instruments under Article 49(1)(p)and 60(n) of the CRR

The following treatment shall apply in the use of special purposes entities for indirect issuance of own funds instruments.

(a) Where the institution or the entities listed in point (p) of Article 49(1) and in point (n) of Article 60 of Regulation xx/xxx [CRR] issues a capital instrument that is subscribed by a special purpose entity, this capital instrument shall not, at the level of the institution or of the above-mentioned entities, receive recognition as capital of a higher quality than the lowest quality of the capital issued to the special purpose entity and the capital issued to third parties by the special purpose entity. Such requirement applies at the consolidated, sub-consolidated and individual levels of application of prudential requirements.

Chapter 3 General Requirements

Section 1: Indirect holdings arising from index holdings

Article 17: Indirect holdings arising from index holdings—extent of conservatism required in estimates for calculating exposures used as an alternative to the underlying exposures under Article 71(1) of the CRR

1. An indirect holding arising from an index holding comprises the proportion of the index invested in the Common Equity Tier 1, Additional Tier 1 and Tier 2 instruments of financial sector entities included in the index. For the purpose of this Article, an index includes, but is not limited to, index funds, equity or bond indices or any other scheme where the underlying instrument is a capital instrument issued by a financial sector entity.

2. Where the monitoring by an institution on an ongoing basis of its underlying exposures to the capital instruments of financial sector entities that are included in indices is deemed by the competent authority to be operationally burdensome, the institution may adopt a structure-based approach to estimating the value of the exposures.

3. When using a structure-based approach, an institution shall ensure in particular by means of the investment mandate of the index, that a capital instrument of a financial sector entity which is part of the index cannot exceed a maximum percentage of the index. This percentage shall be used as an estimate for the value of the holdings that shall be deducted from own funds.

4. In the event that an institution is unable to determine the maximum percentage as referred to in paragraph 3 and the index, in particular in accordance with its investment mandate, includes capital instruments of financial sector entities, the institution shall take into account the full amount of the index holdings for the deduction from own funds.

5. The deduction shall be operated on a corresponding deduction approach. In situations where the institution cannot determine the precise nature of the holding, the value of the holding shall be deducted from Common Equity Tier 1 capital.

17.8 Document 6: Excerpts from the European Commission's CRR-IV

European Council (2013), "Regulation (EU) No 575/2013 of the European Parliament and of the Council of 26 June 2013 on prudential requirements for credit institutions and investment firms and amending Regulation (EU) No. 648/2012," *Official Journal of the European Union*, 27.6.2013 L176. Cited as CRR.

http://ec.europa.eu/internal_market/bank/regcapital/legislation_in_force_en.htm, or
http://eur.lex.europa.eu/LexUriServ/LexUriServ.do?uri=O-J:l:2013:176:0001:0337:EN:PDF

Whereas:

(45) All additional Tier 1 and Tier 2 instruments of an institution should be capable of being fully and permanently written down or converted fully into Common Equity Tier 1 capital at the point of non-viability of the institution. Necessary legislation to ensure that own funds instruments are subject to the additional loss absorption mechanism should be incorporated into Union law as part of the requirements in relation to the recovery and resolution of institutions. If by 31 December 2015, Union law governing the requirement that capital instruments should be capable of being fully and permanently written down to zero or converted into Common Equity Tier 1 instruments in the event that an institution is no longer considered viable has not been adopted, the Commission should review and report on whether such a provision should be included in this Regulation and, in light of that review, submit appropriate legislative proposals.

Article 28. Common Equity Tier 1 instruments

1. Capital instruments shall qualify as Common Equity Tier 1 instruments only if all the following conditions are met:

(a) the instruments are issued directly by the institution with the prior approval of the owners of the institution or, where permitted under applicable national law, the management body of the institution;

(b) the instruments are paid up and their purchase is not funded directly or indirectly by the institution;

(c) the instruments meet all the following conditions as regards their classification:

(i) they qualify as capital within the meaning of Article 22 of Directive 86/635/EEC;

(ii) they are classified as equity within the meaning of the applicable accounting framework;

(iii) they are classified as equity capital for the purposes of determining balance sheet insolvency, where applicable under national insolvency law;

(d) the instruments are clearly and separately disclosed on the balance sheet in the financial statements of the institution;

(e) the instruments are perpetual;

(f) the principal amount of the instruments may not be reduced or repaid, except in either of the following cases:

(i) the liquidation of the institution;

(ii) discretionary repurchases of the instruments or other discretionary means of reducing capital, where the institution has received the prior permission of the competent authority in accordance with Article 77;

(h) the instruments meet the following conditions as regards distributions:

(ii) distributions to holders of the instruments may be paid only out of distributable items;

(v) the conditions governing the instruments do not include any obligation for the institution to make distributions to their holders and the institution is not otherwise subject to such an obligation;

(vi) non-payment of distributions does not constitute an event of default of the institution;

(vii) the cancellation of distributions imposes no restrictions on the institution;

(i) compared to all the capital instruments issued by the institution, the instruments absorb the first and proportionately greatest share of losses as they occur, and each instrument absorbs losses to the same degree as all other Common Equity Tier 1 instruments;

(j) the instruments rank below all other claims in the event of insolvency or liquidation of the institution;

(k) the instruments entitle their owners to a claim on the residual assets of the institution, which, in the event of its liquidation and after the payment of all senior claims, is proportionate to the amount of such instruments issued and is not fixed or subject to a cap, except in the case of the capital instruments referred to in Article 27 [This article deals with capital instruments of mutuals, cooperative societies, saving institutions or similar institutions included among Common Equity Tier 1 items];

(l) the instruments are not secured, or subject to a guarantee that enhances the seniority of the claim by any of the following:

(i) the institution or its subsidiaries;

(ii) the parent undertaking of the institution or its subsidiaries;

(iii) the parent financial holding company or its subsidiaries;

(iv) the mixed activity holding company or its subsidiaries;

(v) the mixed financial holding company and its subsidiaries;

(vi) any undertaking that has close links with the entities referred to in points (i) to (v);

(m) the instruments are not subject to any arrangement, contractual or otherwise, that enhances the seniority of claims under the instruments in insolvency or liquidation.

The condition set out in point (j) of the first subparagraph shall be deemed to be met, notwithstanding the instruments are included in Additional Tier 1 or Tier 2 by virtue of Article 484(3), provided that they rank pari passu.

2. The conditions laid down in point (i) of paragraph 1 shall be deemed to be met notwithstanding a write down on a permanent basis of the principal amount of Additional Tier 1 or Tier 2 instruments.

Article 31

Capital instruments subscribed by public authorities in emergency situations

1. In emergency situations, competent authorities may permit institutions to include in Common Equity Tier 1 capital instruments that comply at least with the conditions laid down in points (b) to (e) of Article 28(1) where all the following conditions are met:

   (a) the capital instruments are issued after 1 January 2014;

   (b) the capital instruments are considered State aid by the Commission;

   (c) the capital instruments are issued within the context of recapitalization measures pursuant to State aid rules existing at the time;

   (d) the capital instruments are fully subscribed and held by the State or a relevant public authority or public-owned entity;

   (e) the capital instruments are able to absorb losses;

   (f) except for the capital instruments referred to in Article 27, in the event of liquidation, the capital instruments entitle their owners to a claim on the residual assets of the institution after the payment of all senior claims;

   (g) there are adequate exit mechanisms of the State or, where applicable, a relevant public authority or public-owned entity;

   (h) the competent authority has granted its prior permission and has published its decision together with an explanation of that decision.

2. Upon reasoned request by and in cooperation with the relevant competent authority, EBA shall consider the capital instruments referred to in paragraph 1 as equivalent to Common Equity Tier 1 instruments for the purposes of this Regulation.

CHAPTER 3: Additional Tier 1 capital

Section 1: Additional tier 1 items and instruments

Article 51: Additional Tier 1 items

Additional Tier 1 items shall consist of the following:

(a) capital instruments, where the conditions laid down in Article 52(1) are met;

(b) the share premium accounts related to the instruments referred to in point (a).

Instruments included under point (a) shall not qualify as Common Equity Tier 1 or Tier 2 items.

Article 52: Additional Tier 1 instruments

1. Capital instruments shall qualify as Additional Tier 1 instruments only if the following conditions are met:

(a) the instruments are issued and paid up;

(b) the instruments are not purchased by any of the following:

(i) the institution or its subsidiaries;

(ii) an undertaking in which the institution has a participation in the form of ownership, direct or by way of control, of 20 % or more of the voting rights or capital of that undertaking;

(c) the purchase of the instruments is not funded directly or indirectly by the institution;

(d) the instruments rank below Tier 2 instruments in the event of the insolvency of the institution;

(e) (same as Article 28(l))

(f) (same as Article 28(m))

(g) the instruments are perpetual and the provisions governing them include no incentive for the institution to redeem them;

(h) where the provisions governing the instruments include one or more call options, the option to call may be exercised at the sole discretion of the issuer;

(i) the instruments may be called, redeemed or repurchased

only where the conditions laid down in Article 77 are met, and not before five years after the date of issuance except where the conditions laid down in Article 78(4) are met; (j) the provisions governing the instruments do not indicate explicitly or implicitly that the instruments would or might be called, redeemed or repurchased and the institution does not otherwise provide such an indication, except in the following cases:

(i) the liquidation of the institution;

(ii) discretionary repurchases of the instruments or other discretionary means of reducing the amount of Additional Tier 1 capital, where the institution has received the prior permission of the competent authority in accordance with Article 77;

(k) the institution does not indicate explicitly or implicitly that the competent authority would consent to a request to call, redeem or repurchase the instruments;

(l) distributions under the instruments meet the following conditions:

(i) they are paid out of distributable items;

(ii) the level of distributions made on the instruments will not be amended on the basis of the credit standing of the institution or its parent undertaking;

(iii) the provisions governing the instruments give the institution full discretion at all times to cancel the distributions on the instruments for an unlimited period and on a non-cumulative basis, and the institution may use such cancelled payments without restriction to meet its obligations as they fall due;

(iv) cancellation of distributions does not constitute an event of default of the institution;

(v) the cancellation of distributions imposes no restrictions on the institution;

(m) the instruments do not contribute to a determination that the liabilities of an institution exceed its assets, where such a determination constitutes a test of insolvency under applicable national law;

(n) the provisions governing the instruments require that, upon the occurrence of a trigger event, the principal amount of the instruments be written down on a permanent or temporary basis or the instruments be converted to Common Equity Tier 1 instruments;

(o) the provisions governing the instruments include no feature that could hinder the recapitalization of the institution;

(p) where the instruments are not issued directly by an institution, both the following conditions shall be met:

(i) the instruments are issued through an entity within the consolidation pursuant to Chapter 2 of Title II of Part One;

(ii) the proceeds are immediately available to the institution without limitation and in a form that satisfies the conditions laid down in this paragraph.

The condition set out in point (d) of the first subparagraph shall be deemed to be met notwithstanding the instruments are included in Additional Tier 1 or Tier 2 by virtue of Article 484(3), provided that they rank pari passu.

2. EBA shall develop draft regulatory technical standards (RTS) to specify all the following: [see the near-final drafts of "all the following" RTS already provided in the preceding document (5)]

Article 53: Restrictions on the cancellation of distributions on Additional Tier 1 instruments and features that could hinder the recapitalization of the institution

For the purposes of points (l)(v) and (o) of Article 52(1), the provisions governing Additional Tier 1 instruments shall, in particular, not include the following:

(a) a requirement for distributions on the instruments to be made in the event of a distribution being made on an instrument issued by the institution that ranks to the same degree as, or more junior than, an Additional Tier 1 instrument, including a Common Equity Tier 1 instrument;

(b) a requirement for the payment of distributions on Common

Equity Tier 1, Additional Tier 1 or Tier 2 instruments to be cancelled in the event that distributions are not made on those Additional Tier 1 instruments;

(c) an obligation to substitute the payment of interest or dividend by a payment in any other form. The institution shall not otherwise be subject to such an obligation.

Article 54: Write down or conversion of Additional Tier 1 instruments

1. For the purposes of point (n) of Article 52(1), the following provisions shall apply to Additional Tier 1 instruments:
(a) a trigger event occurs when the Common Equity Tier 1 capital ratio of the institution referred to in point (a) of Article 92(1) falls below either of the following:
    (i) 5.125%;
    (ii) a level higher than 5.125%, where determined by the institution and specified in the provisions governing the instrument;
(b) institutions may specify in the provisions governing the instrument one or more trigger events in addition to that referred to in point (a);
(c) where the provisions governing the instruments require them to be converted into Common Equity Tier 1 instruments upon the occurrence of a trigger event, those provisions shall specify either of the following:
    (i) the rate of such conversion and a limit on the permitted amount of conversion;
    (ii) a range within which the instruments will convert into Common Equity Tier 1 instruments;
(d) where the provisions governing the instruments require their principal amount to be written down upon the occurrence of a trigger event, the write down shall reduce all the following:
    (i) the claim of the holder of the instrument in the insolvency or liquidation of the institution;
    (ii) the amount required to be paid in the event of the call or redemption of the instrument;

(iii) the distributions made on the instrument.

2. Write down or conversion of an Additional Tier 1 instrument shall, under the applicable accounting framework, generate items that qualify as Common Equity Tier 1 items.

3. The amount of Additional Tier 1 instruments recognized in Additional Tier 1 items is limited to the minimum amount Common Equity Tier 1 items that would be generated if the principal amount of the Additional Tier 1 instruments were fully written down or converted into Common Equity Tier 1 instruments.

4. The aggregate amount of Additional Tier 1 instruments that is required to be written down or converted upon the occurrence of a trigger event shall be no less than the lower of the following:
   (a) the amount required to restore fully the Common Equity Tier 1 ratio of the institution to 5.125%;
   (b) the full principal amount of the instrument.

5. When a trigger event occurs institutions shall do the following:
   (a) immediately inform the competent authorities;
   (b) inform the holders of the Additional Tier 1 instruments;
   (c) write down the principal amount of the instruments, or convert the instruments into Common Equity Tier 1 instruments without delay, but no later than in one month, in accordance with the requirement laid down in this Article.

6. An institution issuing Additional Tier 1 instruments that convert to Common Equity Tier 1 on the occurrence of a trigger event shall ensure that its authorized share capital is at all times sufficient, for converting all such convertible Additional Tier 1 instruments into shares if a trigger event occurs. All necessary authorizations shall be obtained at the date of issuance of such convertible Additional Tier 1 instruments. The institution shall maintain at all times the necessary prior authorization to issue the Common Equity Tier 1 instruments into which such Additional Tier 1 instruments would convert upon occurrence of a trigger event.

7. An institution issuing Additional Tier 1 instruments that convert to Common Equity Tier 1 on the occurrence of a trigger event shall ensure that there are no procedural impediments to that conversion by virtue of its incorporation or statutes or contractual arrangements.

Article 55: Consequences of the conditions for Additional Tier 1 instruments ceasing to be met

The following shall apply where, in the case of an Additional Tier 1 instrument, the conditions laid down in Article 52(1) cease to be met:

(a) that instrument shall immediately cease to qualify as an Additional Tier 1 instrument;

(b) the part of the share premium accounts that relates to that instrument shall immediately cease to qualify as an Additional Tier 1 item.

Section 2: Deductions from additional tier 1 items

Article 56: Deductions from Additional Tier 1 items

Institutions shall deduct the following from Additional Tier 1 items:

(a) direct, indirect and synthetic holdings by an institution of own Additional Tier 1 instruments, including own Additional Tier 1 instruments that an institution could be obliged to purchase as a result of existing contractual obligations;

(d) direct, indirect and synthetic holdings by the institution of the Additional Tier 1 instruments of financial sector entities where the institution has a significant investment in those entities, excluding underwriting positions held for five working days or fewer;

(e) the amount of items required to be deducted from Tier 2 items pursuant to Article 66 that exceed the Tier 2 capital of the institution;

Article 57: Deductions of holdings of own Additional Tier 1 instruments (detail here omitted)

Article 58: Deduction of holdings of Additional Tier 1 instruments of financial sector entities and where an institution has a reciprocal cross holding designed artificially to inflate own funds (detail here omitted)

Article 59: Deduction of holdings of Additional Tier 1 instruments of financial sector entities (detail here omitted)

Section 3: Additional Tier 1 capital

Article 61: Additional Tier 1 capital

The Additional Tier 1 capital of an institution shall consist of Additional Tier 1 items after the deduction of the items referred to in Article 56 and the application of Article 79.

CHAPTER 4

Article 62: Tier 2 items

Tier 2 items shall consist of the following:

(a) capital instruments and subordinated loans where the conditions laid down in Article 63 are met;

(b) the share premium accounts related to instruments referred to in point (a);

(c) for institutions calculating risk-weighted exposure amounts in accordance with Chapter 2 of Title II of Part Three, general credit risk adjustments, gross of tax effects, of up to 1.25% of risk-weighted exposure amounts calculated in accordance with Chapter 2 of Title II of Part Three;

(d) for institutions calculating risk-weighted exposure amounts under Chapter 3 of Title II of Part Three, positive amounts, gross of tax effects, resulting from the calculation laid down in Articles 158 and 159 up to 0.6% of risk weighted exposure amounts calculated under Chapter 3 of Title II of Part Three.

Items included under point (a) shall not qualify as Common Equity Tier 1 or Additional Tier 1 items.

Article 63: Tier 2 instruments

Capital instruments and subordinated loans shall qualify as Tier 2 instruments provided the following conditions are met:

(a) the instruments are issued or the subordinated loans are raised, as applicable, and fully paid-up;

(b) the instruments are not purchased or the subordinated loans are not granted, as applicable, by any of the following:

(i) the institution or its subsidiaries;

(ii) an undertaking in which the institution has participation in the form of ownership, direct or by way of control, of 20% or more of the voting rights or capital of that undertaking;

(c) the purchase of the instruments or the granting of the subordinated loans, as applicable, is not funded directly or indirectly by the institution;

(d) the claim on the principal amount of the instruments under the provisions governing the instruments or the claim of the principal amount of the subordinated loans under the provisions governing the subordinated loans, as applicable, is wholly subordinated to claims of all non-subordinated creditors;

(f) the instruments or subordinated loans, as applicable, are not subject to any arrangement that otherwise enhances the seniority of the claim under the instruments or subordinated loans respectively;

(g) the instruments or subordinated loans, as applicable, have an original maturity of at least five years;

(h) the provisions governing the instruments or subordinated loans, as applicable, do not include any incentive for their principal amount to be redeemed or repaid, as applicable by the institution prior to their maturity;

(i) where the instruments or subordinated loans, as applicable, include one or more call options or early repayment options, as applicable, the options are exercisable at the sole discretion of the issuer or debtor, as applicable;

(j) the instruments or subordinated loans, as applicable, may be called, redeemed or repurchased or repaid early only where the conditions laid down in Article 77 are met, and not before five years after the date of issuance or raising, as applicable, except where the conditions laid down in Article 78(4) are met;

(k) the provisions governing the instruments or subordinated loans, as applicable, do not indicate explicitly or implicitly that the instruments or subordinated loans, as applicable, would or might be called, redeemed, repurchased or repaid early, as applicable by the institution other than in the insolvency or liquidation of the institution and the institution does not otherwise provide such an indication;

(l) the provisions governing the instruments or subordinated loans, as applicable, do not give the holder the right to accelerate the future scheduled payment of interest or principal, other than in the insolvency or liquidation of the institution;

(m) the level of interest or dividend payments, as applicable, due on the instruments or subordinated loans, as applicable, will not be amended on the basis of the credit standing of the institution or its parent undertaking;

Article 64: Amortization of Tier 2 instruments

The extent to which Tier 2 instruments qualify as Tier 2 items during the final five years of maturity of the instruments is calculated by multiplying the result derived from the calculation in point (a) by the amount referred to in point (b) as follows:

(a) the nominal amount of the instruments or subordinated loans on the first day of the final five year period of their contractual maturity divided by the number of calendar days in that period;

(b) the number of remaining calendar days of contractual maturity of the instruments or subordinated loans.

17.9 Document 7: Excerpts from Final Rules Issued by OCC and Fed

OCC and Fed (2013b), "Regulatory Capital Rules: Regulatory Capital, Implementation of Basel III, Capital Adequacy, Transition Provisions, Prompt Corrective Action, Standardized Approach for Risk-weighted Assets, Market Discipline and Disclosure Requirements, Advanced Approaches Risk-Based Capital Rule, and Market Risk Capital Rule; Final Rule," *Federal Register,* Vol. 78, No. 198, October 11, 2013, Part II, pp. 62017–62291.

http://www.gpo.gov/fdsys/pkg/FR-2013-10-11/pdf/2013-21653.pdf

V. Definition of Capital
A. Capital Components and Eligibility Criteria for Regulatory Capital Instruments

2. Additional Tier 1 Capital

Consistent with Basel III, the agencies and the FDIC proposed that additional tier 1 capital would equal the sum of: Additional tier 1 capital instruments that satisfy the criteria set forth in section 20(c) of the proposal, related surplus, and any tier 1 minority interest that is not included in a banking organization's common equity tier 1 capital (subject to the proposed limitations on minority interest), less applicable regulatory adjustments and deductions. The agencies and the FDIC pro-

posed the following criteria for additional tier 1 capital instruments in section 20(c):

(1) The instrument is issued and paid in.

(2) The instrument is subordinated to depositors, general creditors, and subordinated debt holders of the banking organization in a receivership, insolvency, liquidation, or similar proceeding.

(3) The instrument is not secured, not covered by a guarantee of the banking organization or of an affiliate of the banking organization, and not subject to any other arrangement that legally or economically enhances the seniority of the instrument.

(4) The instrument has no

maturity date and does not contain a dividend step-up or any other term or feature that creates an incentive to redeem.

(5) If callable by its terms, the instrument may be called by the banking organization only after a minimum of five years following issuance, except that the terms of the instrument may allow it to be called earlier than five years upon the occurrence of a regulatory event (as defined in the agreement governing the instrument) that precludes the instrument from being included in additional tier 1 capital or a tax event. In addition:

(i) The banking organization must receive prior approval from its primary Federal supervisor to exercise a call option on the instrument.

(ii) The banking organization does not create at issuance of the instrument, through any action or communication, an expectation that the call option will be exercised.

(iii) Prior to exercising the call option, or immediately thereafter, the banking organization must either:

(A) Replace the instrument to be called with an equal amount of instruments that meet the criteria under section 20(b) or (c) of the proposed rule (replacement can be concurrent with redemption of existing additional tier 1 capital instruments); or

(B) Demonstrate to the satisfaction of its primary Federal supervisor that following redemption, the banking organization will continue to hold capital commensurate with its risk.

(6) Redemption or repurchase of the instrument requires prior approval from the banking organization's primary Federal supervisor.

(7) The banking organization has full discretion at all times to cancel dividends or other capital distributions on the instrument without triggering an event of default, a requirement to make a payment-in-kind, or an imposition of other restrictions on the banking organization except in relation to any capital distributions to holders of common stock.

(8) Any capital distributions on the instrument are paid out of the banking organization's net income and retained earnings.

(9) The instrument does not have a credit-sensitive feature, such as a dividend rate that is reset periodically based in whole or in part on the banking organization's credit quality, but may have a dividend rate that is adjusted periodically independent of the banking organization's credit quality, in relation to general market interest rates or similar adjustments.

(10) *The paid-in amount is classified as equity under GAAP.*

(11) The banking organization, or an entity that the banking organization controls, did not purchase or directly or indirectly fund the purchase of the instrument.

With regard to Criterion (10) above for inclusion in AT1 Capital:

Commenters also noted that proposed criterion (10), which requires the paid in amounts of tier 1 capital instruments to be classified as equity under GAAP before they may be included in regulatory capital, generally would prevent contingent capital instruments, which are classified as liabilities, from qualifying as additional tier 1 capital.

These commenters asked the agencies and the FDIC to revise the rules to provide that contingent capital instruments will qualify as additional tier 1 capital, regardless of their treatment under GAAP. Another commenter noted the challenges for US banking organizations in devising contingent capital instruments that would satisfy the proposed criteria, and noted that if US banking organizations develop an acceptable instrument, the instrument likely would initially be classified as debt instead of equity for GAAP purposes. Thus, in order to accommodate this possibility, the commenter urged the agencies and the FDIC to revise the criterion to allow the agencies and the FDIC to permit such an instrument in additional tier 1 capital through interpretive guidance or specifically in the case of a particular instrument.

The agencies continue to believe that restricting tier 1 capital instruments to those classified as equity under GAAP will help to ensure those instruments' capacity to absorb losses and further increase the quality of US banking organizations' regulatory capital. The agencies therefore have decided to retain this aspect of the proposal. To the extent that a contingent capital instrument is considered a liability under GAAP, a banking organization may not include the instrument in its tier 1 capital under the final rule. At such time as an instrument converts from debt to equity under GAAP, the instrument would then satisfy this criterion.

6. Agency Approval of Capital Elements

[O]ver time, capital instruments that are equivalent in quality and capacity to absorb losses to existing instruments may be created to satisfy different market needs.

Therefore, the agencies and the FDIC proposed to create a process to consider the eligibility of such instruments on a case-by-case basis. Under the proposed rule, a banking organization must request approval from its primary Federal supervisor before including a capital element in regulatory capital, unless: (i) Such capital element is currently included in regulatory capital under the agencies' and the FDIC's general risk-based capital and leverage rules and the underlying instrument complies with the applicable proposed eligibility criteria for regulatory capital instruments; or (ii) the capital element is equivalent, in terms of capital quality and ability to absorb losses, to an element described in a previous decision made publicly available by the banking organization's primary Federal supervisor.

In the preamble to the proposal, the agencies and the FDIC indicated that they intend to consult each other when determining whether a new element should be included in common equity tier 1, additional tier 1, or tier 2 capital, and indicated that once one agency determines that a capital element may be included in a banking organization's common equity tier 1, additional tier 1, or tier 2 capital, that agency would make its decision publicly available, including a brief description of the capital element and the rationale for the conclusion.

The agencies continue to believe that it is appropriate to retain the flexibility necessary to consider new instruments on a case-by-case basis as they are developed over time to satisfy different market needs. The agencies have decided to move the agencies' authority in section

20(e)(1) of the proposal to the agencies' reservation of authority provision included in section 1(d) (2)(ii) of the final rule. Therefore, the agencies are adopting this aspect of the final rule substantively as proposed to create a process to consider the eligibility of such instruments on a permanent or temporary basis, in accordance with the applicable requirements in subpart C of the final rule (section 20(e) of the final rule).

Section 20(e)(1) of the final rule provides that a banking organization must receive its primary Federal supervisor's prior approval to include a capital element in its common equity tier 1 capital, additional tier 1 capital, or tier 2 capital *unless* that element: (i) Was included in the banking organization's tier 1 capital or tier 2 capital prior to May 19, 2010 in accordance with that supervisor's risk based capital rules that were effective as of that date and the underlying instrument continues to be includable under the criteria set forth in this section; or (ii) is equivalent, in terms of capital quality and ability to absorb credit losses with respect to all material terms, to a regulatory capital element determined by that supervisor to be includable

in regulatory capital pursuant to paragraph (e)(3) of section 20. In exercising this reservation of authority, the agencies expect to consider the requirements for capital elements in the final rule; the size, complexity, risk profile, and scope of operations of the banking organization, and whether any public benefits would be outweighed by risk to an insured depository institution or to the financial system.

Criteria for Tier 2 Instruments

Consistent with Basel III, the agencies and the FDIC proposed the following criteria for tier 2 capital instruments:

(1) The instrument is issued and paid in.

(2) The instrument is subordinated to depositors and general creditors of the banking organization.

(3) The instrument is not secured, not covered by a guarantee of the banking organization or of an affiliate of the banking organization, and not subject to any other arrangement that legally or economically enhances the seniority of the instrument in relation to more senior claims.

(4) The instrument has a minimum original maturity of at least five years. At the beginning of each of the last five years of the life of the instrument, the amount that is eligible to be included in tier 2 capital is reduced by 20% of the original amount of the instrument (net of redemptions) and is excluded from regulatory capital when remaining maturity is less than one year. In addition, the instrument must not have any terms or features that require, or create significant incentives for, the banking organization to redeem the instrument prior to maturity.

(5) The instrument, by its terms, may be called by the banking organization only after a minimum of five years following issuance, except that the terms of the instrument may allow it to be called sooner upon the occurrence of an event that would preclude the instrument from being included in tier 2 capital, or a tax event. In addition:

(i) The banking organization must receive the prior approval of its primary Federal supervisor to exercise a call option on the instrument.

(ii) The banking organization does not create at issuance, through action or communication, an expectation the call option will be exercised.

(iii) Prior to exercising the call option, or immediately thereafter, the banking organization must either:

(A) Replace any amount called with an equivalent amount of an instrument that meets the criteria for regulatory capital under section 20 of the proposed rule; 79 or

(B) Demonstrate to the satisfaction of the banking organization's primary Federal supervisor that following redemption, the banking organization would continue to hold an amount of capital that is commensurate with its risk.

(6) The holder of the instrument must have no contractual right to accelerate payment of principal or interest on the instrument, except in the event of a receivership, insolvency, liquidation, or similar proceeding of the banking organization.

(7) The instrument has no credit sensitive feature, such as a dividend or interest rate that is reset periodically based in whole or

in part on the banking organization's credit standing, but may have a dividend rate that is adjusted periodically independent of the banking organization's credit standing, in relation to general market interest rates or similar adjustments.

(8) The banking organization, or an entity that the banking organization controls, has not purchased and has not directly or indirectly funded the purchase of the instrument.

(9) If the instrument is not issued directly by the banking organization or by a subsidiary of the banking organization that is an operating entity, the only asset of the issuing entity is its investment in the capital of the banking organization, and proceeds must be immediately available without limitation to the banking organization or the banking organization's top-tier holding company in a form that meets or exceeds all the other criteria for tier 2 capital instruments under this section.

(10) Redemption of the instrument prior to maturity or repurchase requires the prior approval of the banking organization's primary Federal supervisor.

(11) For an advanced approaches banking organization, the governing agreement, offering circular, or prospectus of an instrument issued after January 1, 2013, must disclose that the holders of the instrument may be fully subordinated to interests held by the US government in the event that the banking organization enters into a receivership, insolvency, liquidation, or similar proceeding.

The agencies and the FDIC also proposed to eliminate the inclusion of a portion of certain unrealized gains on AFS equity securities in tier 2 capital given that unrealized gains and losses on AFS securities would flow through to common equity tier 1 capital under the proposed rules. As a result of the proposed new minimum common equity tier 1 capital requirement, higher tier 1 capital requirement, and the broader goal of simplifying the definition of tier 2 capital, the proposal eliminated the existing limitations on the amount of tier 2 capital that could be recognized in total capital, as well as the existing limitations on the amount of certain capital instruments (that is, term subordinated debt) that could be included in tier 2 capital.

18

Conclusions and Recommendations for Cocos Design and Evaluations

On New Year's Day, 2014, the *New York Times* carried a story that wondered why "Ski Helmet Use Isn't Reducing Brain Injuries." Such helmets have been getting ever better in shock absorbtion, but the rate of serious head injury has reportedly not declined; only lesser injuries like scalp lacerations, have been reduced. We may similarly ask ourselves why it is that capital has become ever more loss absorbing, yet the rate of financial crises has not declined. Perhaps it will turn out that excessive risk taking is hard to restrain when managers have no intention to help in doing so and are inclined to rate regulations by their nuisance value rather than by any stabilization benefits. Greater capital buffers might just stimulate higher risk taking, and the eventual damage could be just as great as before.

While some disappointment is thus inevitable, promoting and defending capital adequacy—not only with regulatory measures but also with new market instruments—is still the most promising focus for reform. No matter how well a bank is capitalized right now, it is likely to find itself less than adequately capitalized someday, and when that happens, many other banks are likely to be in difficulties too. Then all the usual remedies available to banks in isolation to de-risk and de-leverage (e.g., through asset sales and new equity issues) will become very expensive if they remain viable at all.

18.1 Cocos by Design

Even being very well capitalized before the start of a financial crisis cannot protect an individual banking institution entirely from being engulfed by the liquidity and funding crises first felt

241

by weaker institutions. Yet would the growth of mutual distrust, the freezing up of interbank and wholesale money-markets—in short, increasing-correlation risk, no-longer-stable funding risk, and illiquidity risk—be as likely to spread and be as devastating if financial institutions on the whole were better capitalized? A crisis brought on by the collapse of an asset price bubble and "over-lending" affects most financial institutions at the same time and in a similar way. Even if the origins of such a crisis were to lie to some extent outside the banking system, if that system is very well capitalized, it might help brake the common shock's downward-spiraling dynamic for the financial sector. Assured access to more equity capital in a crisis would allow more banks to take care of themselves, thereby diminishing the adverse spillovers to other banks.

Cocos prove their merit at that point as they are meant to be a prompt and reliable provider of equity through debt forgiveness to troubled banks on preset terms. Having cocos equal to 2% of a bank's total asset exposures (as defined in the leverage ratio) on their balance sheet by the start of 2019 would be a worthy goal. Regulators should encourage, but not require, all except the smallest banks to meet it. If these cocos are all T1, they would get full credit for boosting the leverage ratio T1/TA and partial credit—for up to 1.5% of risk weighted assets—as AT1/RWA. The rest could be credited to the T2 component of the risk-based capital ratio as laid out in Table 1 before.

The corresponding trigger levels of going-concern cocos should be no less than the actual or proposed future minima for CET1/RWA and for the leverage ratio, which by 2019 would be 7% and 3%, respectively, and 9.5% and 5% for the largest SIFIs. Logically, multiple minima require multiple cocos trigger concepts to make sure that assistance is available through conversion to help meet each of the minima imposed. Since the leverage ratio is meant to serve as a backstop for the CET1 ratio, a leverage ratio trigger should also back the CET1 ratio trigger.

18.2 Setting the Replacement Rate to Appropriately Manage Incentives

The replacement rate is equal to the percentage of the principal of cocos that can be recovered from the sale of the common stock received upon conversion. If stock quotations are not deep and resilient at the time of conversion or industry effects and contagion become dominant in stock price formation, the estimate of the replacement rate at conversion on a date yet uncertain will become very loose.

To recapitulate briefly: formally, the replacement rate [ρ] can be expressed as the ratio of two prices. The one in the numerator is the market price of common stock at which business can be done after the completion of conversion [MP_c]. Conversion is due within one month from the time it has been determined that a trigger event has occurred. The variable in the denominator is the conversion price [CP]. It is a control variable that can either be fixed or bounded absolutely in advance, or linked to the market price in the numerator that prevails upon conversion as just described. Once the conversion price has been set, subject only to anti-dilution adjustments, it fixes the number of shares to be issued in conversion because the product of that number of shares and the conversion price is identically equal to the face value of the cocos being converted.

In the case of write-down-only cocos, the replacement rate is zero because conversion does not actually take place. Given that $\rho = MP_c/CP$, it has also been said that one can instead imagine that conversion does take place even when $\rho = 0$, but at a CP of infinity. A zero replacement rate for cocos holders is surely the wrong set-up because it lowers the cost of excessive risk taking by existing shareholders. It also potentially exposes cocos holders to very large losses that could spill back into banking systems through the networks of institutional cocos holders who are loan clients of banks or counterparties to such clients who might be drawn in. On the other side, if the market price at conversion were to exceed the conversion price, cocos holders would enjoy a replacement rate in excess of 1 in the event of conversion.

Giving cocos holders reason to expect such an outcome is unde-sirable, as it would sap their incentives to exercise debt discipline. Pre-existing shareholders, anticipating that cocos holders would be overcompensated at their expense, would oppose cocos from ever being issued by the bank in the first place.

Between the ρ values of 0 and 1—which can be considered extremes in that with ρ of 0 cocos holders lose everything upon conversion while with ρ of 1 they lose nothing—a replacement rate of about 0.8 is most commendable. It is sufficient to preserve debt discipline by giving cocos holders an incentive to use their influence with management to steer clear of conversion. At the same time it would give pre-existing shareholders no more than a small consideration at conversion. That would be just enough to keep them interested in having cocos issued without inviting excessive risk taking that might end badly and risk triggering conversion. Because cocos conversion is an exchange-of-claims accounting act, it does not affect the return on the total assets of firm or the size of its balance sheet. Hence its direct effects can only be distributive, primarily between pre-existing shareholders and cocos holders. If the replacement rate is 1 because CP has been specified to be equal to whatever MP_c turns out to be upon conversion, there is no such redistribution. Stockholders then bear the entire loss from the adverse developments that have lowered the value of their shares while cocos holders are fully compensated for giving up their claim.

The next question is how the conversion price, and hence the number of shares to be issued upon conversion of a given face value [FV] of cocos, should be set *ex ante* to achieve an expected replacement rate of 0.8 if that is the chosen target. Already fixing the number of shares received in conversion at the time of cocos issue, and hence CP, is desirable for hedging and pledging purposes. The guiding principle here is that the better an institution is capitalized at the time of cocos issue, the lower the probability that cocos will be converted prior to being called, or before reaching maturity, on account of a trigger event. The reason why this is to be expected is that these cocos start out when the bank is far away from the trigger point. Hence, the bank's capitalization, and with it the price of its shares, would have a long way to fall before reaching the trigger point and observing MP_c. The ratio of CP to the market price of its shares at the time of cocos issue $[MP_0]$ should therefore be *lower* the higher the excess capital buffer at that time.

The results in column 4 of Table 6 above are broadly compatible with setting a CP equal to 50% of MP_0 because MP_c was estimated to be only about 40% of MP_0 by the time the cocos would be triggered. Such a conversion price would promise a replacement rate of about 0.8 in the event of conversion if the bank is very well capitalized to start with. For a bank to be in such a comfortable position requires an initial CET1 capital ratio 4 percentage points or more above the trigger level, which is normally still 7% for going-concern cocos. If the bank was well, but not very well, capitalized, that initial CET1/RWA ratio at the time of cocos issue would be at least 2% but less than 4% above the trigger level. The conversion price should then be set at around 70% of the level of the stock price at the time of cocos issue. It should be set at around 90% of that price if the bank were only adequately capitalized, with a CET1 capital ratio buffer of less than 2% above the trigger level. The conversion price is relatively high here because not much more decline in CET1 (and thus also in the stock price) would be needed to activate the trigger. As in the other cases, for a replacement rate of 0.8, the conversion price would always be 25% above the expected market price at conversion (and that market price 20% below the conversion price) recalling that $\rho = MP_c/CP$. The formula is a reminder that any percentage change in the estimate of MP_c relative to MP_0 must be matched with an equal percentage change in CP relative to MP_0 to stabilize ρ at its target level $\underline{\rho}$.

18.3 How to Better Secure the Targeted Replacement Rate

Taking account of the inverse relation between MP_c/MP_0 and the size of the initial capital buffer of the bank is surely a step in the right direction. However, the market price of the bank's shares to be expected post-conversion—and thus the actual replacement rate to be had—remain highly uncertain because that price $[MP_c]$

depends not only on the condition of the individual bank but also on the financial sector as a whole. The question then arises whether investors should have a stop-loss option to convert if the (average volume-weighted weekly) market price, instead of ending up 20% below the conversion price at conversion and yielding a 0.8 recovery rate, ends up, say, 40% below the conversion price.

Putting a floor of 0.6 in this way on the replacement rate actually obtained would make achievement of the 0.8 target at least on average more secure by staunching the distribution of outcomes upward from its extended lower end. Since a bank that is very well capitalized at the time of cocos issue would have expected MP_c to be $0.4MP_0$ when it set CP equal to $0.5MP_0$, setting the trigger MP_c of the proposed option 25% below that would make it equal to $0.30MP_0$. That trigger price in relation to MP_0 shows that the shareholders would already have lost 70% by that time, while cocos holders would recover at a minimum 60% of the principal value of cocos. If the value of cocos equaled as much as one-quarter of shareholders' equity on the bank's balance sheet, book value per share would rise from cancellation of the cocos debt by 10%, from $0.30MP_0$ to $0.33MP_0$. Cocos conversion would thus make only a modest contribution to reducing the losses to shareholders, but their losses remaining after cocos conversion and cancellation would still be proportionately much greater than those of cocos holders who expect, on average, to attain a replacement rate of 80% with a 60% floor under this proposal. Normal principles of seniority would be respected, principles which require at the very least that common stock holders should absorb proportionately greater losses than holders of subordinated debt, including cocos, even when claims are reshuffled outside of bankruptcy.

Regarding the regulatory treatment of options contained in cocos, Document 4 in Chapter 17 allows for holders' right to convert [cocos] into shares to be considered as an "open option." Article 52(h) of Document 6 states, however, that if an AT1 instrument contains one or more call options, "the option to call may be exercised at the sole discretion of the issuer." Even so, regulators may have an open mind on the matter of granting cocos holders' an option to trigger the conversion to shares on the downside, although—guided by the principles explained in the Introduction—I would not favor an option for issuers to exercise.

It thus appears worth considering either adding a stop-loss event to the several other (e.g., tax and regulatory) "events" that can cause a whole class of cocos to be converted, or to use the stop-loss option approach to conversion that must be exercised by cocos holders individually. I remain opposed to embellishing cocos with upside-conversion features because they could act perversely to take capital insurance through cocos away from the bank in good times, thereby making it unavailable in bad times. Such an option has already been added to one such issue by setting not only a minimum but also a maximum on the conversion price with an option to trigger conversion when profitable to do so because the market price has risen above the conversion price. Adhering to the principle that cocos should be issued to private holders in good times, to be available for contingent conversion in bad times, is essential if cocos are to help stabilize the financial system by serving as a brake on the financial accelerator and its self-aggravating dynamic in an approaching crisis. This principle has also been violated when severely troubled banks in Portugal and Spain issued cocos to their government as an off-budget "investment" with the understanding that these cocos were to be re-purchased by the banks as soon as their funding situation improved.

18.4 The Level of the Conversion Risk Premium and its Determinants

Together with the chosen trigger level, the size of the initial capital buffer or "excess" above required levels is among the factors that determines the annual probability of conversion $[\pi]$. This variable and the replacement rate target $[\rho]$ then combine to determine the size of the conversion risk premium. Here the estimate of that premium represents the least that must be added under risk neutrality to the 'riskless' rate, from the Treasury yield curve, to cover the loss expected in the event that the cocos are triggered for conversion. Table 5 above showed that if $\pi = 0.02$ and ρ is 0.8, this risk premium should be only 40–50 bps, but twice as high if π is 0.04 or 4%. However, if the expected recovery rate is 0, as it is for the write-down-only cocos to be avoided, the appropriate "conversion" risk premium should be 200 to 210 bps if π = 0.02 and 410 to 430 bps if π = 0.04. Hence the replacement rate is critical to how much the conversion risk premium would cost issuers; firming up ρ's target level and expected value, and determining how to secure that value, should prove rewarding for issuers and investors.

Cocos with a zero or very low replacement rate are not only expensive but also asking for abuse by their issuers; should they ever be triggered they are thus not likely to be replaceable anytime soon. The triggering of high-trigger cocos with high expected replacement rates would leave no such black mark and bad memories. Because of this, only high-trigger cocos are likely to be sustainable.

18.5 Three Pleas: Better Tax, Rating, and Qualification Treatment for Cocos

Each of the three previous chapters in this Part identified at least one issue relating to the treatment of cocos that appears amenable to change. This has resulted in the following pleas:

18.5.1 Tax Authorities to Clarify Status of Interest Paid on Cocos Where Needed

One of the requirements for the success of cocos is the deductibility of interest paid on them from taxable corporate income. Allowing the interest deduction would prevent cocos from being severely handicapped against otherwise comparable unsecured long-term (but not contingently convertible) debt. Leaving this issue unresolved in some major advanced countries is needlessly harmful, insofar as it could discourage the use of a financial instrument that promises to deliver significant private and public benefits. The following quotation from HM Revenue and Customs (2011, p. 5) no longer applies to the United Kingdom, nor, since April 2014, to Germany but is still apt for the United States:

[T]he equity/liability project is currently on hold... Even minor changes could have a significant impact upon the classification of instruments which are at the boundaries of equity/liability classification (which may include some additional Tier 1 instruments)... In view of this uncertainty, it may be difficult in the short term (at least the next 12 months) to give any certainty over the future accounting treatment of possible Additional Tier 1 capital instruments.

If determining the debt/equity mix of cocos for tax purposes is such a subtle and tangled business, tax authorities should at least start (or continue?) to work with potential cocos issuers through a pre-approval process. In that process, the tax status of interest payments on a planned issue of cocos of some proposed design could then be decided on a case-by-case basis. A formal ruling on the features which cocos would need to possess for tax deductibility of the interest paid on them to be granted should then follow in the US, Germany, and any other country in which that tax treatment is still unclear to potential issuers.

18.5.2 Moody's to Step Up to Rating Going-Concern Cocos

Moody's rating considerations for contingent capital securities, at least until February 2014, have consisted of a "yes", a "no", and "maybe not" as follows:

- Moody's will rate where loss absorption is tied to triggers that are credit-linked, objective, and measurable, but such triggers do not exist so far

- Will not rate where loss absorption occurs: 1) at the bank's option or 2) is tied to triggers unrelated to the bank's financial health such as the bank's stock price

- May not rate where loss absorption is subject to regulatory discretion and/or the breach of regulatory capital triggers.

The last of these three considerations expresses Moody's reluctance to rate going-concern cocos, i.e., the majority of the cocos issued so far.

Moody's proposed in April 2013 that it would rate only contractual non-viability securities. It would be illogical to continue to justify Moody's reluctance to rate going-concern cocos with a regulatory capital-ratio trigger by basing this reluctance on the difficulty in predicting when loss absorption would be triggered in rapidly changing regulatory and political environments. Going-concern cocos worthy of their name are governed by the contractual terms of their covenant. It is extremely unlikely that regulators would (or even could) declare a non-viability event before high-trigger cocos had already been triggered automatically and converted on their own terms to raise CET1. Except in the event of a surprise "jump" process—perhaps associated with the discovery of large trading losses, supported by egregious accounting irregularities or massive fraud, and posing an immediate risk of bankruptcy—the authorities would have no reason to activate this high trigger on their own before the accounting for regulatory capital could catch up.

Moody's should face no great inherent difficulty assessing the conversion risk exposure and the prospective replacement rate and to translate the resulting estimates into issue ratings for cocos, since it already rates the issuers and their subordinated debt in most cases anyway. I sympathize with Moody's (2014) conclusion that AT1 securities must still be examined as a unique offering on account of a lack of product harmonization, and the absence of trigger standards, and loss absorption features: this absence of standard features lowers their attractiveness compared with other hybrids, increases risk premiums and may harbor unexpected losses. In my opinion, it is the methods used to determine π and estimate ρ, and what the target value of ρ should be and how it should best be protected, that have the highest priority for making cocos issues—and the implications of the choice of their key parameter values—better understood.

18.5.3 US to Allow AT1 Cocos and BCBS and National Regs: Hands Off High-Trigger Cocos but Discourage Issuance of Write-Off-Only Cocos

The trio of US bank regulators have let treatment of cocos as debt or equity under GAAP—irrespective of their treatment under international financial reporting standards [IFRS]—decide whether they should be classified as equity or as debt. Classification as equity would then make them eligible for inclusion in AT1. But because GAAP treats cocos as debt, they are not accepted as part of AT1 in the United States.

It is curious that a country that contains a major center of world finance would refer solely to its own accounting standards to settle such matters, rather than work towards mutual recognition or adoption of a single standard with other advanced countries. There is also the question of internal consistency between the different agencies of the US Government. The IRS has avoided specifying precisely what debt-like features cocos would need to possess to be deductible for tax purposes, but it is not necessarily inclined or obligated to defer to their treatment under GAAP on such matters. Otherwise the interest paid on cocos, on account of being classified as debt, would clearly have to be deductible. Basel III has made room for qualifying cocos to be given credit towards AT1, and the United States should do likewise.

The BCBS in its collective wisdom, with national regulators included, might also choose to reconsider a few matters. In particular, all officials concerned should abrogate their claimed right to interfere with the application of the trigger and conversion mechanism built into high-trigger cocos, except in extraordinary and exigent circumstances which would pose a threat to the financial system as a whole if not immediately addressed,. They should also stop encouraging write-off-only cocos whose perverse incentives and contingent perdition without recovery could leave holes between the counterparties so deep as to further destabilize the financial system once a crisis has begun.

References

Admati, Anat and Martin Hellwig, 2013, *The Bankers' New Clothes: What's Wrong with Banking and What to Do About It*, Princeton and Oxford: Princeton University Press.

Allen & Overy LLP, 2013, "Tax Treatment of Additional Tier 1 Capital under Basel III," Global Tax Practice. http://www.allenovery.com/SiteCollection-Documents/Tax%20Treatment%20of%20Additional%20Tier%201%20 Capital%20under%20Basel%20III.pdf

American Bankers Association (cited as ABA), 2010a, "Dodd-Frank Wall Street Reform and Consumer Protection Act (Dodd-Frank Act), Title I: Financial Stability, Full Title I Summary." https://www.aba.com/Issues/RegReform/ Pages/RR1_overview.aspx

ABA, 2010b, "Dodd-Frank Act, Title II: Orderly Liquidation Authority, Full Title 2 Summary." https://www.aba.com/Issues/RegReform/Pages/RR2_overview.aspx

Atkinson, Tyler, David Luttrell and Harvey Rosenblum, 2013, "How Bad Was It? "The Costs and Consequences of the 2007–09 Financial Crisis," *DallasFed Staff Papers*, No. 20, July.

Bank of Cyprus Group, 2011, "Notice of Shareholders' Extraordinary General Meeting," Nicosia, March 1. http://www.bankofcyprus.com.cy/Documents/ Cyprus/News/20110301-EGM-Notice.pdf

Bank of Cyprus Group, 2013, "Group Financial Results for the Year ended 31 December 2012," Announcement, Nicosia, October 11.

Barth, James R., Gerard Caprio, Jr., and Ross Levine, 2012, *Guardians of Finance: Making Regulators Work for Us*, Cambridge, MA: MIT Press.

BBVA Citi Research, 2013, "Funding Models of Banks and Corporates: Implications of the Euro Crisis, Banking Union and Bail-in," October 8.

Bank for International Settlements (cited as BIS), 2013, "CoCos: A Primer," *BIS Quarterly Review*, September, pp. 43–56.

Basel Committee on Banking Supervision (cited as BCBS), 2010, "Basel III: International Standards for Liquidity Risk Measurement, Standards and Monitoring," December. http://www.bis.org/publ/bcbs188.pdf

BCBS, 2011a, "Basel III Definition of Capital—Frequently Asked Questions," December update. www.bis.org/publ/bcbs211.htm.

BCBS, 2011b, "Final Elements of the Reforms to Raise the Quality of Regulatory Capital Issued by the Basel Committee," *BIS Press Release*, January 13. http://www.bis.org/press/p110113.pdf

BCBS, 2011c, "Basel III: A Global Regulatory Framework for More Resilient Banks and Banking Systems," December 2010, revised June 2011. http://www.bis.org/publ/bcbs189.pdf

BCBS, 2011d, "Global Systemically Important Banks: Assessment Methodology and the Additional Loss Absorbency Requirement: Rules Text," November. http://www.bis.org/publ/bcbs207.pdf ; update published July 2013. http://www.bis.org/publ/bcbs255.pdf

BCBS, 2013a, *Charter*, January. http://www.bis.org/bcbs/charter.htm

BCBS, 2013b, "Regulatory Consistency Assessment Programme (RCAP)— Analysis of Risk-Weighted Assets for Market Risk," January, rev. February. http://www.bis.org/publ/bcbs240.htm

BCBS, 2013c, "Compilation of Documents that Form the Global Regulatory Framework for Capital and Liquidity," July (continuously updated from 2006 on). http://www.bis.org/bcbs/basel3/compilation.htm

BCBS, 2013d, "Revised Basel III Leverage Ratio Framework and Disclosure Requirements," Consultative Document, June. https://www.bis.org/publ/bcbs251.pdf

BCBS, 2014, "Basel III Leverage Ratio Framework and Disclosure Requirements," January. http://www.bis.org/publ/bcbs270.pdf

Black, Thomas, 2008, "Mexico Bailout Mistakes May Provide Lessons for US Lawmakers," Sept. 25. http://www.bloomberg.com/apps/news?pid=newsarchive&sid=a995IUbqAcaM/

Bolton, Patrick and Frédéric Samama, 2012, "Capital Access Bonds: Contingent Capital with an Option to Convert," *Economic Policy*, 27(70), April: 275–317.

Calomiris, Charles W. and Richard J. Herring, 2011, "How and Why to Design a Contingent Convertible Debt Requirement," available at http://ssrn.com/abstract=1815406

Caprio, Gerard, Jr., 2003, Episodes of Systemic and Borderline Financial Crises: Dataset, January 22. http://go.worldbank.org/5DYGICS7B0

Congressional Budget Office, cited as CBO, 2012, *Report on the Troubled Asset Relief Program—March 2012*. http://www.cbo.gov/publication/43138

CRR, 2013, see EC.

Curtis, Polly, 2011, "Reality Check: How Much did the Banking Crisis Cost Taxpayers?" *The Guardian News Blog*, September 12. Available via http://www.guardian.co.uk/politics/reality-check-with-polly-curtis/2011/sep/12/reality-check-banking-bailout?INTCMP=SRCH

Deutsche Bank, 2013, "CoCos: Interesting Market Trends," Deutsche Bank Research, September 23.

ECM, 2013, "Credit Market Summary," December 6. www.ecm.com/commentaryfiles/06_December_2013_ECM_Credit_Market_Summary.pdf

Economic Report of the President, Transmitted to the Congress March 2013 together with the Annual Report of the Council of Economic Advisers, 2013, Washington, D.C.: US Government Printing Office.

European Banking Authority (cited as EBA), 2011a, Excerpts from "Annex II: Capital Buffers for Addressing Market Concerns over Sovereign Exposures," and "Annex III: Buffer Convertible Capital Securities: Common Term Sheet," in *EBA Recommendation on the Creation and Supervisory Oversight of Temporary Capital Buffers to Restore Market Confidence* (EBA/REC/2011/1), December 8.

http://www.eba.europa.eu/documents/10180/16460/EBA+BS+2011+173+Recommendation+FINAL.pdf/b533b82c-2621-42ff-b90e-96c081e1b598

EBA, 2011b, "The EBA Details the EU Measures to Restore Confidence in the Banking System," October 26. http://www.eba.europa.eu/-/the-eba-details-the-eu-measures-to-restore-confidence-in-the-banking-sector

EBA, 2013a, "Interim Results of the EBA Review of the Consistency of Risk-Weighted Assets: Top-down Assessment of the Banking Book," February 26. http://www.eba.europa.eu/documents/10180/15947/Interim-results-EBA-review-consistency-RWAs_1.pdf

EBA, 2013b, "EBA draft Regulatory Technical Standards-Near Final Version on Own Funds [Part 1] under the draft Capital Requirements Regulation (CRR), EBA-RTS-2013-01 (near final)," 5 June, pp. 23–28.

http://www.eba.europa.eu/documents/10180/16058/EBA-RTS-2013-01(Near-final+Draft+RTS+on+OF+Part+1).pdf

European Commission (cited as EC), 2011, *Proposal for a Regulation of the European Parliament and of the Council on Prudential Requirements for Credit Institutions and Investment Firms*, Part III, Brussels: 20.7.2011 COM(2011) 452 final.

EC, 2013, "Regulation (EU) No 575/2013 of the European Parliament and of the Council of 26 June 2013 on prudential requirements for credit institutions and investment firms and amending Regulation (EU) No. 648/2012." *Official Journal of the European Union*, 27.6.2013 L176 (Capital Requirements Regulation CRR IV).

http://ec.europa.eu/internal_market/bank/regcapital/legislation_in_force_en.htm , or

http://eur.lex.europa.eu/LexUriServ/LexUriServ.do?uri=O-J:l:2013:176:0001:0337:EN:PDF

Federal Deposit Insurance Corporation (cited as FDIC), n.d., *Resolutions Handbook*, www.fdic.gov/bank/historical/reshandbook/

FDIC, 2011, "Feature Article: The Orderly Liquidation of Lehman Brothers Holdings Inc. under the Dodd-Frank Act," *FDIC Quarterly* 5(2): 1–19.

Financial Stability Board (cited as FSB), 2012, *Peer Review of Switzerland: Review Report*, January 25. http://www.financialstabilityboard. org/publications/r_250112.pdf

FSB, 2013, "Update of Group of Global Systemically Important Banks (G-SIBs)," November 11. http://www.financialstabilityboard.org/ publications/r_131111.pdf

Financial Stability Oversight Council, 2012, *Report to Congress on Study of a Contingent Capital Requirement for Certain Nonbank Financial Companies and Bank Holding Companies*, July. http://www.treasury.gov/initiatives/fsoc/ studies-reports/Documents/Co%20co%20study[2].pdf

FitchRatings, 2009, "Rating Hybrid Securities," Corporate Finance, December 29.

http://www.scribd.com/doc/38018911/Fitch-Ratings-Rating-Hybrid-Securities

FitchRatings, 2011a, "Treatment of Hybrids in Bank Capital Analysis," Global Sector-Specific Criteria Report: Banks, July 11.

http://www.fitchratings.com/creditdesk/reports/report_frame.cfm?rpt_ id=641269

FitchRatings, 2011b, "Pricing and Calibration of Contingent Capital with a Structural Approach," Fitch Solutions / Products & Services / Quantitative Research.

http://www.fitchratings.com/creditdesk/reports/report_frame.cfm?rpt_ id=647903

FitchRatings, 2012, "Assessing and Rating Subordinated and Hybrid Securities," Sector-Specific Rating Criteria / Banks / Global, December 5. http:// www.fitchratings.com/creditdesk/reports/report_frame.cfm?rpt_id=695542

FitchRatings, 2014, "Basel III Common Equity Tier 1: Early Delivery," Macro Credit Research, January 29.

Flannery, Mark J., 2005, "No Pain, No Gain? Effecting market discipline via 'Reverse Convertible Debentures,'" in Hal S. Scott, ed., *Capital Adequacy Beyond Basel: Banking, Securities, and Insurance*, New York: Oxford University Press, 171–195.

Flannery, Mark J., 2009, "Stabilizing Large Financial Institutions with Contingent Capital Certificates." Available at http://ssrn.com/abstract=1485689

Flannery, Mark J. and Enrico Perotti, 2011, "CoCo Design as a Risk Preventive Tool," *Vox*, 9, February.

Goodhart, Charles A.E., 2011, "The Squam Lake Report: A Commentary," *Journal of Economic Literature* 49(1): 114–119.

Hammer, Viva and John Bush, 2011, "The Taxation of Dodd-Frank," *Tax Notes, Special Report*, July 11.

Hammer, Viva, Sam Chen and Paul Carman, 2011, "United States: Tax Treatment of Contingent Convertible Bonds," *Derivatives & Financial Instruments*, May/June, pp. 97–106.

HM Revenue & Customs, 2011, "The Tax Treatment of Regulatory Capital Instruments," HM Revenue & Customs Discussion Paper. http://www.hmrc. gov.uk/basel3/discussion.pdf

Independent Commission on Banking, cited as ICB, 2011, "Interim Report: Consultation on Reform Options," UK, April. http://bankingcommission.s3.amazonaws.com/wp-content/uploads/2011/04/Interim-Report-110411.pdf

Internal Revenue Service (cited as IRS), 2010, "Application of Section 382 to Corporations Whose Instruments are Acquired and Disposed of by the Treasury Department Under Certain Programs Pursuant to the Emergency Economic Stabilization Act of 2008," *Internal Revenue Bulletin; 2010-2*, January 11. http://www.irs.gov/irb/2010-02_IRB/ar09.html

KPMG, 2011, "An Introduction to the Tax Implications of the Dodd-Frank Wall Street Reform and Consumer Protection Act," Washington National Tax and Americas' FS Center of Excellence, May.

Miller, Merton H., 1995, "Do the M & M Propositions Apply to Banks?" *Journal of Banking & Finance*, 19(3–4), June: 483–489.

Montiel, Peter J., 2014, *Ten Crises*, London and New York: Routledge.

Moody's Investors Service (cited as Moody's), 2011, "Corporate Defaults and Recovery Rates, 1920–2010," Global Corporate Finance: February 28. http://www.naic.org/documents/committees_e_capad_vos_c1_factor_review_sg_related_docs_moodys_corporate_default.pdf

Moody's, 2013, "Moody's Proposed Approach for Rating Certain Bank Contingent Capital Securities and Update to Approach for Rating Bank Subordinated Debt: A Proposed Update to Moody's Consolidated Global Bank Rating Methodology," Global Credit Research, Apr. 10.

http://www.moodys.com/research/Moodys-Proposed-Approach-for-Rating-Certain-Bank-Contingent-Capital-Securities-PBC_150964

Moody's, 2014, "Additional Tier 1 Contingent Capital: Securities Have Common Features, but Structural Differences Pose Degrees of Credit Risk to Investors," February 13.

National Audit Office, HM Treasury, 2011, *The Comptroller and Auditor General's Report on Accounts to the House of Commons*, National Audit

Office, July 13. http://www.nao.org.uk/wp-content/uploads/2011/07/HMT_account_2010_2011.pdf

Oakes, Jeffrey and Connie Milonakis, 2013, "Considerations when Issuing CoCos into the US." http://www.iflr.com/Article/3210360/Considerations-when-issuing-CoCos-into-the-US.html

Office of the Comptroller of the Currency (cited as OCC), 2003, *Comptroller's Licensing Manual: Subordinated Debt*, Washington D.C., November. http://www.occ.gov/publications/publications-by-type/licensing-manuals/subdebt.pdf

OCC and Federal Reserve System (cited as OCC & Fed), 2013a, "Regulatory Capital Rules: Regulatory Capital, Implementation of Basel III, Capital Adequacy, Transition Provisions, Prompt Corrective Action, Standardized Approach for Risk-Weighted Assets, Market Discipline and Disclosure Requirements, Advanced Approaches Risk-Based Capital Rule, and Market Risk Capital Rule." http://www.occ.gov/news-issuances/news-releases/2013/2013-110a.pdf

OCC & Fed, 2013b, "Regulatory Capital Rules: Regulatory Capital, Implementation of Basel III, Capital Adequacy, Transition Provisions, Prompt Corrective Action, Standardized Approach for Risk-weighted Assets, Market Discipline and Disclosure Requirements, Advanced Approaches Risk-Based Capital Rule, and Market Risk Capital Rule; Final Rule," *Federal Register*, Vol. 78, No. 198, October 11, 2013, Part II, pp. 62017–62291.

http://www.gpo.gov/fdsys/pkg/FR-2013-10-11/pdf/2013-21653.pdf

OCC, Fed & FDIC, 2012a, "Regulatory Capital Rules: Standardized Approach for Risk-Weighted Assets; Market Risk and Disclosure Requirements." http://www.fdic.gov/news/board/2012/2012-06-12_notice_dis-d.pdf

OCC, Fed & FDIC, 2012b, "Regulatory Capital Rules: Regulatory Capital, Implementation of Basel III, Minimum Regulatory Capital Ratios, Capital Adequacy, Transition Provisions, and Prompt Corrective Action." http://www.occ.gov/news-issuances/news-releases/2012/nr-ia-2012-88a.pdf

Office of Superintendent of Financial Institutions, cited as OSFI, 2011, "Advisory on Non-Viability Contingent Capital," *The OSFI Pillar* 5(3), Autumn. Available at http://www.osler.com/NewsResources/Details.aspx-?id=3680

Osler, 2011, provides access to the draft of "Advisory: Non-Viability Contingent Capital" of February 2011 with changes marked ("blacklined") August 18, 2011. The direct link is given below. http://www.osler.com/uploadedFiles/OSFI_Advisory_NVCC_Blackline.pdf

Paulson, Henry M., Jr., 2010, *On the Brink*, New York: Business Plus.

PricewaterhouseCoopers (cited as PwC), 2009, "Debt Restructurings and Bankruptcy: Accounting, Tax and FAS 109 Considerations," Tax Accounting Services.

PwC, 2011, *Basel III and Beyond*. The Trillion Dollar Question: Can Bail-in Capital Bail Out the Banking Industry?" November. http://www.pwc.com/en_JG/jg/publications/basel-and-beyond-trillion-dollar-question.pdf

Rajan, Raghuram G., 2010, "Too Systemic to Fail: Consequences, Causes, and Potential Remedies," *BIS Working Papers*, No. 305.

Raviv, Alon, 2004. "Bank Stability and Market Discipline: Debt-for-Equity Swaps versus Subordinated Notes," Available at http://ideas.repec.org/p/wpa/wuwpfi/0408003.html

Reinhart, Carmen M., Vincent R. Reinhart and Kenneth S. Rogoff, 2012, "Public Debt Overhangs: Advanced-Economy Episodes since 1800," *Journal of Economic Perspectives*, 26(3), Summer: 69–86.

Reinhart, Carmen M. and Kenneth S. Rogoff, 2009a, "The Aftermath of Financial Crises," *American Economic Review: Papers and Proceedings*, 99(2), May: 466–472.

Reinhart, Carmen M. and Kenneth S. Rogoff, 2009b, *This Time is Different: Eight Centuries of Financial Folly*, Princeton and Oxford: Princeton University Press.

Reinhart, Carmen M. and Kenneth S. Rogoff, 2010, "Growth in a Time of Debt," *American Economic Review: Papers and Proceedings*, 100(2), May: 573–578. Statement No. 303.

Sgard, Jérôme, 2013, "Bankruptcy, Fresh Start and Debt Renegotiation in England and France," pp. 223–235 in Thomas Max Safley, ed., *The History of Bankruptcy: Economic, Social and Cultural Implications in Early Modern Europe*, London and New York: Routledge.

Shadow Financial Regulatory Committee (cited as SFRC), 2010, "The Case for a Properly Structured Contingent Capital Requirement," Statement No. 303.

Skeel, David A. Jr., 2001, *Debt's Dominion: A History of Bankruptcy Law in America,* Princeton and Oxford: Princeton University Press.

SolarWorld, 2013, *First Half 2013 Consolidated Interim Report Solarworld AG.* http://www.solarworld.de/fileadmin/downloads_new/ir/2013/2013_q2_en_web.pdf

Sorkin, Andrew Ross, 2009, *Too Big to Fail*, London: Viking Penguin.

Standard & Poor's (cited as S&P), 2011a, "2010 Annual Global Corporate Default Study and Rating Transitions," March 30. http://www.standardandpoors.com/ratings/articles/en/us/?assetID=1245302234237

S&P, 2011b, "Bank Hybrid Capital Methodology and Assumptions," *Global Credit Portal* RatingsDirect, Criteria / Financial Institutions / Banks: November 1.

http://img.en25.com/Web/StandardandPoors/BankHybridCapital_Methodology_11_1_11_4216.pdf

S&P, 2011c, "Banks: Rating Methodology and Assumptions," *Global Credit Portal*, RatingsDirect, Criteria / Financial Institutions / Banks: November 9. http://www.standardandpoors.com/spf/upload/Ratings_EMEA/2011-11-09_CBEvent_CriteriaFIBankRatingMethodologyAndAssumptions.pdf

S&P, 2012, "Issuer Credit Profiles for the Top 100 Banks Globally," April 20. http://www.standardandpoors.com/ratings/articles/en/us/?articleType=HTM-L&assetID=1245332401015

von Furstenberg, George M., 1969, "Default Risk on FHA-Insured Home Mortgages as a Function of the Terms of Financing: A Quantitative Analysis," *Journal of Finance* 24(3), June: 459–477.

von Furstenberg, George M., 2009, "US Executive-Branch Transgressions in the Depth of the 2007–09 Financial Crisis," *Journal of Financial Transformation,* Vol. 37: 69–73.

von Furstenberg, George M., 2011a, "Contingent Capital to Strengthen the Private Safety Net for Financial Institutions: Cocos to the Rescue?" Discussion Paper Series 2: Banking and Financial Studies, No. 01/2011, Frankfurt a.M.: Deutsche Bundesbank. http://www.bundesbank.de/Redaktion/EN/Downloads/Publications/Discussion_Paper_2/2011/2011_02_07_dkp_01.pdf?_blob=publicationFile

von Furstenberg, George M., 2011b, "Concocting Marketable Cocos." HKIMR Working Paper No. 22/2011, Hong Kong Institute for Monetary Research, July. Available at SSRN: http://ssrn.com/abstract=1895984

von Furstenberg, George M., 2012a, "Mega-Banks' Self-Insurance with Cocos: A Work in Progress," *Global Credit Review,* Vol. 2, July: 53–78.

von Furstenberg, George M., 2013a, "Who or What has been Hobbling Cocos: Three Essentials for Making Cocos a Success," *Journal of Financial Transformation,* Vol. 36: Global Finance and Regulation, The Capco Institute, February: 95–105. http://www.capco.com/insights/capco-journal/journal-36-global-finance-and-regulation

von Furstenberg, George M., 2013b, "Determinants of the Interest-Rate Premium on Contingent Convertible Bonds (Cocos)," *Journal of Financial Perspectives* 1(2), Part II: 1–12, EY Global Financial Services Institute, July:1–12. www.gfsi.ey.com/the-journal-of-financial-perspectives/volume/1/issue/2/determinants-of-the-interest-rate-premium-on-contingent-convertible-bonds-cocos_45

Whelan, Karl, 2012, "ELA, Promissory Notes and All That: The Fiscal Costs of Anglo-Irish Bank," University College Dublin, Revised Draft, September. http://www.karlwhelan.com/IrishEconomy/Whelan-PNotes-September2012.pdf

Index

Printed in the United States
By Bookmasters